DRAMATURGY OF SOUND
IN THE AVANT-GARDE AND POSTDRAMATIC THEATRE

Contents

DRAMATURGY of SOUND in the AVANT-GARDE and POSTDRAMATIC THEATRE

MLADEN OVADIJA

McGill-Queen's University Press
Montreal & Kingston • London • Chicago

ISBN 978-0-7735-4173-3 (cloth)
ISBN 978-0-7735-4588-5 (paper)
ISBN 978-0-7735-8866-0 (ePDF)
ISBN 978-0-7735-8867-7 (ePUB)

Legal deposit third quarter 2013
Bibliothèque nationale du Québec
First paperback edition 2016

Printed in Canada on acid-free paper that is 100% ancient forest free (100% post-consumer recycled), processed chlorine free.

This book has been published with the help of a grant from the Canadian Federation for the Humanities and Social Sciences, through the Awards to Scholarly Publications Program, using funds provided by the Social Sciences and Humanities Research Council of Canada.

McGill-Queen's University Press acknowledges the support of the Canada Council for the Arts for our publishing program. We also acknowledge the financial support of the Government of Canada through the Canada Book Fund for our publishing activities.

Library and Archives Canada Cataloguing in Publication

Ovadija, Mladen, 1947–
Dramaturgy of sound in the avant-garde and postdramatic theatre / Mladen Ovadija.

Includes bibliographical references and index.
ISBN 978-0-7735-4173-3 (bnd). – ISBN 978-0-7735-4588-5 (paper)
ISBN 978-0-7735-8866-0 (ePDF). – ISBN 978-0-7735-8867-7 (ePUB)

1. Theaters – Sound effects. 2. Experimental theater – History and criticism. 3. Avant-garde (Aesthetics). I. Title.

PN2091.S6093 2013 792.02'4 C2013-902121-3

This book was typeset by True to Type in 10.5/13 Sabon

Acknowledgments

My biggest gratitude goes to Christopher Innes, my postdoctoral research mentor and Mark Abley, my acquisition editor at McGill-Queen's University Press who were closely involved in the creation of this book and who strongly believed in its purpose. They offered a much-needed understanding of my endeavours and of the matter I have been dealing with. Innes spared no effort to read and talk over most of the material I wrote: his advice was invaluable for the successful completion of the book. Abley, for his part, knew how to lead me through the challenges of the publishing process: his encouragement went far beyond the professional support of an editor.

I would like to thank Stephen Johnson, Domenico Pietropaolo, and Veronika Ambros who remained on my side all the way through.

I also thank Joanne Mackay-Bennett, Martin Townsend, and Kathryn Simpson for their editorial assistance.

I am grateful to Biljana, Perla, Jelena, my family, friends, and colleagues for their healthy and healing cheer that never stopped.

Parts of chapters 1 and 7 in their initial versions have been published in *Theatrical Blends*, Gdansk: Slowo/Obraz Terytoria, 2010, and *Futurist Dramaturgy and Performance*, New York/Ottawa/Toronto: Legas, 2011.

DRAMATURGY OF SOUND
IN THE AVANT-GARDE AND POSTDRAMATIC THEATRE

Introduction

This book, strictly speaking, belongs to the field of theatre studies, but to be true to its subject, which is theatre sound, it adopts a multidisciplinary approach and includes discussion of the aural principles and methods of poetry, performance, painting, and music developed in the historical avant-garde and applied subsequently in contemporary theatre. It explores the dramaturgy of sound – at first glance an oxymoronic and paradoxical term that escapes its own verbal root "drama," thought of as a literary discipline, and connects it to a purely material phenomenon of sound. Indeed, if dramaturgy's customary concern is the temporal and spatial disposition of the plot in a dramatic text and its staging – an orderly and ordering enterprise par excellence – then how can it possibly be paired with something disorderly, something as transient, delicate, but powerful as the sound of wind through leaves, as emotional as a sigh or cry, as disruptive as a clap of thunder? Fluid, erotic, immediate, and signifying through its own materiality, sound is not an arbitrary signifier denoting a thing or an act; it *is* a thing and/or an act in itself. It is an aural object thrown onstage through a performative act – utterance or gesture – that "betrays" the text of literary drama. "Representation and interpretation," alleges Jim Drobnik, "are issues in which sound shares with pictures and text, yet sound reconfigures these very issues by inflecting representation with affect, and interpretation with embodiment … [and] challenges the conventions of visual and textual models."[1] The immanence, fluidity, and sensuality of the human voice and the expressiveness of stage sound – traditionally considered secondary to the primacy of the text – are essential elements of the performativity and scenic dynamics that propel dramaturgy in contemporary theatre. Here, sound reveals – or perhaps more appropriately, *is* – performance. The dramaturgy of sound, therefore, reads/writes another type of text (one of physical theatricality) by the temporal and spatial disposition of aural objects/acts of performance. It displays voice – not only as a carrier of speech but also as an emotional, pulsional,[2] gestural expression in excess of speech, and sound – not only as supporting music or incidental noise but also as an autonomous stage-building material. Discussing Robert Wilson's "theatre of images," an epitome of "postdramatic" staging, Patrice Pavis notes that it "plays simultaneously 'on both panels' [visual and auditory] according to the two rhythms peculiar to each system, and particularly that such a theatre needs music [or organized sound/silence, as John Cage would have it] and the voice to 'cement' the images."[3]

One can consider dramaturgy in the sense of Eugenio Barba's description of the term as a live process of drama-ergon, that is, "work of actions" in the performance, which is based on the understanding of "text" in its pre-verbal sense of "weaving together" that characterizes a ritual process of discovery of a never-decipherable world.[4] In contemporary theatre practice, this "weaving" becomes simultaneously available for theatrical and dramaturgical use. It does not stop at the representation of a play, if such really exists, but offers a flexible matrix for the performance. It does not stop even at a director's creation of a *mise-en-scène*, or its factual incarnation by the performers' stage presence, but stretches into an interactive environment of the theatrical event, which aims to solicit the audience's participation. Naturally, a prime example of such a dramaturgy is the use of immersiveness of sound in theatre. For Barba, the process of transforming the play text into the textuality of stage performance is threefold. It starts with "*narrative dramaturgy*" (1) that through "*organic or dynamic dramaturgy*, (2) of the rhythms and dynamisms affecting the spectators on a nervous, sensorial and sensual level," evolves into "*dramaturgy of changing states* (3) when the entirety of what [is shown] manages to evoke something totally different, similar to when a song develops another sound line through the harmonics."[5] One should note that while the first type of dramaturgy still holds to the Aristotelian concept of drama, the last two remind us of the avant-garde methods of assaulting the audience with deliberate sensory overload and immersing spectators in a performance sound/event. Indeed, the theatrical event lives and dies with the lights and sounds of a stage inhabited by moving bodies that expose their perceptible materiality. Its ergonomics depends as much on visceral, concrete, and abstract qualities – of suffering/joyful human bodies and kinetic masses of stage objects, changing lights, colours, voices, noises, sounds, and silences felt, seen, and heard – as on plot development.

In a theatre of "drama-ergon" dramaturgy is not exhausted in the realm of the dramatic plot of interwoven characters' actions, which as Aristotle admits, does not necessarily require spectacle/staging (*opsis*) since it is complete in itself. Elinor Fuchs notes: "If we are approaching the end of character [and plot] on the postmodern stage, what is replacing it? Perhaps a flux of Aristotle's six famous elements, with Character and Action no longer holding dominion over Music, Diction, Thought, and Spectacle. Indeed the independence Aristotle assigned to these aspects of theater almost makes him sound like the first anticipator of the postmodern … In the theater of difference,[6] each signifying element – lights, visual design, music, etc., as well as plot and character elements – stands to some degree as an independent actor. It is as if all the Aristotelian elements of theater had survived, but had slipped the organizing structure of their former hierarchy."[7] The clash of independent material elements, although received as dramatic or significant, breaks the rules of dramatic representation. Indeed in Hans-Thies Lehmann's "dramaturgy on shifting grounds" [a postdramatic term obviously borrowed from Barba], "the traditional hierarchy of theatrical elements has almost vanished: as the text is no longer the central and superior factor, all the other elements like space, light, sound, music, movement and gesture tend to have an equal weight in the performance process."[8] It is in this counterpoint of the performative and the theatrical, the corporeal and the figurative, the visceral and the architectural that the dramaturgy of sound operates.

I argue that the initial probes into anti-textual sonority made by the historical avant-garde have a viable and germane relationship with the auditory semiotics of postdramatic theatre. Consequently, a new concept of theatre sound coalesces in a twofold, simultaneously oral and aural, dramaturgy that emerges from the ideas and practice related to sound in different historical movements including Futurism, Expressionism, Dadaism, and the Bauhaus. This book, therefore, describes such a theatrical style as developed in an interplay of the corporeal, vocal, gestural, and incantational elements of the performance (in an arc from Antonin Artaud to Jean-François Lyotard) and the abstract/concrete architecture of the stage sound (from the Bauhaus to Wilson). Thus, charting a history of the early twentieth-century innovative conceptions and practices of sound poetry, arts, and performance – that prove to be in line with most recent theoretical discourse – my study makes a case for the centrality of sound as a both performative and architectural constituent of contemporary theatre. It also sheds light on another "weaving together" that happens in contemporary arts and theatre – an amalgamation of performance, conceptual, and installation art and their reflections in theatre proper recognized by Erika Fischer-Lichte as the "performative turn" and by Lehmann as "postdramatic theatricality."

Lehmann's *Postdramatic Theatre* (German edition 1999, English translation 2006) reads as a proposal for contemporary discourse based on an autonomous theatricality of "states and of scenically dynamic formations." In his *Theory of the Modern Drama* (1956) Peter Szondi conceives of these states and formations as an answer to "the crisis of drama" that he diagnoses in the works of Henrik Ibsen, Anton Chekhov, August Strindberg, Maurice Maeterlinck, and Gerhart Hauptmann. These modern playwrights abandoned the absolute correlation of content and form in the ideal Hegelian "Drama," whose historical source Szondi traces to the Renaissance, when "a bold intellectual effort [was] made by a newly self-conscious being [... to] mirror himself on the basis of interpersonal relationships alone" – relationships that in effect dictate the dialogical structure of drama. "Man entered the drama only as a fellow human being, so to speak ... Most radical of all was the exclusion of that which could not express itself – the world of objects – unless it entered the realm of interpersonal relations."[9] Szondi finds that the representational capacity of such character/plot/action-driven situational drama is seriously challenged by the intrusion of epic features in modernist drama. Coming soon after modernists, the historical avant-gardes started harshly to question the integrity of the "newly self-conscious being" and the representational techniques of his illusionistic, bourgeois drama by refusing to serve mimetic reconstructions of the literary text and instead shifting emphasis to the theatricality and materiality of performance. Another intrusion, an explosion of hybridized artistic techniques and forms, various audiovisual installations, and media presentations – cinematic, electronic, and digital – flooded the stage from the 1960s onwards and, reintroducing "the world of objects," brought about a further disruption of dramatic form. Acknowledging this development in a way "different from Szondi who only discusses modern theatre in negative terms – as an art form in crisis, a becoming-problematic of drama – Lehmann maps out an affirmative aesthetics of postdramatic theatre and provides a catalogue of ideas that allow describing and analyzing that kind of theatre in positive terms."[10] He allows the world of objects and energies (and thus of sound) to re-enter independently the stage that so far, in dramatic theatre, had been exclusively reserved for a dialogic interaction of characters.

Presenting a "plethora of phenomena in the theatre landscape of the last few decades" as the outcome of the heterogeneous "dramaturgies beyond the representation," Lehmann inscribes a new paradigm of the postdramatic in the contemporary theoretical discourse. His paradigmatic theatre landscape, which appears after three centuries of dominantly dramatic theatre, incorporates "the enormous variety of theatre work: from a theatre of images to a theatre of voices, from choral and monologic structures to durational performance."[11] In line with my own research, Lehmann acknowledges the role of the materiality of sound in the disruption of visual and textual orders in both avant-garde and postdramatic theatre. Furthermore, his concepts of "auditory semiotics," "theatre as music," "turn to performance," and "scenic dynamic as opposed to dramatic dynamic" coincide with my exploration of a dramaturgy of sound as a vital element of an all-embracing deconstruction of literary drama by postdramatic theatricality. Nevertheless, Lehmann warns: "Today a Gotthold Ephraim Lessing, who could develop 'the' dramaturgy of postdramatic theatre, is unthinkable."[12]

Dramaturgy of Sound in the Avant-garde and Postdramatic Theatre explores the oral/aural aspect of such a multifaceted dramaturgy and reveals that most of its compositional methods concerning use of sound in the postdramatic theatre were already at work in poetry and performance of the early-twentieth-century avant-gardes. The avant-garde's focus on sound and voice as the autonomous materials led to the disruption of the logocentric, rational framework of the traditional literary and dramatic form. Understanding sound not as subordinate to linguistic sense or visual gesture, but as equal in every respect, it opened paths for a theatre of the postdramatic age that works synaesthetically, promoting a unified sense of experience. The book illuminates this development through the discussion of a large corpus of contemporary works that distance themselves from dramatic representation by sonically, visually, or kinetically embodying postdramatic structures and "narratives."

Establishing the lineage of performative and theatrical aspects of corporeal vocal gesture, the book traces its historical sources from Filippo Tommaso Marinetti's "lyrical intoxication with matter," onomatopoeia, destruction of syntax, liberation of words, and *bruitist* declamations at the Futurist *serate* to simultaneous poetry performances at the Dadaist Cabaret Voltaire, Hugo Ball's *verse ohne worte* (wordless verse), Raoul Hausmann's "optophonetic" poetry, and Tristan Tzara's poetics of indeterminacy. *Dramaturgy of Sound* also reveals a line of development that goes from Luigi Russolo's *The Art of Noises* to *musique concrète* and contemporary theories of music not as tonal composition but rather as organized sound. This includes John Cage's durational concept of music as a continuum of silence, sound, and noise and the spread of his ideas in the new American avant-garde, notably its theatre. At the same time, examining sources of the abstractionist tendencies of the dramaturgy of sound, the book looks into Wassily Kandinsky's synaesthetic theory of "inner sound" as a lead toward synthetic and intermedial theatre. Similarly, it describes the Expressionist *Geist* acting/staging method conceived by Lothar Schreyer as a confluence of vocal performance and abstract/concrete stage sound. Furthermore, the book identifies the principles of Alexei Kruchenykh's and Velimir Khlebnikov's beyond sense (*zaum*) poetry and language as formative factors in the theatricality of the Russian Futurist stage works *Victory over the Sun* and *Zangezi*, produced by Kazimir Malevich, Mikhail Matiushin, and Vladimir Tatlin. On the Italian side, it documents a parallel path leading from sound poetry to abstract theatre in a number of Futurist synthetic theatre pieces in which sound makes an independent building block of a scenography that incarnates the "plastic moto-rumorist complex," a precursor of the Bauhaus's synacoustic and synoptic stage architecture.

Finally, the last chapter looks at the historical avant-garde sources of the dramaturgy of sound through the rear-view mirror of postdramatic theatre. It offers a series of short case analyses of the dramaturgical use of sound in more recent performances, including works of the Living Theatre, Peter Brook, Tadeusz Kantor, Robert Wilson, Caryl Churchill, Christoph Marthaler, Einer Schleef, Sound & Fury, the Sòcietas Raffaello Sanzio, and the Theatregroep Hollandia. The book ends with a coda to the opening discussion of the performativity of voice and sound, which connects their corporeal and concrete with architectural and abstract aspects in poetry, music, visual arts, and performance. Thus, in conclusion, *Dramaturgy of Sound* not only evidences the "echo" of avant-garde experiments with sound in the pronounced orality/aurality of postdramatic theatre productions and re-evaluates their legacy, but also espouses a novel approach to theatre based on the dramaturgy of sound as a viable reference for performance analysis in general.

1

The Performativity of Voice and Sound in Theatre

The breakthrough of the dramaturgy of sound is not an issue of artistic technique or craftsmanship. It is a consequence of the avant-garde's recognition of the materiality of sound, the revision of the conventional referentiality of artistic means, and the establishment of a new aesthetic that deals with sound as matter, form, and an independent constituent of the work of art. No longer is the question how to produce, by means of sound, a work of art that would represent an object, signify something, or express an aesthetic idea formulated elsewhere in culture, language, or theory. Rather, the question is how to deal with sound itself as an actor in the drama of things – either as an erotic material of vocal performance, or as an element of a new theatricality in which sound interacts independently with lights, objects, and stage design. Conceiving a method of theatrical composition or construction that tells its own "plot" through the process of an oral/aural *semiosis*, the dramaturgy of sound has become constitutive of a theatre that places more emphasis on performance, *mise en scène*, and the audio-visual architecture of the stage than it does on dramatic text. Its story, recounted in this book, begins with the historical avant-garde's exploits in the field of orality/aurality of performance.

The topic of theatre sound has been overwhelmingly neglected in contemporary critical and scholarly discourse. Theatre historians have by and large ignored the seminal role of the historical avant-garde's treatment of sound in the development of contemporary performance. Likewise, theoreticians of sound poetry and audio art – Douglas Kahn, Steve McCaffery, and Klaus Schöning, to name three – have identified the Futurists and Dadaists as pioneers of acoustic art, but they have generally not examined the sustained and multifaceted impact that the exploratory work of these forerunners has had on theatre. Philosophers and theorists such as Adriana Cavarero, Martin Jay, and Steven Connor have discussed the aurality paradigm that has recently gained currency in postmodern cultural discourse, but have left its theatrical aspect mostly unexplored. The same lack of theatre topics is noticeable in recently published studies that otherwise offer a profound analysis of sound perception, sound art, and a new philosophy and aesthetics of listening, like those by Casey O'Callaghan, Brandon LaBelle, and Salomé Voegelin.

Meanwhile, general studies of theatre art have assigned sound a mainly illustrative role, as a sort of aural *coulisse* for a performance/production. Stagecraft manuals consider sound design in a context of the practical application of other artistic disciplines such as architecture, sculpture, painting, and music. Conceptually and pragmatically, sound has remained limited to its relational role – as a means that, together with stage setting and lighting, defines the location of the action and the mood of the scene, marks the passage of time, and announces actors' entrances and exits. The 2006 *Routledge Companion to Theatre and Performance* reads: "Lighting and sound may be indispensable elements of performance events but they are often overlooked by the public, critics and academics alike. An explanation for this invisibility is the fact that they usually have supplementary or supporting rather than dominant roles. Used often to provoke emotional responses or create mood in a subliminal rather than overt way, they are mostly employed non-figuratively. They thus need to be considered in relation to other aspects of the *mise en scène* or production rather than just by themselves."[1]

More encouragingly, and in contrast to this summary description of the illustrative function of sound, some theatre scholars, notably Hans-Thies Lehmann and Erika Fischer-Lichte, the most cited theatre theoreticians of the last decade, have begun to give theatre sound its due. Lehmann, in his *Postdramatic Theatre*, acknowledges the substantiveness of stage sound and the emergence of an auditory semiotics, while Fischer-Lichte, in her work *The Transformative Power of Performance*, conceives of a "performative generation of materiality" in which sound again plays a major role. Their central argument in the approach to contemporary theatre builds on the historical avant-garde's rejection of the literary/dramatic text in favour of the performance, either as an immediate event or as an art installation. In this context, my book analyses the historical avant-garde's recognition of the materiality of sound and the development of an ensuing dramaturgy of sound that secured theatrical sound the current position of a non-figurative element participating in the synaesthetic, synacoustic, synoptic, and syncretic forms of today's performance.

The discourse on orality/aurality has been revived lately in theatre journals such as *Performance Research* and *Modern Drama* and in academia, for instance at the University of London's Central School of Speech and Drama. The latter is a home to sound design teacher Ross Brown, whose comprehensive book *Sound: A Reader in Theatre Practice* appeared in 2010, and a site of the conference "Theatre Noise: The Sound of Performance" held in 2009 (followed by the book of the same name edited by Lynne Kendrick and David Roesner in 2012).[2] Likewise, the book *Composed Theatre: Aesthetics, Practices, Processes* (2012) appeared as a result of an Arts and Humanities Research Workshop Series: "Processes of Devising Composed Theatre" led by David Roesner and Matthias Rebstock.[3] *Sound*, a collection of essays edited by Caleb Kelly in the series Documents of Contemporary Art, and *Dramatic Theories of Voice in the Twentieth Century*, a study by Andrew M. Kimbrough, both published in 2011, also witness the recent rediscovery of the topic of theatre sound.

But what is sound to theatre, or theatre to sound? What would be the motive and the cue for our cry for sound? Whatever the answers to this quasi-Shakespearean question, it holds true that sound has become the subject of renewed interest in recent theatre discourse.

In theatre, as in life, sound is born and dies with action. The transitory life of sound is essentially dramatic.[4] It becomes audible only when a moving mass of gaseous, liquid, or solid matter encounters an obstacle to create whistling, trumpeting, hums, shrills, babbles, gurgles, shrieks, drumbeats, rings, and the like. Sound emanates from the stage in the form of vocal utterances (speech, chanting, and singing), instrumental renditions (music), and the clamour of environmental onstage and offstage events (noise). We perceive it as a sensory attraction caused by a movement of air coming from an animate source (such as a performer) or an inanimate source (perhaps a part of stage setting). We perceive sound directly without necessarily knowing its source or meaning: it simply escapes mere denotative function. Sound, thus, not only reveals dramatic performance: it is perhaps more appropriate to say, sound *is* performance.

Sound by its very nature contradicts and destabilizes the objectivity, certainty, and distinctiveness of sight on which Cartesian logocentrism relies. It has thus become a part of the weaponry in the struggle of the historical avant-garde against the closure of representation of the dramatic text, which Jacques Derrida analyzes. However, highlighting the role of sound in theatre does not mean that we ought to consider aurality as the preferred sense of performance and reception. Quite the contrary, the spatiotemporal reality of the stage is an area where sight and sound overlap in a complex relationship. David Burrows notes that "at the same time that the viewer in each of us is stepping back from the world and sorting its contents out into discrete entities, the listener in each of us is merging with a range of its activity."[5] Experiencing theatre (listening/watching/being there) is like stepping across a crevasse without looking down; we hear sound emanating from an "opaque" depth and moving toward a "clear" horizon of meaning. Theatre sound presupposes our emotional and cognitive engagement: our sensual immersion in the event and reflection on its possible meaning. But what appears as a tidy resolution, a dialectic unity of opposites that build the dramatic story, is undone by a series of constantly renewed dichotomies in performance. It is the dichotomies of sound and meaning, speech and language, time and space, body and sense, performance and text, which lie at the core of theatre theory and practice, layered with ancient history and contemporary urgency. Sound, always associated with the first members in these pairs, had been a subject of intense discussion in the historical avant-garde, particularly among Futurists, Expressionists, and Dadaists, who largely focused their arguments on two material aspects of sound: its corporeality and its abstract form. Hence, in the early years of the twentieth century, the recognition of the materiality of sound, first taking place in Futurist poetry and performance, prompted the formulation of a genuine aesthetic and dramaturgy of sound. The radical shift from the words' meaning to their sound was coupled with the dissociation of vocal utterance from syntactical language. Coinciding with the avant-garde's critical rejection of narrative and figurative pretensions in literature, art, and theatre, Futurist change of perspective provided the conceptual grounds for the development of sound-text poetry, *musique concrète*, abstract and objectless painting, and antitextual theatre. Clearly, all of these artistic trends were more concerned with material – sound, noise, colour, painterly mass, and theatre physicality – than with signification.

Patrice Pavis argues that the materiality of theatrical signs arises when the spectator perceives various sensory attractions acting alongside the signifier with no attempt to reach the signified. Spectators/listeners enjoy the corporeality of the actor, the texture of the spoken voice, music, sounds, colours, and rhythms emanating from stage: "they do not have to reduce this experience to words; they savour rather the 'erotic in the theatre act' without trying to reduce the performance to a series of signs."[6] Thus, through their perceived oral/aural materiality, voice and sound (no longer necessarily vocal) reclaim their own structural value in a synergetic relationship with movement, light, and other stage elements of theatre.

Robert Wilson, whose work epitomizes a dominant performance trend in postdramatic theatre of the last few decades, produces his pieces as kinetic constellations of aural and visual icons. He insists on switching channels between auditory and visual sensations, traditionally framed as separate entities, and conceives of a method of juxtaposition of "a radio image over the film's voice" that allows both to maintain their autonomy. As he explains, this criss-crossing of aural and visual sensations bring together the power of radio plays to suggest limitless images and the power of silent films to provoke our unbounded imagination of sounds. Still, in his theatre music and visuals do not illustrate each other. They "make balance between what you hear and what you see, so that perhaps you can do both at the same time."[7] Sergei Eisenstein similarly conceived his method of "the montage of attractions," in which sound, movement, space, and voice do not accompany each other but function as elements of equal significance. In his description of the exemplary experience of Kabuki theatre, Eisenstein compares the audience to a man who perceives vibration of light as sound, and tremors of air as colour; that is, he *hears light* and *sees sound*. Wilson relieves us from listening to words, which are in any case meaningless, and encourages us: "Just enjoy the scenery, the architectural arrangements in time and space, the music, the feeling they all evoke! Listen to the pictures!"[8]

True experiences of the power of theatre are rare, but I remember one such moment when director Paolo Magelli created an immersive aural space based on the purely physical sensation of sound in his 1998 staging of *The Phoenician Women*.[9] Long before the actors entered the stage, we, the audience, were sucked into an intensely aural performance space. As we entered the theatre (the audience were seated on the stage) and took our seats, we were deluged by a tidal wave created by the constant wailing of a boat siren, gradually increasing in volume. Our initial shock of disbelief was soon replaced by sensory overload and discomfort as we struggled to keep our heads "above water" in this huge wave of sound. We had no choice but to swim. We felt a heavy, wet burden around and in us as our bodies slowly began to resonate with the overwhelming pressure of sound that for some was physically nauseating. When the first footsteps sounded in an acoustic hole created by the sudden retreat of the siren and when, in pitch darkness, we heard the clear echo of actors' cothurni, this distinct percussive sound on the empty stage brought relief from the physical burden and the deafening opacity of the siren. But calming as the new aural configuration seemed, the eerie echo and imminent staccato of the scurrying steps of the chorus announced further turmoil. Our immersion in a sensual (although involuntary) sound bath of the boat siren anticipated the coming bloodshed at the Theban court. Rendered vulnerable by sheer sound, we listened to the actors' voices, ears tuned to hear what they had to say. But what they uttered was again primarily defined by sound – the phonetic material of speech.

The effective use of sound and voice in theatre, apart from the textual content of drama, dates back to antiquity. In embryonic theatre events, religious rituals, tribal rites, and shamanistic séances, the magic power of sound was used to heal and celebrate, to lament and mourn, to attract the good spirits and scare the evil ones. The rhythms of drums and the melodies of primitive euphonic instruments prompted chant and dance that united all participants in a ceremony. This ability of raw sound to renew the communality of the event and to escape the dominance of the text was recognized by poets, painters, and theatre artists of the avant-garde who returned to "primitive" chant and dance, and the patterns of Balinese and African masks. Even a classical source of Western text-based dramaturgy, Greek tragedy, displays an aural/rhythmical structure that points to its oral and ritual provenance. Thanos Vovolis, known for his restoration of the acoustical resonance mask used in Greek theatre, found that tragic verses contained phonetic fragments (vowels, diphthongs, and syllables) inherited from the repertory of ecstatic lamentations. A substantial part of actors' speech material consisted of the ritual lamentation cry (*ololygmos*) rooted in the performance tradition of the Eleusinian mysteries. In Aeschylus' *Persians*, for instance, there are more than one hundred such occurrences.[10] The rendition of these archetypal sounds – incomprehensible vocal remnants from Dionysian rites – required a technique of voice formation and speech articulation entirely different from the psychological and intellectual manipulation of the actor's expressive powers in naturalistic theatre. Hence, the tragic actors' voices carried not only the textual content of the tragedy but also an aural texture travelling toward spectators engaged in communal listening to an oral performance of *mythos*. Their performance did not mean a mere articulation of the rhythmic structure of iambic or trochaic verses shaped by prosodic and rhetorical rules. When director Andrei Serban explored, with his actors, how to create "a sound which grows and turns into a cry," he turned to a classical example: "What is it then that touches us in *Electra*? What does Electra say during her long lament? It is difficult to determine … She repeats: 'eee.' It is simply what one hears: a prolonged 'e.' What does this continual repetition of a vowel mean? Nothing that can be translated; 'e' means nothing other than 'e.' The meaning is in the sound itself. The fundamental character of the tragedy can be rediscovered in this unique sound – impossible to translate."[11] Apparently, underneath the *mythos* ran an opaque story, embodied in the voices, verbal gestures, and actions of the actors. It is an aural tale of the world created from the magmatic state of matter by a strife of chthonic forces, Titans, Olympic gods, and men. As a primal story, still unrefined by literature, it could only be told through a visceral oral performance that stems from Dionysian inebriation with music, which Friedrich Nietzsche regarded as a source of tragedy. Phenomenologist of sound Don Ihde characterizes the immediacy of music (or sound) as a dense presence in which there is no purity of conceptual meaning. In doing so he follows Sören Kierkegaard, who describes primordial sound as the "pure sensuous," the "demonic," or the pregnancy of meaning that presents itself as music.

No words could put the audience of Magelli's *The Phoenician Women* in the centre of Thebes, burdened with the expectation of unavoidable tragedy, with the armies surrounding the city, the way the wailing siren did. Although it could be comprehended as mere incidental music that supports a dramatic situation, the long call of the siren, which is indeed an alarm, created an immersive space whose meaning could not be exhausted in its signalling function. Although its tone was sorrowful, what the audience heard was not only an atmospheric enhancement of the scene. The emotional urgency of its "tune" – a single elongated note – combined with the physical ability of the sound to form an auditory space, forced us to be there – that is, forced us into a ritual and sensorial co-presence. "Auditory space is very different from visual space," testifies sound artist, composer, and theoretician of sound environments R. Murray Schafer; he claims that "we are always at the edge of visual space, looking in with the eye. But we are always at the centre of auditory space, listening out with the ear."[12]

Ihde regards our involvement with sound through voice and listening as a pervasive bodily experience, and claims: "Phenomenologically I do not merely hear with my *ears*, I *hear* with my whole body … This may be detected quite dramatically in listening to loud rock music. The bass notes reverberate in my stomach, and even my feet 'hear' the sound of the auditory orgy … The bodily involvement comprises the range from soothing pleasure to the point of insanity in the continuum of possible sound in music and noise."[13] This ontological continuum of sound is what Maurice Merleau-Ponty calls the "singing of the world." Through our sensory and bodily presence in the world we are, in the Bergsonian sense, always already immersed in this "singing." "We *never* completely escape from the realm of perceptual reality," Merleau-Ponty writes, "and even the seemingly independent structures of categorical thought (of 'rationality') are ultimately founded in perception. We are always immersed in the world and perceptually present to it."[14] Interacting with the surrounding world, we discover phenomena through our body and our perceptive faculties before they become conceptualized in our consciousness.

Attending to the fluidity, temporality, and transience of theatrical events, and acknowledging sound as the material that best supports these traits, recent theatrical studies have begun to prioritize the aural paradigm in performance analysis. David Roesner, for example, points out "the musicalization of theatre" as a significant trend in contemporary staging and performance. In *Theater als Musik* (Theatre as Music, 2003), Roesner analyzes the work of Christoph Marthaler, Einar Schleef, and Robert Wilson and finds that they place rhythm, sound, tonality of speech, and musicality of performance at the centre of the aesthetic organization of their theatre pieces. Roesner's assertion that theatre should be considered as music goes beyond the comparison of a theatre piece to a musical composition. It is not the narrative or programmatic features of a specific performance that theatre shares with music, but rather the immediacy, materiality, and transience of sound. In other words, it is the dramaturgy of sound – that is, a compositional approach to the creation and structure of performance – that makes theatre music.

One particular occurrence of such dramaturgy that can be traced back to the avant-garde methods of sound-text poetry and physical performance is found in Marthaler's *Stunde Null oder Die Kunst des Servierens* (Zero Hour or The Art of Public Service, 1995), a work commemorating the fiftieth anniversary of the end of the Second World War. In a stage space designed by Anna Viebrock, reminiscent of a large school gymnasium, a recording studio, or a bunker, middle-aged German state functionaries are taught how to shake hands, deliver speeches and slogans through microphones, cut ribbons, roll out red carpets, and perform other routines that public servants should know. Undressed for exercise, these sorry-looking individuals in singlets and shorts go through an exhausting physical and vocal drill interspersed with nostalgic singing numbers. In one of the most impressive scenes, actor Graham Valentine delivers a long verbal cavalcade in which the official four-language text of the 1945 Allies Control Council regulations gradually dissolves into the incomprehensible sound poetry of Dadaist Kurt Schwitters. A London reviewer described it thus: "a crescendo of sound and fury signifying nothing – and everything … As his speech becomes more and more nonsensical, turning towards gibberish and pure vocal sound, it actually makes more and more 'sense,' shifting from bureaucratic jargon, meaningless in its edited form, to a vocal evocation of the war's soundscape (through the syllables of Kurt Schwitters: trucks, machine guns, bombs, crackling radio reception, etc.), which becomes easily comprehensible as an eerie echo with a fifty year delay."[15] Marthaler's skewed perspective on "zero hour" (a military term for the beginning of an operation), with all its socio-political and historical ramifications, obviously resonated with German spectators, but the show became a hit not primarily for its ironic historical content but for its sovereign display of theatricality. Marthaler's *mise en scène* for *Zero Hour* offers "new cohesive strategies and elements: the investigation of voices, the musical [rhythmic] development of a visual or acoustic motif, the experience of time, or the sonority of space."[16] In this perspective, his deliberate shift from a strictly referential language to an oral and physical travesty of celebratory routines can be regarded as a legacy of the dramaturgy of sound introduced by Futurist and Dada sound poetry and performance.

In her prolegomena for a new aesthetics of theatre, *The Transformative Power of Performance*, Erika Fischer-Lichte identifies a process of the "performative turn" that "redefined the relationship between the *materiality* and the *semioticity* of the performance elements, between signifier and signified."[17] Started in the historical avant-garde and enriched in the neo-avant-garde of the 1960s, this process reached its fruition in postdramatic theatre. Clearly, experiments with the aural substance of words were among the early manifestations of this shift. Filippo Tommaso Marinetti's poetics of onomatopoeia and "lyrical intoxication with matter" and Nikolai Burliuk's notion of "verbal texture," for example, shifted the focus from the meaning of words to their sound, favouring sensory attraction over communicational clarity. Their sound poetry of incomprehensible words, cries, breathing, whispering, glossolalia, and onomatopoeic vocalizations of noise was designed to provoke the audience's subliminal reflexes rather than to create a mimetic illusion or deliver a message. The gravity and opacity that these avant-garde poets added to their idiom by favouring pure sound prompted the vigorous emergence of materiality in theatre. This was nothing but a "performative generation of materiality," which, as Fischer-Lichte suggests, contemporary theatre artists attain primarily by the "corporeality, spatiality, and tonality of performance."[18] It was this avant-garde insistence on the materiality of the theatrical sign/sound and the immediacy of oral/aural performance that had instigated the push toward the phenomenological, as opposed to the semiotic, approach in theatre studies. Thus, leaning much more toward a phenomenological than a semantic analysis of performance, Fischer-Lichte embarks on a thorough investigation of voice and sound that inspired an "acoustic" or "sonic turn" in the more recent theoretical discourse.[19]

Similarly, Lehmann admits the dramaturgy of sound into his concept of postdramatic theatre, when envisioning "a theatre of states and of scenically dynamic formations ... [in which] there is a *scenic dynamic* as opposed to the dramatic dynamic."[20] The idea of "scenic dynamic" coalesces with the method of juxtaposition of aural and visual masses and intensities first employed in the avant-garde's hybridization of art forms and experiments with sound as an independent scenic element beyond its illustrative dramatic role. Lehmann acknowledges the significance of this legacy in his discussion of the audiovisual scenic dynamic of John Cage's *Roaratorio: An Irish Circus on Finnegans Wake* (1979), a sound/dance/theatre work performed by the Merce Cunningham Dance Company at the Avignon Festival in 1985. In this performance Cage's vocal rendition, in the manner of a sound poetry reading, represented a counterpart of Joyce's writing "that opened up a new era of ways of dealing with language material: transgressions of the boundaries between national languages, condensations and multiplications of possible meanings, and musical-architectonic constructions. Postdramatic theatrical signs are situated in the tradition of such textures."[21]

In addition to the "roar oration" of the script, the piece included live music by an Irish traditional band and recordings of concrete sounds of pub crowds, radio broadcasts, street traffic, barking dogs, and crying babies captured at numerous locales of the novel, which culminated in an excessive cacophony. As Robert Bean claims, *Roaratorio* "engages such heterogeneity of sounds and noises that disruption and disorientation are paramount ... [It] requires a distinct mode of auditory experience – what I call *polyphonic aurality*. This term, implying simultaneously the opening of numerous ears and the production of an incomprehensible sound collage, also alludes to a renewal of collective hearing ... *Roaratorio* can be best described as sixty minutes of *prepared noise*. This creates an aesthetic of both anxiety and pleasure ... [where] we witness the 'activity of sounds.'"[22]

In *Roaratorio*'s stage version, its dense aural material served not as a ballet score to be choreographed but as a soundscape to be counterpointed by dancers' movements and figures. Here the usual dramatic scheme, relying on program music, choreographed dance, and written libretto, was replaced by the scenic dynamic of a postdramatic sound/dance/theatre work. The signs of this conceptual and practical change are abundantly present in the corpus of Futurist and Dadaist sound poetry, manifestos, and performance. They reveal a dynamic range of sonic creation, from an intuitive onomatopoetic vocal utterance to the use of sound as the autonomous material of theatre production. Thus, following the historical avant-garde's experimentation, sound came to be understood and dealt with as substance rather than as a means of signification and communication. As such, it prompted the emergence of an "independent auditory semiotics" in postdramatic theatre that I refer to as the "dramaturgy of sound."

Another facet of avant-garde sound poetry's expressive power builds on the endless conflicting relationship between visuality and aurality reflected in the clash between the shape of letters and the sound of phonemes, between written/printed text and vocal utterance. Avant-garde poets consciously played on the interstice between the poem's graphic representation and its oral performance. An example of such practice is Filippo Tommaso Marinetti's *Zang Tumb Tumb*, a verbo-voco-visual book/sound poem with a title drawn from the noise of howitzer fire. On its pages, the visual force attained by the typographical revolution unleashes the vocal force of *parole in libertà*, whose dynamic declamation will echo the noises of the modern battlefield. Letters of different shapes, sizes, and levels of boldness, printed, written, drawn, or stenciled confront the irregular gaps of white space on the paper. Graphic symbols thus achieve an uneven visual rhythm of redundancy and sparseness, triggering a cacophonous vocal interpretation. Words explode on the page just as the sounds of war burst onstage in Marinetti's famous onomatopoeic rendition.

It is such verbo-voco-visual clash that ignites Steve McCaffery's frantic vocal performance at a Glasgow festival of experimental sound, Instal 09, in March 2009.[23] It originates from the chaotically "organized" visual space of the poems *Carnival I* and *II*, written in the 1970s. The poems consist of typewriter-generated graphic tables in which the textual matrix, represented by swarms of letters – at times in the shape of readable sequences, at times utterly deformed in blotches – animate the visual play of words and figures. As McCaffery admits, "language units are placed in visible conflict, in patterns of defective messages, creating a semantic texture by shaping interference within the clear line of statement."[24] However essentially visual McCaffery's sound-text pages appear, when their swarming letters move into vocal performance, like the exploding letter-formations of Marinetti's *Zang Tumb Tumb*, they reach the audience as sounds and noises. In the end, it is the voice/sound that is at stake in performance. Thus, on the video of his vocal performance at Instal 09, we see and hear the poet obsessed with sound. His utterances encompass everything from the corporeal sounds of inhaling and exhaling to the articulation of standard speech elements, phonemes, syllables, and words – along with the emphatic production of the consonant sounds of sibilants, fricatives, and explosives – to the onomatopoeia of inanimate sounds, the mechanical tearing of material, shrieks, scrapes, and blows. A poetry reading becomes an energetic transfer of sounds in which all sound-producing capabilities of the performer's body are engaged. "Voice is the polis of mouth, lips, teeth, tongue, tonsils, palate, breath, rhythm, timbre and sound ... Enjoying such complexity, even a single voice resonates as simultaneity of corporeal, acoustic events,"[25] claims the poet.

The members of the Italian theatre company Socìetas Raffaello Sanzio, whose performances alongside compelling visual images contain a no-less-impressive layer of acoustic sensations, searched for the "lungs" of the words in preparing their *Tragedia Endogonidia*. One of the authors, Chiara Guidi, explains the kind of sound she is looking for in her letter to sound designer, composer Scott Gibbons, at the laboratory stage of the production: "None of the words I'd like to use have any necessity ... What type of voice do you think could bring out that obscure and hidden sound that accompanies the entrance of the audience, which only later might be recognizable as belonging to a voice? ... I am not thinking about texts but emulsions of sound, built up rhythmically and then covered with their own breath. I want to get between the folds of the specific sound ... or get inside the cry of an animal and move it and shake it in a dramaturgical key."[26]

Tragedia Endogonidia, a theatrical project in eleven installments, was produced in the course of two years in different European cities. In its second part, performed at the 2002 Avignon Festival, the authors wanted to excavate a language, a voice, or a living sound of the mythological animal *tragos*, which pulsates throughout the entire tragic poetry of humankind. A live goat that appears physically onstage in one of the later episodes of *Tragedia* needed an oral/aural reality. Therefore, the company put together the *tragos*'s "text" by rehearsing grammatical drills with scattered letters/phonemes drawn from the names of twenty amino acids, the chemical components responsible for carrying the energy of living creatures. Their inhaling/exhaling exercises were conceived as gymnastics for the throat that would deliver bodily secrets through vocal utterance and give voice to a possible oral "writing" of the endogenous growth of the human tragedy. This ritual digging deep into the human/animal body in search of vocal expression, hidden underneath verbal signification and the graphic appearance of letters, reveals workings of the dramaturgy of sound and comes close, at least as a formal practice, to the ideas and methods of Marinetti's parole in libertà and McCaffery's performance poetry.

Using another technique of avant-garde sound poetry, the structural counterpoint of different verbal textures, Austrian playwright Elfriede Jelinek, in place of dialogue, creates a collage of "speech/language plates" (*Sprachflächen*) by manipulating texts of different (low and high) styles and juxtaposing blocks of their verbal sound to each other. Her juxtaposition of "language surfaces" inaugurates sound/speech as an independent, both visceral and constructive, theatrical material used in contrast to the dramatic dialogue. The method of such oral/aural composition in Jelinek's plays "corresponds to the turning point of painting in modernity when, instead of the illusion of three-dimensional space, what is being 'staged' is the picture's plane-ness, its two-dimensional reality, and the reality of colour as an autonomous quality,"[27] observes Lehmann. The "planeness" here does not mean flatness or artistic impoverishment. On the contrary, it means an enrichment of the substantial artistic form and matter by the avant-garde shift away from the illusionistic, narrative, and figurative methods of bourgeois art. It means a turn toward the "creation of painterly forms as ends in themselves," shaping a new painterly realism that would liberate "colour oppressed by common sense, enslaved by it," and let it live as "a painted surface – a real living form,"[28] as pioneer of abstraction Kazimir Malevich put it. His friends, Russian Cubo-Futurist sound poets, conceived of "language texture," borrowing the term from contemporaneous painters who treated paint as palpable mass rather than as a mere carrier of pigment. In their poetic language beyond sense called zaum, words were treated as clusters of sounds bearing aural density amassed in a poem in a way comparable to the use of thick strokes of paint on canvas. Consequently, the theatrical language of Russian Futurists was to be exclusively valued not as the speech of characters, but as an oral/aural structure in which sound appears on an equal footing with the other elements of theatre. There is hardly a better example of such cross-fertilization between artistic disciplines than the collaboration between Suprematist painter Malevich, zaum poet Alexei Kruchenykh, and composer and painter Mikhail Matiushin, in the 1913 production of the first Futurist opera, *Victory over the Sun*.

Italian and Russian Futurists, together with other historical avant-gardes, adopted a dual oral/aural idiom of theatre that merges the sensuality and corporeality of the performers' voice with the structural disposition of the concrete and abstract sound on stage. These two inextricably intertwined aspects of theatrical creation determined the evolution of the avant-garde dramaturgy of sound based on the orality of the performer's vocal exposure and the aurality of the stage's sonic composition and construction. The first aspect, which draws from the power of vocal sound to express inner emotional, libidinal intensity, and the performer's bodily presence, marks the orality of performance. Beginning with Futurist "lyrical intoxication with matter," in poetry, and *fisicoffolia* (body madness), in theatre, it includes Expressionist *Schrei* (scream) acting and the incantational idiom of Antonin Artaud's theatre of cruelty. It promotes a performance style that celebrates the performer's presence, on the stage and in the world, through his/her self-realization in/by a non-discursive language. More recent epitomes of this style, which communicates the body/voice straight to the audience's senses, are performances of New York's Living Theatre, Peter Brook's *Spurt of Blood*, and Herman Nitsch's *Theatre of Orgies and Mysteries*. Their visceral performance idiom attempts to erase the liminal line between life and stage (life's double) by unrestrained physicality of stage presence, which Artaud called "the encounter of one epidermis with another in a timeless debauchery."[29] It falls in line with postmodern discourse on theatre's corporeality, exemplified by Roland Barthes's notion of "the grain of the voice," a sensual bridge between the body and the performance, and Jean-François Lyotard's plea for an energetic theatre that produces forces, intensities, and affects as "pulsional displacements" instead of "representational replacements."

In its second aspect, the dramaturgy of sound focuses on the materiality of sound *per se* as an independent, simultaneously concrete and abstract element of theatre that Marinetti envisioned as "an abstract and alogical pure drama of pure elements ... and surprising combination of blocks of typical sensations."[30] It was in this theatrical tradition that sound was conceived as palpable matter and used as malleable mass, comparable to paint or clay. This allowed sound to participate in the building of the spatio-temporal reality of the stage, either as a sonic/sculptural mass determined/liberated by its temporal flux – in the manner of Art Informel, or as a series of aural formations, blocks of sound/noise/silence available for techniques of collage and juxtaposition – in the manner of Cubist and Constructivist art. A similar transgression of sound into the sphere of plastic arts is notable in the experimental stage designs of Giacomo Balla, Fortunato Depero, and Enrico Prampolini. These designs are associated with the concept of the *complesso plastico motorumoristo* (the plastic motorumorist complex), which was initially invented to describe the creation of robot-like "polyexpressive artificial living beings." Adopting a broad approach to the audio-visual hybridity of art, these authors synthesized all that was seen and heard on the stage into an abstract, noisily kinetic compound of scenic action and architecture. All the structural elements of the Futurist stage – including sound understood as physical matter – thus acquired a dramaturgical value. Consequently, a dramaturgy of matter (objects, colour, light, and sound) supplanted customary dramatic plot and character development to create an audio-visual, kinetic theatre regarded today as postdramatic. Futurist discoveries, together with Kandinsky's abstract synaesthesia, prefigured the Bauhaus's "theatre of totality" as well as more recent theatre forms, such as Robert Wilson's "theatre of images" and ensuing stage experiments by the Socìetas Raffaello Sanzio, the Theatregroep Hollandia, and Christoph Marthaler – to mention but a few protagonists of postdramatic theatre whose works will be discussed later in the book. First, in the next chapter, we need to examine the conceptual change, in the approach to sound as artistic material in the cultural and historical context of the twentieth century, that made this theatrical development possible.

2

Avant-garde and Postmodern Conceptions of Aurality

A CENTURY OF SOUND SATURATION

The art of the early avant-garde emerged in the first decades of the twentieth century when the peaceful soundscape of countryside and unspoiled nature, a welcoming refuge for the artist's lyrical soul, had been overwhelmed by the cacophonic, soiled sound of expansive technology, speedy communications, political strife, and frantic city life. In the century that broke out with noise brought about by the surge of industrialization, sheer sound, a most affective/effective[1] sensory attraction became a substantial element of all the arts. In *Noise, Water, Meat*, Douglas Kahn avows: "Sound saturates the arts of this century, and its importance becomes evident if we can hear past the presumption of mute visuality within art history, past the matter of music that excludes references to the world, past the voice that is already its own source of existence, past the phonetic taskmastering of writing."[2]

Indeed, the present discourse in visual arts has been finally "un-muted" by the inclusion of the temporality, kinetics, and aurality of a work of art in its vocabulary. Listening to these terms we can hear reflections of Futurist and Dadaist ideas of fluidity, simultaneity, and "the painting of sounds, noises, and smells." Listening to contemporary musique concrète we can hear extensions of Luigi Russolo's art of noise, which introduced an ocean of raw, non-harmonic sounds to the sphere of music. In the sound-text poetry of today, we attend to the interplay of graphemes, phonemes, and vocal gestures instigated by Filippo Tommaso Marinetti's onomatopoeia and Velimir Khlebnikov and Alexei Kruchenykh's language beyond sense, *zaumny yazyk*, that deals with the "word as such" and its phonetic roots rather than its conceptual meaning. In the most recent performance events and theatre productions, we hear an interplay of live, recorded, and electronically treated sounds that transcends vocal expression and dramatic writing to reach toward a pure acoustic art. All of this marks a breakthrough of aurality in the arts at the beginning of the twenty-first century that initially appeared as the historical avant-garde's genuine answer to the twentieth-century phenomenon – sound saturation. Confronted with the din of the industrialized world, the avant-gardes chose to immerse themselves in the swirl of here and now rather than look for an idyllic hideout of serenity and the sublime, celebrated by the *passéist* poetics of the Belle Époque. It fell to the Futurists, the self-proclaimed knights of merciless change, speed, and violence, to be first to embrace the excitement of the burning dynamism and cacophony of a new age, and to announce the renewal of the sensibility of modern humankind.

"The Founding and Manifesto of Futurism," written by Filippo Tommaso Marinetti and published on 20 February 1909 as a paid advertisement on the front page of *Le Figaro*, the most influential daily of Paris, broke the news of the movement's birth to the world. Marinetti was an accomplished free-verse poet and strident declaimer of poetry (collected in *La Conquête des Étoiles* and *Destruction*); an internationally acclaimed publisher of the journal *Poesia* in Milan; a rather notorious playwright of scandalous theatre pieces in the style of Alfred Jarry (*Le Roi Bombance* and *Poupées Électriques*); and a brilliant polemicist famed as "the caffeine of Europe." His proclamation of the new poetics was fashioned as a calculated bang, a provocation typical of Futurist aggressiveness: "We intend to sing the love of danger, the habit of energy and fearlessness … Up to now literature has exalted a pensive immobility, ecstasy and sleep ... The poet must spend himself with ardor to swell the enthusiastic fervor of the primordial elements … We want to free this land from its smelly gangrene of professors, archeologists, ciceroni and antiquarians."[3] In numerous, similarly intoned manifestos that followed, Marinetti kept calling for subversive changes in art and life: these included a "re-construction of the universe" based on a new sensibility; admiration for the modern age of industry, machinery, electricity, speedy communications and traffic; and even praise for "war as the only hygiene of the world."

The explosive power of social, commercial, and technological development had been best felt in a modern industrial city, a hitherto unknown hive of activities in which a buzz produced in the clench between machines and men never stopped. Writing about a megalopolis, painting it, and echoing its noise in music and performance, all avant-gardes acquired an urban and, consequently, international character. Metropolitain in spirit, Marinetti's first manifesto soon spread from Paris to London, Berlin, New York, and Tokyo. Many artists of these world centres were captivated by the birth of the metropolis, a place of toil and joy, a Moloch-like beast devouring working people, a glittering attraction for a new urban personality, a *flâneur*, and a place "where thousands of actors of different temperament, habit and character competed for the major parts."[4] In his writings that precede Futurist immersion in life, Jules Romains remembers how he felt lost in the rhythm and noise of the crowd and traffic at the Parisian Rue d'Amsterdam. Carried by metropolitan "feverish pulsations," in the 1908 book of poetry *La vie unanime* he exclaims: "I am a joyous intersection of rhythms, a condenser of universal energies … The *unanime* vibrates in my brain: the city becomes my body." Romains feels his sensual aura dispersing through the city, its barracks, factories, offices, cafés, carriages, trams, and boulevards full of people, in which passersby "join each other and join my body." Becoming one soul with a mass of city dwellers, he feels *unanime* (unanimous) with the pulsation of the metropolis that is "nothing but a stream of force in which the rhythms are steeped."[5] Romains's Unanimist perception of the buzzing metropolis laid a setting for Marinetti's manifestos and poetry of a "lyrical intoxication with matter," and for Luigi Russolo's composition for noise intoners, "Awakening of a City," which was a response to the wonderment of the metropolitan life expressed exclusively by means of sound.

Symptomatically, Marinetti's founding manifesto of Futurism begins with a lyrical neo-Romantic story that tells of a night of "feverish insomnia" suffered by the poet and his friends, exhausted with the boredom of petit bourgeois life. Responding to the call of "the mighty noise of the huge double-decker trams" and the "famished roar of automobiles," they rush out to the streets of the metropolis, enchanted by its clamour. Prophets of speed and noise for whom "a roaring car that seems to ride on grapeshot is more beautiful than the *Victory of Samothrace*," they jump in their cars, "snorting beasts" with "torrid breasts … like serpents of explosive breath."[6] Marinetti's vocabulary, loaded with auditory implications, determines the character of the manifesto: it is definitely noisy. Its noisiness arises from the artist's intuitive and sensual confrontation with the new type of sound ushered into the world by new technology. Steven Conor claims: "The artificial amplitude of sound is one of the great inventions of the 20th century. Modernity may be defined as the coming of the human capacity to make inhuman noise. The great shock of the modern city and of the modern warfare that was in extrapolation were not so much the experiences of their disorientating energy and speed, as their sheer noisiness, the appalling, exhilarating, omnipresence of man-made or mechanical sound: of cars, sirens, gramophones, loudspeakers, cannons, airplanes and industrial machinery; all the dinning cacophony of the modern."[7]

For the Futurists the convulsions of the emerging industrial world materialized as a shrill noise that was hard to listen to and a red-hot sight that was difficult to watch. This sound image is conveyed in the depiction of the volcano crater that figures significantly in Marinetti's later writings. Such an unbearable vista (or soundscape) represents an equivalent to the primeval sight of chaotic magma that the old Titanic gods had been facing before the Earth solidified in the shape available to the Apollonian gaze of the new Olympian gods. Friedrich Nietzsche wrote in *The Birth of Tragedy from the Spirit of Music* that the powerful sight of world creation could be captured only by the Dionysian music of intoxication, still unrefined by reason. Music, he thought, was superior to all other arts because it did not represent a phenomenon but rather the "world will" itself. It served as a non-representational bridge between the world of the unknown and the creative impulse, which, as Sören Kierkegaard put it, brings about a demonic pregnancy of meaning that presents itself as music. Nietzsche's notion of Dionysian music undeniably inspired Futurists' dealing with life's "sound and fury" through the onomatopoeic mimesis of worldly noise. "The Futurist Synthetic Theatre" manifesto of 1915, thus, reads: "reality vibrates around us, hitting us with *bursts of fragments*, with events among them embedded one within the other, confused, entangled, chaotic ... Just as the painter and composer discover, scattered through the outside world, a narrower but more intense life, made up of colours, forms, sounds and noises, the same is true *for the man gifted with theatrical sensibility, for whom a specialized reality exists that violently assaults his nerves*: it consists of what is called THE THEATRICAL WORLD."[8]

Therefore, we can consider Marinetti's inflammatory founding manifesto programmatic for the acoustic turn in the arts and theatre of the twentieth and twenty-first centuries. "We will sing of great crowds excited by work, by pleasure, and by riot; we will sing of the multicolored, polyphonic tides of revolution in the modern capitals; we will sing of the vibrant nightly fervor of arsenals and shipyards blazing with violent electric moons; greedy railway stations that devour smoke-plumed serpents ... adventurous steamers that sniff the horizon; deep-chested locomotives whose wheels paw the tracks like the hooves of enormous steel horses bridled by tubing; and the sleek flight of planes whose propellers chatter in the wind like banners and seem to cheer like an enthusiastic crowd."[9]

THE SUBVERSIVE POWER OF NOISE

The avant-garde artists of early-twentieth-century Europe rebelled against history, the permanence of aesthetic values, and art as an institution. They questioned the existence of masterpieces and renounced the myth of the progress of civilization, declaring it a spurious advancement to an ersatz apex achieved only by imitating and replicating past paradigms. Their manifestos were thundering indictments against tradition. The Italian Futurists announced: "We must shake the gates of life, test the bolts and hinges ... Come on! Set fire to the library shelves! Turn aside the canals to flood the museums!"[10] The Russian Cubo-Futurists claimed: "The horn of time blows through us in the art of words ... Pushkin, Dostoevsky, Tolstoy, etc. etc., must be thrown overboard from the Ship of Modernity."[11] And Dadaist Hugo Ball insisted: "Our cabaret is a gesture. Every word that is spoken and sung here says at least one thing: that this humiliating age has not succeeded in winning our respect. What could be respectable and impressive about it? Its cannons? Our big drum drowns them ... Our spontaneous foolishness and our enthusiasm for illusion will destroy them."[12]

The anti-bourgeois tendency of the avant-garde was a reaction to the inadequacy of traditional art confronted with an increasingly fractured, mechanized, and conflicting world. Faced with "the shock of modernity" and a fragmented world picture – with what Marinetti called "the cinematic experiences of daily life" – modern artists rejected the passéist escape into the sublime and the production of illusions. Their offensive vocabulary often outraged members of European artistic circles. Composer Camille Saint-Saëns wrote to Marinetti after reading his founding manifesto:

> Sir,
> You predict that in ten years you will be thrown in the wastebasket;
> in my opinion one could do so now!
> Unleash the forces of the *unknown*!
> Open the floodgates of the impossible!
> Add to the fervor of primordial elements!
> All this rigmarole is perfectly ridiculous and
> I beg you not to continue sending me your review.
> I fear fisticuffs, which you extol;
> I am seventy years old and I wish to die in peace.[13]

Unfortunately, in the social reality there was no peace. The overriding narrative of bourgeois art – confirming the teleological path of historical progress carried out by the bourgeois state – had already produced a disappointing result: after only a decade of the promising twentieth century, the European nations were about to begin a mass slaughter of their own people in the First World War. The time was ripe for a riot against the establishment. Dissatisfaction with the existing state was tangible in the artistic manifestos and happenings that mushroomed across Europe. Expressionists portrayed a world where "man explodes in front of man."[14] Futurists energetically propagated the nationalist war frenzy. Dadaists refused to serve in the carnage and opted for anarchism, absurdism, and nihilism. This was "the moment when socially 'alienated' artists felt a need to disrupt and completely overthrow the whole bourgeois system of values, with all its philistine pretensions to universality,"[15] argues Matei Calinescu.

Meanwhile, institutional theatre moved along. Mainstream Parisian theatres kept producing Eugène Scribe's well-made plays. The Milanese audience enjoyed the grandiloquence and the pathetic heroism of Giuseppe Verdi, Giacomo Puccini, and Gabriele D'Annunzio. Richard Wagner's music drama, or *Gesamtkunstwerk* (total work of art), continued to hold sway with the Germanic theatre world, while Konstantin Stanislavski directed naturalist pieces of fine psychological detail for the Moscow Art Theatre. True, Aurélien Lugné-Poë, André Antoine, Georg Fuchs, Edward Craig, Vsevolod Meyerhold, and Sergei Eisenstein had shifted to experimental styles of mise en scène, promoting "director's theatre." But the avant-garde artists were far more vociferous in their demands. They wanted to put an end to bourgeois art as an institution organized into disciplines and removed from real life. They sought existence in a world where art and life are no longer separated.

The artistic uprising signalled by Italian Futurists almost immediately spread to Russia and Germany, where Cubo-Futurists and Expressionists participated in the germination of a proletarian revolution, and to Switzerland, where Dadaists took it over to a level of an absolute negation of any sense-making, even its own. Ball defined this artistic riot against the social and cultural status quo in a seemingly paradoxical but actually quite apt manner: "Dada is a farce of nothingness in which all higher questions are involved."[16] At the turn of the century, Nietzsche's and Henri Bergson's merciless critique of the "higher questions" of bourgeois creed – Cartesian logic and positivist science – brought the two philosophers to the cusp of European thought. European culture needed a Nietzsche and a Bergson to ventilate its brain, and Futurism and Dadaism to ventilate its lungs, so that it could think and breathe freer. Inspired by Nietzsche's "philosophy of the future," the Futurists embraced lyrical intoxication with matter. They bravely looked in the eye of the big turmoil of modern times, like a Dionysian chorus of satyrs watching *theomachia* in *The Birth of Tragedy*. They opted for *bruitism*, the cacophonic, onomatopoeic vocal reflection of the din of reality, instead of illusionistic musical or literary expression. At the same time, inspired by Bergson, Futurists strove for an art that reflects an intuitively experienced dynamic flux of "constant becoming." They, as Marinetti acknowledged, even considered "dynamism," a key word from Bergson's vocabulary, for a name with which to christen the new movement.

Italian Futurism, perhaps one of the boldest and most disruptive art movements of the time, was surely the noisiest. It was the noisiest not only for its uncompromising art-action happenings – public battles against old bourgeois art norms – but also for its *bruitist* performance style. Francesca Bacci even argues: "The real common thread of Futurism is not speed or dynamism, as long maintained by scholars, but the element of noise."[17]

Dadaists shared their performance-poetry methods with Futurists. Standing for an intuitive involvement in the world, a disruption of logic, and a creative irrationalism, noise figured prominently in the poetry and performance of both movements. Thus, Richard Huelsenbeck emphasizes: "*bruitism* is a view of life which, strange as it may seem at first, compels men to make an ultimate decision. There are only bruitists and others!"[18] From this, one might conclude that Futurists and Dadaists were, at the time, real brothers in arms.

Huelsenbeck, well known as Cabaret Voltaire's Dada Drummer, understood the Futurist obsession with the concrete. Accepting Marinetti's and Russolo's concepts, he suggested that, contrary to the abstract artists, who "maintained the position that a table is not the wood and nails it is made of but the idea of all tables," the Futurists wanted to immerse themselves in the angularity of things. "Along with tables there were houses, frying pans, urinals, women, etc. Consequently, Marinetti and his group love war as the highest expression of the conflict of things, as a spontaneous eruption of possibilities, as movement, as a simultaneous poem, as a symphony of cries, shots, commands, embodying an attempted solution of the problem of life in motion."[19] Thus, despite the two movements' opposite ideological sides in the First World War – Futurists siding with nationalist warmongers, Dadaists with internationalists and pacifists – Huelsenbeck, who in the 1920s promoted Dada as German Bolshevism, did not deem the Futurist love of war an inexcusable political attitude. He saw it as a consequence of their inclination toward the dynamism of life and its materiality. Later, he drew a line between Dada and Futurism, which was revered by "some imbeciles," as he put it. However, his idea of noise as a "direct call for action" connected two essentially activist, anarchic, and rebellious movements. As a result, many Futurist bruitist works made it into the repertory of the Cabaret Voltaire soirées while Dadaists' noisy nonsense of "rejecting normal logic and trusting to instinct," testifies Huelsenbeck, helped us "realize the existence of a structure in ourselves."[20]

In spite of the two movements' opposite socio-political positions, the artistic bond between Futurism and Dadaism hatched similar poetry/performance methods, which deserve to be explored in parallel. In spite of its significant artistic achievements, Futurism has been left in obscurity by critiques that focus on Benito Mussolini's appropriation of the movement for the glorification of the Fascist cause. But an analysis that would tackle the formal/material structure of poetry and performance in Futurism, instead of searching for its political misgivings, is seriously missing. However, plenty of Futurist artistic merits have been now discovered and accepted by the neo-avant-garde, in postmodern art, and in postdramatic theatre.

The shift in contemporary theatre historiography began with the writings of Michael Kirby, a leading American neo-avant-garde artist and theorist of the 1960s who encouraged this kind of formal/structural analysis. Applying his critical method, in 1971 Kirby published a seminal study on Futurist performance illustrated by an exemplary selection of manifestos and play scripts. More recently, in her keynote lecture for the Yale Futurist Conference (October 2009), Marjorie Perloff stressed, "A hundred years after its inception, Futurism remains a curiously misunderstood movement. The reviews of the recent Tate Gallery exhibition dismiss Futurism as inferior to Cubism and tainted by its Fascist connections." In her lecture, Perloff reevaluates the historical and aesthetic merits of Italian and Russian Futurism, asserting that they represent essentially one double-faced movement, a movement that ends with the First World War – in Russia with the victory of the proletarian revolution, and in Italy with Marinetti's alliance with the Fascists. She even claims that Marinetti was the only major Futurist who seriously tried to take Futurism into the Fascist mainstream. Perloff finds numerous, thus far largely disregarded, congruencies between the poetic principles and artistic methods of the Russian and Italian Futurists. In the same vein, the evidence gathered in my research of the dramaturgy of sound points to shared features of poetry, art, and performance in both varieties of Futurism, and in Dada, that originate from their formal rather than ideological aspects. Besides, if we examine the historical development of Italian Futurism, Russian Cubo-Futurism, and Dadaism, we shall see that in the 1920s all three of them were swallowed by ideology. While Italian Futurism was acknowledged by the Fascist academy as stately art, Russian avant-gardes around the journal *Left Front of the Arts* (LEF) and Constructivist groups soon started to serve the practical needs of the Soviet communist cause. A bit later, in France, André Breton's "Surrealist Revolution" and his agenda of liberating the subconscious absorbed Tristan Tzara's Dadaism. This political tendency ended up in Louis Aragon's blind leftist engagement. The appropriation of avant-garde artistic ideas on both ends of the political spectrum, and their practical inclusion in the political struggle, bore ambiguous and controversial consequences. Still, in spite of their contribution to the value of different ideological currencies, the formal features and aesthetic methods of the avant-garde art movements have been carried ahead and reached today's artistic practice. One should not consider these surviving features as merely formal. Futurist noisiness and Dadaist nihilism should be taken as signs of the inherent heteroglossia of the avant-garde idioms. Thus their sound poetry and performance, one may say, voiced an ideological stance as well. Their heteroglossia spilled over to the postmodern notion of ambiguity, not as an escapist strategy, but as a firm defence of genuine humanity against the big narratives of ideology and history. Or, as Ann Smock and Phyllis Zuckerman argued beautifully: "If the Revolution could be spoken, it would only be with a discourse that cannot assume a coherent position of truth, with a series of contradictory voices that cannot know themselves, which do not constitute a point of view, which repeat themselves and fall apart, only in order to be able to begin again."[21]

SOUND AND NOISE UNDER SCIENTIFIC SURVEILLANCE

In practical terms of economics and controllability, sound can be divided into three areas: the vocal sound of language communication, regulated by phonetics; musical sound, organized by its tonal and rhythmic composition; and noise, generally an unordered, wasteful aural mass. The third area is subject to a "negative" control, a pest-control-like sound abatement designed to protect human environments from noise pollution. The artistic embrace of noise was a significant factor in the avant-garde's attempted dethronement of traditional literature and music. As much as Marinetti's verbo-vocal experiments with onomatopoeic noise in parole in libertà (words set free) contributed to sound-text and performance poetry, Luigi Russolo's contemporaneous invention of the art of noises (one might think of *suoni in libertà* – sounds set free) contributed to the liberation of modern music from the dictates of tonality. "As it [sound] grows ever more complicated today, musical art seeks out combinations more dissonant, stranger, and harsher for the ear. Thus it comes closer to the noise-sound," asserts Russolo.[22]

Inclusion of noise in music is a still-viable artistic gesture adopted by contemporary composers, sound artists, and theorists. One of them, Torben Sangild, chooses noise as the prime subject of his aesthetics. He reminds us of the etymological root of "noise" in the Greek word *nausea*, which stands not only for sound of roaring sea but also for seasickness, and points to our unavoidable corporeal involvement with sound. Sangild interprets noise according to three aspects: acoustic, communicative, and subjective. In the acoustic sense, noise is defined "as impure and irregular, neither tone nor rhythm – roaring, pealing, blurry sound with a lot of simultaneous frequencies, as opposed to a rounded sound with a basic frequency and its related overtones."[23] Then, in communication theory, noise is defined as the distortion or impediment of the message whose quality depends on the signal/noise ratio. Communicational noise, that is, an obstruction of the signal, gets an aesthetic dimension when infused in music as a bearer of tension and dramatic power. Finally, from the subjective, emotional perspective of the listener, noise is usually deemed unpleasant. However, when addressing the contemporary art of sound, one should take into account the pleasure of discovery, and sensory fulfillment, induced for the listener by the ostensibly unpleasant amplification and diversification of aural attractions. In effect, all three aspects find their place in the dramaturgy of sound that consciously employs the acoustic and communicational impurity of theatrical signs/messages.

Jacques Attali's *Noise: The Political Economy of Music* sheds light on this phenomenon from another angle. It considers noise as a counterpart of music whose ritual ("primitive"), scored, and recorded forms reflect the historical socio-political changes that shaped the consumerist culture of modern capitalism. "Listening to music is listening to all noise," explains Attali, "realizing that its [noise's/sound's] appropriation and control is a reflection of power that is essentially political."[24] Consequently, he explores noise in the context of its colonization and cultivation by music. The ordering and transformation of raw noise into discernible tonal forms, claims Attali, is a perpetual historical process, almost as important for society as the development of means of production: "More than colors and forms, it is sounds and their arrangements that fashion societies. With noise is born disorder and its opposite: the world ... Everywhere codes analyze, mark, restrain, train, repress, and channel the primitive sounds of language, of the body, of tools, of objects, of the relations to self and others. All music, any organization of sounds is then a tool for the creation or consolidation of a community, of a totality."[25] Consequently, Attali describes the cultural conditioning of sound as a historical process that passes through several sequential phases of turning noise into music: (a) listening, (b) sacrificing, (c) representing, (d) repeating, and (e) composing. Attali, in the end, believes in the struggle against the political use of music as a commodity and as entertainment. He envisions the socially positive outcome of the channeling of noise's subversive powers into the last phase of the historical process, which he calls "a true composition." This new epoch, Attali claims, "heralds the emergence of a formidable subversion, one leading to a radically new organization"[26] that will put an end to the establishment of a society of consumption and repetition ushered in by normative music. Although Attali's prediction comes close to Russolo's proposition of "the art of noises," his "formidable subversion" is of quite another sort: it pertains to the discourse of contemporary critical theories and cultural studies developed by the descendants of the Frankfurt School of social research. In contrast, the subversion initiated by Futurist onomatopoeic performance and Dadaist simultaneous sound poetry grew out of artists' intuitive response to surrounding noise and a pragmatic struggle with the raw sound material – a din of machines, traffic, communications, and warfare – rather than out of a conscious effort to impose a liberating sociocultural agenda.

However, Attali remains aware of the vital force of noise: "Our science has always desired to monitor, measure, abstract, and castrate meaning, forgetting that life is full of noise and that death alone is silent: [It has forgotten the] noise of work, noise of man, and noise of beast. Noise bought, sold, or prohibited. Nothing essential happens in the absence of noise."[27] Futurists, who understood that very well, reacted to noise noisily and to life with live performance. Marinetti and friends threw onomatopoeic sound bombs and vocal bursts of shrapnel fire at their audiences, who responded with rotten tomatoes – a fair exchange between anarchistic avant-garde artists and bourgeois audiences. At least, in performances at the Futurist serate, there was no fake representing, repeating, and selling of passéist goods to the consumerist public. As Balilla Pratella wrote in his

"Manifesto of Futurist Musicians": "*well-made music* [is] the falsification of all that is true and great, a worthless copy sold to a public that lets itself be cheated by its own free will."[28]

Noise has always been kept under the surveillance of the dominant culture that preferred verbal syntax and musical harmony. The understanding of sound at the turn of the century was based on the ideology of the Enlightenment and on scientific positivism, which held that all phenomena are detectable, observable, and explicable in terms of Cartesian logic. As Jonathan Sterne observes in *The Audible Past*, despite new dimensions of hearing and listening that erupted with modernity, traditional science remained definitely under the spell of rationality: "As there was an Enlightenment, so too was there an 'Ensoniment.' A series of conjunctures among ideas, institutions, and practices rendered the world audible in new ways and valorized new constructs of hearing and listening. Between about 1750 and 1925, sound itself became an object and a domain of thought and practices, where it had previously been conceptualized in terms of particular idealized instances like voice or music. Hearing was reconstructed as a physiological process, a kind of receptivity and capacity based on physics, biology, and mechanics. Through listening techniques people harnessed, modified, and shaped their powers of auditory perception in the service of rationality."[29]

In 1863, one of the most notable scientists of the nineteenth century and a pioneer of the philosophy of science, Hermann Ludwig Ferdinand von Helmholtz (1821–1894), published a book called *On the Sensations of Tone as a Physiological Basis for the Theory of Music*, a canonical resource of traditional musicology. Helmholtz conceived his theory of music as an amalgamation across "the boundaries of *physical and physiological* acoustics on the one side and *musical science and aesthetics* on the other."[30] His theory of music stemmed from a belief in the civilizing, cultural power of science and empiricist philosophy that correlates aesthetic perception and the laws of nature. Exploring physical acoustics in detail, Helmholtz defended a theory that sound arises from the motion of elastic bodies. Additionally, he investigated physiological and psychological aspects of perceived sensorial stimuli produced by sound.

Devoted to the experimental method, Helmholtz even constructed experimental devices (such as Helmholtz's resonator) that enabled him to demonstrate how series of physical impulses produce vibrations of the air that result in audible sensations. If repeated with sufficient rapidity, these impulses generate sounds, which, if the impulses recur with perfect regularity and in precisely equal time, become musical tones. Interpreted mathematically as ratios of small whole numbers, such tones provide syntactic material for musical composition based on harmonic intervals. In contrast, irregular agitation of the air produces only noise, considered undesirable for musical composition. Helmholtz's theory of harmony and musical scales, intervals, consonances, and so forth pertain to the field of physical acoustics. But it is his exploration of the physiological and psychological processes of the perception of musical sounds in the human ear that has earned him prominence in musicology. Connecting physical acoustics with the theory of sensations, Helmholtz was able to analyze the perception of sound as a formative element of human emotions caused by the sensory reception of musical movements. "The properties of musical movements which possess a graceful, dallying, or a heavy, forced, a dull, or a powerful, a quiet or excited character, and so on, evidently chiefly depend on psychological action,"[31] argued Helmholtz. His discovery of the interdependence of the physical movement of sound and its aural, psycho-physiological reception introduces Helmholtz's discussion into the field of aesthetics. Thus, his book became the foundation of a modern theory and aesthetics of music.

From the contemporary perspective, however, a weak point of Helmholtz's theory is that he considered music as an art consisting exclusively of concordant or harmonic sounds rhythmically ordered in time. His scientific tools were designed to analyze only physically measurable elements of sound used in music: pitch (including melody and harmony); rhythm (including tempo and meter); and the sonic qualities of timbre, articulation, dynamics, and texture. This approach, overtaken by the musicology and aesthetics of music at the turn of the century, was awaiting the Futurists' furious renewal of sensibility and the breakthrough of the art of noise.

ORALITY AND LITERACY: THE AURAL/TEMPORAL VERSUS THE VISUAL/SPATIAL

Don Ihde criticizes positivist scientists for having forgotten that sound is strictly speaking invisible. He warns, "The scientific study of sound makes sound rational or measurable … reduced to or transformed into a visual pattern that becomes scientifically intelligible" while a real truth is that "visual phenomena tend to be spatially oriented; auditory phenomena tend to be temporally oriented."[32] Positivists' efforts to access experiential phenomena by discursive means remained consistent with the visual paradigm of the world favoured by Cartesian logic and the philosophy of the

Enlightenment. The acoustics of the nineteenth century could easily measure the intensity, pitch, tempo, reverberation, and diffusion of sound in a way that conformed to a spatial concept of the world, but it could hardly cope with sound in its permanent becoming, its fleeting presence on the brink between birth and death. Apparently, bonded to the visual/spatial paradigm of the world, positive science approached sound without due attention to its fluidity, transient character, and imminence – quintessential features of the aural/temporal paradigm of the world.

Our chirographic culture that writes/reads encoded graphic symbols (letters and words) to grasp phenomena – objects, creatures, actions, and qualities – has been developed on the power of a visual metaphor of the world. In his influential 1982 book *Orality and Literacy*, Walter J. Ong charts a distinction between oral and chirographic cultures. In terms of cultural theory, Ong adheres to the Toronto School of Communication Theory. Its members Harold Innis and Eric Havelock argued: "The introduction of handwriting as a mode of communication in ancient Greek civilisation prompted changes in the way philosophers conceived of truth and knowledge ... [while] before philosophical discourse and education transpired as an oral activity ... The media of writing and print shaped Western philosophic tradition from Plato down to the twentieth century."[33] Orality, on the other hand, imposes total sensory experience of the environment perceived in the immersive, omnidirectional, and synaesthetic field of sound. "People dwelling within acoustic space rely upon knowledge that they can remember and retell rather than upon visual proofs of observation and measurement that have to be referenced elsewhere ... They are kept open to discontinuities and mysteries as they are rooted in tradition, not in the empiricism of the visual space of print."[34]

Ong, obviously, prioritizes the oral culture paradigm insofar as it maintains an authentic contact with the world. He finds the term "oral literature," a customary name for the creative verbo-vocal practice of the not-yet-literate, somewhat oxymoronic: "Oral expression can exist and mostly has existed without any writing [literature] at all, writing never without orality."[35] But prior to the analysis of its implications in literature, Ong describes physical features of sound, such as its temporality and materiality: "There is no way to stop sound and have sound. I can stop a moving picture camera and hold one frame fixed on the screen. If I stop the movement of sound, I have nothing – only silence and no sound at all. All sensation takes place in time, but no other sensory field totally resists a holding action, stabilization, in quite this way. Vision can register motion, but it can also register immobility. Indeed, it favours immobility, for to examine something closely by vision, we prefer to have it quiet ... There is no equivalent of a still shot for sound. An oscillogram is silent. It lies outside the sound world."[36]

With this discussion of spatio-temporal distinction, which is sustained by the physical features of sound and vision, a significant cleavage between the visual and aural paradigms in the interpretation of the world (and consequently of the arts) opens. The awareness of two opposing but never-fully-separated aspects of the phenomenal world (sound and silence, movement and immobility, time and space) is what allowed for a renewal of aurality in postmodern aesthetics and cultural studies. This renewal first gained prominence in the philosophical work of Henri Bergson, who criticized the essentially static Cartesian world-view that relies on the sense of sight. The classic Cartesian notion of measurable, spatialized time is represented by a chronometer that shows its succession mechanically as visually discerned units (seconds, minutes, hours). Bergson, on the other hand, speaks of the phenomenal world as a single space-time continuum determined by "duration" (*la durée*), a constant flux of the phenomena that indicates our being in time. He imagined the unbreakable process of "coming into being" as a continual interpenetration of time and space in which we live so that it can only be grasped as a duration seen/felt from the inside and not observed from the outside.

Bergson invoked an aural paradigm of the world that profoundly influenced the art of the historical avant-garde, specifically its dealings with sound. In fact, Bergson himself used the metaphor of musical flow to illustrate his idea of the world in constant flux. Hearing, he thought, provides the experience of temporal duration that, like music, intertwines past, present, and future. In his ever-changing world, "there is neither an immutable substratum nor are there distinct states that appear and pass like actors on a stage. There is simply the continuous melody of our interior life, a melody that runs and will run indivisible, from the beginning to the end of our conscious existence."[37] Taking a cue from Bergson, Ihde elaborates his phenomenology of sound: "The ever-changing presence of sound is time-full. Sound is never static. It is coming into being and its passing from being is continual in its variations ... The constant temporality of sound presence is almost total."[38]

Nevertheless, the visual paradigm of the world based on a stable and discernible picture of reality has a long philosophical tradition. In his *Metaphysics* Aristotle affirmed: "Above all, we value sight; disregarding its practical uses, we prefer it, I believe, to every other sense, even when we have no material end in view. Why? Because sight is the principal source of knowledge and reveals many differences between one object and another."[39] René Descartes reinforced the authority of vision as our most truthful sense with his belief that the cognition of distinct phenomena constitutes humankind's only source of knowledge. Hence, he praised sight: "All the management of our lives depends on the senses ... [and] that of sight is the most comprehensive and the noblest of these."[40] The classic prevalence of visual perspective is most notable in the metaphor contained in the name "Enlightenment." This historical epoch, which strove to spread knowledge and establish an optimistic, positive, and rational view of the world, was named after a visual phenomenon – the shedding of light upon what was thought to have previously been a mystified, dark picture of reality.

Contrary to the Cartesian interpretation of the world in Apollonian visual terms of clarity and distinctness, in Futurist art sound lived its Dionysian predisposition for disturbance, creating a blurred but no less true image of reality. It lived not only on the brink of the aural and the visual – instinctual and cognitive – but also in the divergent inclinations in the artistic creation between noise-music and music proper. The latter dichotomy has its roots in ancient Greek mythology. In *The Birth of Tragedy*, Nietzsche describes a contrasting instrumental symbolism in the musical accompaniment of the performance where "the *aulos* reed-pipe represented Dionysean rudeness and the crafted, stringed lyre represented Apollonian serenity and order."[41] There is a myth that the first known player of the *aulos* was Marsyas, the satyr who after losing a musical contest to the lyre-playing Apollo was flayed alive for his hubris in challenging a god. The story of Marsyas links the tension between freedom and tyranny, moderation and excess, inebriation and sobriety, primitivism and culture to a significant opposition in the approach to noise/sound/music making. Nietzsche finds the lyre, or cithara, representative of "Doric architecture expressed in sound," stresses Steven Connor. "In a sense, Nietzsche seems to be saying, the music of the lyre is no longer music at all, but only the symbol of the higher, more abstract kind of music of mathematical relations. The lyre is identified with reason and measure, presumably because it includes within itself the regularly spaced intervals of the mode, or the octave. The strings arrayed in parallel approximate to the abstract picture of music provided by the stave."[42] In addition, plucking the strings on the lyre meant operating the instrument at a distance, while blowing in the aulos meant an immediate corporeal contact – its shrill sound was a direct result of the performer's physical efforts, an extension of his vocal gesture of excessive pain or joy.

As we see, vocal gesture, utterance, dramatic speech, and even blowing into an aulos all expose specific carnal and libidinal values of the performer/performance. It is because the vocal sound, produced by movements, frictions, and explosions of air in the body, always already exhibits its somatic aspects. But Connor alleges that it holds true for any sound: "Sound, wrote Aristotle (*De anima*, II. 8), is a kind of pathos, a suffering. The air is battered, stretched, percussed when there is sound. The voice never simply appears, but is expressed, its shape formed out of resistance. What resists the voice? The heaviness, the reluctant inertia of things, the world's weary wish to hold its peace. The voice must overcome this lethargy deep down things. It is a striving, and a disturbance: it subjects the world to strain."[43] Sound in its pure materiality – a physical disturbance of the air made audible, as Helmholtz explains, when thought of as a carnal emanation of the human spirit (breath or *pneuma*) – becomes an emotional, sensorial, and spiritual substance. That is what compelled postmodernist Connor to paraphrase Aristotle's musing on the aural pathos.

In a similar fashion, Roland Barthes's writing on "the grain of the voice" became paradigmatic for the actor's bodily presence in theatre performance. Barthes defines "the grain of the voice" as "a dual posture, a dual production of language and of music," a locus of "the encounter between a language and a voice," that is, a medium uniting performance and the performer's body.[44] For him, a vocal interpretation of an aria is a wider and more concrete phenomenon than a mere reproduction of a text or rendition of a musical phrase. It is, Barthes says, "a cantor's body brought directly to your ears ... from deep down in the cavities, the muscles, the membranes, and the cartilages ... The grain is that: the materiality of the body speaking its mother tongue."[45]

So what Aristotle describes as the pathos and suffering of physical sound becomes a *jouissance*, an erotic exchange between the performer and spectator conveyed by voice. The sound of the actor's voice gives a corporeal, sensuous dimension to the performance; it achieves an erotic reciprocity in an extra-textual communication, a communication in excess of the linguistic one. "Reciting or singing in front of others entails showing them something of one's body," suggests French psychoanalyst Pierre Fédida; "it also means discovering, in a flash, a given diffuse sensibility of our body. The voice is bodily matter – a pre-objective element quite unlike the objectivity of our ocular relation to the person and their capacity to represent themselves."[46]

Clearly, the presentational ability of voice/sound, in contrast to the representational features of the visual, coheres with Ong's distinction between the oral and the written. It lies at the root of the antitextual orientation in the sound poetry and theatre of the historical avant-garde. The onomatopoetic mime and bruitist declamations at Futurist serate, the return to the sound substance of language in the Russian beyond sense poetry of zaum, and the alogical verbal and vocal practices of Dadaist simultaneous poetry – all followed this very impulse toward a pre-objective quality of voice and its material realization in the sound of speech and performance.

SYNTHETIC THEATRE AND THE SYNAESTHETIC POTENTIAL OF SOUND

The popularity of synaesthesia in artistic circles at the beginning of the twentieth century was impelled by the mystical teachings of Esoteric Buddhism, Anthroposophy, and Theosophy promulgated by Madame Helena Blavatsky and Rudolf Steiner. The Symbolists were the first to thoroughly consider the potential of synaesthetic artistic expression based on chromatic or tonal features of sound and colour. They celebrated the *audition colorée*, of which Arthur Rimbaud's poem "Voyelles" (Vowels) provides a well-known case in point:

> A noir, E blanc, I rouge, U vert, O bleu: voyelles,
> Je dirai quelque jour vos naissances latentes:
> A, noir corset velu de mouches éclatantes
> Qui bombinent autour des puanteurs cruelles ...
>
> A black, E white, I red, U green, O blue: vowels,
> Someday I'll explain your burgeoning births:
> A, a corset, black and hairy, buzzing with flies
> Bumbling like bees around a merciless stench ...[47]

The Futurists and other avant-gardes soon adopted the idea of sound-colour correspondence. Thus, Nikolai Kublin, impresario of the Russian avant-garde and one of very few Cubo-Futurists to welcome Marinetti's 1914 visit to Moscow, wrote a manifesto entitled "What Is the Word?" in which he assigned each vowel its own pitch and each hard consonant its own colour. The poets Kruchenykh and Khlebnikov joined in by applying tactile and spatio-temporal qualities of vowels and consonants to the formation of words in zaumny yazyk. They understood "vowels as time and space (a characteristic of thrust), and consonants as color, sound and smell."[48]

On the side of the visual arts, Mikhail Larionov, inventor of Rayonism, argued: "Obviously, a blue spread evenly over the canvas vibrates with less intensity than the same blue put on more thickly. Hitherto this law has been applicable only to music, but it is incontestable also with regard to painting."[49] Similarly, Enrico Prampolini wrote a manifesto titled "Chromophony – The Color of Sounds," in which he claimed: "We conceive painting as an aggregation of chromatic vibrations ... The aim will be to encourage the optical appreciation of fine distinctions, atmospheric subtleties, and rhythmic influences of the atom, and to be able to express in chromatic terms the sound waves and the vibrations of all movements within the atmosphere."[50]

Obviously, both Larionov and Prampolini tried to give some scientific credibility to their artistic theories. However, although the idea of the vibrational nature of sound and colour has been established by experimental physics, in the arts it has been interpreted in a more mystical way as a fluid correspondence of sensory attractions aimed at the mutual reinforcement of the expressiveness of aural and visual material. Wassily Kandinsky, for example, who attended several of Steiner's lectures in 1908 and wrote about his appreciation for Mme Blavatsky in his 1911 essay "On the Spiritual in Art,"[51] advocated the dominance of spirituality in arts through his pseudo-scientific speculations on the nature of sound, colour, and form. He regarded aural and visual sensory attractions as conduits of "inner sound" (*innerer Klang*), the mystical vibration that reverberates between the artist, its object, and the spectator, and between soul and nature. Kandinsky contrived the idea of the "inner sound," an intrinsic fluid content that a painter senses in each object and reproduces for the viewer, from his experience working on canvas. He wanted to develop an abstract painting technique that would function in the same way as "musical sound [that] acts directly on the soul and finds an echo there." Arnold Schönberg, Kandinsky's composer friend, who was also a painter, likewise noted this affinity between music and painting: "Kandinsky and Oskar Kokoschka paint pictures in which the external object is hardly more to them than a stimulus to improvise in color and form and to express themselves as only the composer expressed himself previously."[52] This observation is just a step away from a claim in postdramatic theory that dramatic plot is no more than a stimulus for an audio-visual scenic structure created in the manner of music composition or kinetic sculpture.

In his memoir Kandinsky recounts that once, in the years of his youth, during a concert of Richard Wagner's *Lohengrin* at the Moscow Court

Theatre, he heard/saw, in a sort of hallucination, musical sounds as an abstract composition of colours. "The violins, the deep tones of the basses, and especially the wind instruments at that time embodied for me all the power of that pre-nocturnal hour. I saw all my colors in my mind; they stood before my eyes. Wild, almost crazy lines were sketched in front of me. I did not dare use the expression that Wagner had painted 'my hour' musically."[53]

This fascination inspired Kandinsky's practical exploration of synaesthesia through his experiments with links among colour, music, and human movement in theatre. Therefore, in 1909, he started to write plays named by sound-colour correspondences: *The Green Sound*, *The Black Sound*, *The White Sound*, *The Violet Sound*. For one of them, *The Yellow Sound*, Kandinsky engaged Russian Futurist composer Thomas De Hartmann to write "a radically antidiatonic, polychromatic score for his minimalist stage piece."[54] However, although published in 1912 in the *Blaue Reiter Almanach* in Munich, the work waited seventy years for its 1982 premiere performance at the Guggenheim Museum in New York.[55]

The Yellow Sound is an abstract play of colour and sound in six stage pictures. Its performers move on stage merely as bearers of colour, sculptural mass, and form, and produce indiscriminate sounds, as is evident from the original stage directions:

> The people resemble marionettes ... First there appear gray, then black, then white, and finally different-colored people. The movements of each group are different. Many of the groups are illuminated from above with stronger or weaker lights of different colors ... The background becomes dark blue in time with the music. Behind the stage we hear a chorus, without words, which produces an entirely wooden and mechanical sound without feeling. After the chorus finishes, a general pause: no movement, no sound. Then darkness. Lights. Five bright yellow giants (as big as possible). Very slowly, they turn their heads toward one another. The giants' very low singing, without words, becomes audible.[56]

"The sound of the human voice," Kandinsky insisted, has "to be pure, i.e.: without being obscured by words or meaning of the words."[57] This resulted in the almost complete absence of dialogue, plot, and sequential action in his play. It is obvious that music and noise together with light and movement were supposed to create, not a drama, but a kinetic performance bordering on visual and aural art installation.

In the introductory essay to *The Yellow Sound*, titled "On Stage Composition," Kandinsky elaborates a theatrical theory behind his staging. He argues that every art has its own language, externally discernible by the means it uses – sounds, colours, actions, and words – but internally these arts retain essentially the same idiom, one of the abstract attractions that the human soul attains as vibrations of the "inner sound." To Kandinsky, there are three distinct external elements used primarily for their inner value: "(1) musical sound and its movement; (2) bodily spiritual sound and its movement, expressed by people and objects; (3) color-tones and their movements (a special resource of the stage). Thus, ultimately, drama consists here of the complex of inner experiences (spiritual vibrations) of the spectator."[58] In spite of their idiomatic differences, these elements together create a play's dynamic structure, emanating its inner vibration that resonates in the spectator's soul.

Kandinsky's theory of stage composition made a significant contribution to avant-garde theatre in two respects. First, it established a dramaturgy of music, body/spirit (united in performer's presence), and colour in their kinetic relationships as three compatible stage elements; and, second, Kandinsky's theory left the ultimate sense of the play to the spectator's imagination. It provided an argument for the aural, kinetic, and sculptural dramaturgy later developed by Futurists, Dadaists, and the Bauhaus into a theatrical technique antecedent to postdramatic staging. *The Yellow Sound* was a pioneering application of Kandinsky's idea of abstract structuring of sound, image, and movement in theatre. It has been said that Expressionist and Bauhaus theatre innovator Lothar Schreyer "built a whole theory of performance on the expressive process first suggested in *The Yellow Sound*."[59]

Kandinsky's stage theory stood in stark contrast to the plot-and-character-based configuration of nineteenth-century theatre. He found the naturalist, slice-of-life theatre insufficient since it represented "in general the more or less refined and profound narration of happenings of a more or less personal character," while "the cosmic element was completely lacking."[60] Hence he banished anecdotal dramatic plot from theatre. Similarly, one of the first of Marinetti's theatre manifestos emphasized the Futurist disgust "with the contemporary theatre (verse, prose, and musical) because it vacillates stupidly between historical reconstruction (pastiche or plagiarism), psychology, and photographic reproduction of our daily life; a finicky, slow, analytic, and diluted theatre worthy, all in all, of the age of the oil lamp." As an alternative, Marinetti extolled a theatre of "all the new significations of light, sound, noise, and language, with their mysterious and inexplicable extensions into the least explored part of our sensibility."[61]

As much as psychological aspects of the performance-reception loop of theatre in general, whether dramatic or postdramatic, are relevant for performance analysis, they are not so sharply articulated in the historical avant-garde. Actually, the avant-garde developed a substantial disregard for individual psychology, pronounced above all in Futurist and Dadaist experiments with sound. Aside from the disrespect for psychologically motivated acting that mimed everyday human behaviour, Marinetti and Kandinsky had further motivations to remove psychology from their creative process. Their reasons were both corporeal and spiritual. Futurists wanted to immerse the audience in noise, to expose it to sensory overload without any pretension to create an understanding or empathy among spectators but simply to trigger their instinctual revolt – Futurists' oral/aural performance communicated on the psychosomatic rather than psychological level. Kandinsky, on the other hand, encapsulated the audiovisual and kinetic essence of the stage in emanations of "inner sound"; his abstract theatre pieces named after sounds conveyed spiritual energies of synaesthesia rather than psychological truths.

Kandinsky did not hide his ambition to create a *Gesamtkunstwerk* although he clearly expressed his disapproval of Wagner's work as the foremost promoter of the total work of art. He criticized the representational mode in Wagner's theatre as too programmatic, and his use of leitmotifs as too repetitive. While admitting that Wagnerian musical drama "created a link between movement and progress of music," Kandinsky argued that "the inner sound of movement did not come into play … [because] in the same artistic but still external fashion Wagner subordinated music to the libretto, that is … the hissing of red-hot iron in water, the sound of the smith's hammer, etc., were still represented musically."[62] Instead of the musical representation of something behind an action, Kandinsky sought the use of sound in its unmediated form, in which sound constitutes an action in itself. His interest in concrete sound was notable in the specific treatment of the human voice in *The Yellow Sound*, where he demanded actors utter pure concrete sound not "obscured by words and meaning." Kandinsky thus rejected the psychologically motivated exaltation, weeping, and emotional speech of characters that was habitual in naturalistic theatre in favour of the vibration of bodily sound and its movement as the basic elements of stage performance. Kandinsky's focus on the concreteness (or materiality) of sound and the dismissal of the anecdotal and the psychological represent two facets of the disruptive tendency of the avant-garde, leading away from the logic and discursive language of literature and art, which is a dominant line of the dramaturgy of sound reaching to the present.

AVANT-GARDE HYBRIDIZATION: TOWARD AN INTERMEDIAL THEATRE

The historical avant-garde appeared at a "climactic moment of rupture … the moment when the integrity of the medium, of genre, of categories such as 'prose' and 'verse' [as well as drama and theatre] and most importantly, of 'art' and 'life' were questioned,"[63] claims Marjorie Perloff. Clearly, the theatre of the avant-garde spoke this language of rupture and dissociation with existing cultural and artistic practice. It refused to obey distinctions of medium, genre, and artistic form. It developed an antitextual idiom no longer dominated by the literary drama, which focuses on the performance and the multimedia structure of the theatrical event (happening/kinetic installation). Consequently, it opted for an anti-art form based on the poetics of discontinuity and hybridization. Futurist evenings, *serate futuriste*, and Dadaist soirées at the Cabaret Voltaire are prime examples of the hybrid mixed-media events that made an early impact on avant-garde theatre. They contained declamations of parole in libertà, simultaneous renditions of sound poetry, readings of manifestos, installations of paintings, posters, and sculptures, and presentations of the new noise music, all assembled in the form of a happening. These *arte-azione* (action art) events soon became rallies at which poets, painters, sculptors, and musicians fought with all expressive means at their disposal against the *passatismo* of conventional art. Upon Marinetti's demand, from the first manifesto of Futurist playwrights, artists performed for the "pleasure of being booed," causing quarrels, riots, and physical conflicts. The unexpected sound of onomatopoeic poetry and eccentric verbalization of manifestos constituted part of their offensive arsenal. In the belief that "only theatrical entertainment is worthy of the true Futurist spirit," they staged these bombastic evenings in grand theatres all across Italy. *Grande Serata* at the Teatro Costanzi in Rome on 2 March 1913 exemplified a typical serata, containing a Molotov cocktail of agitations, invectives, extravagant theories, and provocative art. Its program included Giovanni Papini's speech against the city of Rome, Umberto Boccioni's talk on Futurist painting and sculpture (exhibited onstage), and Marinetti's bruitist declamation of poetry. The *eroiche serate* offered a controversial mixture of symphonic music – like *Inno alla vita* (Hymn to Life) by maestro Balilla Pratella, on later occasions joined by the machine music of Russolo's *intonarumori* (noise intoners) – and onomatopoetic poetry. Marinetti's own bellicose declamation of *Zang Tumb Tumb* was inevitably staged as the event's highlight, especially on the European tours of the Futurist "circus." The audiences, who came to hear a lecture or a poetry reading, would at once see an exhibition, listen to onomatopoeia of mechanical noise, and watch a synthetic theatre piece: they would find themselves immersed in a provocative hybrid of sound poetry, installation, happening, and performance.

An often-quoted case of transgression across the borders of conventional artistic genres is Oskar Kokoschka's *Murderer, the Women's Hope*, performed at the Vienna Kunstschau in a courtyard on 4 July 1909.[64] Kokoschka's hybrid piece was a sign of the avant-garde "performative turn" that liberated theatre from its representational mandates. The audience was scandalized and disgusted by the illicit cruelty of the performance, announced in advance by the visual rawness of two graphic posters for the piece. One of these posters, based on Kokoschka's already notorious self-portrait in Fauvist colours, was actually transposed into the performance itself. Its lines and colours were transferred to thick traces of paint smeared on the performers; nerves and blood vessels appeared on their bodies as if their skin had been literally turned inside out. This extroversion of man's inner self, executed by pragmatic use of visual means, not only adhered to the Expressionist theatre's demand that on the stage "man explodes in front of man" but also showed the artist's preoccupation with the materiality of his art. In the same vein, rather than clearly pronounced lines of verbal dialogue, actors – with their faces made up as masks from "primitive" cultures – produced wild cries, moans, and grunts. Kokoschka's emphasis on the visceral physicality of vocal gestures was intended to communicate performers' corporeal presence while omitting the figural and narrative procedures of drama. The auditory aspect of the performance represented not only an instant of Expressionist Schrei acting, but also a deeper plunge into pre-verbal vocal sound and art practice. The vocal gestures of the performers were amplified by the sound of archaic instruments, dissonant and rough, closer to noise than to music, expressing an uncomfortable mixture of pleasure and pain. Thus, besides relying on Fauvist colours, Kokoschka's piece drew on untamed sound, that is, on the expressive potential found in sound's materiality. It is important to highlight that *Murderer, the Women's Hope* was a play by a painter, and that this was typical of the historical avant-garde, where visual artists, poets, and musicians had often produced stage performances outside the institutional theatre. The creators of such performances were more concerned with the material of their art, sounds, objects, and images, and the kinetic sculptural environment of the stage, than with the plot, character, dénouement, and other elements of traditional drama. Hence, they turned to the interpolation of heterogeneous aural and visual materials in a work of art that would replace the linear narrative structure of the naturalistic theatre.

The concept of the hybridization of the aural and visual arts was put forward by Futurist synaesthetic theories like Carlo Carrà's "The Painting of Sounds, Noises, and Smells" and Enrico Prampolini's "Chromophony – The Colors of Sounds." Drawing their vocabulary from theories of sound and music, Futurist painters introduced primarily aural features of fluidity, loudness, temporality, and the interpenetration of time and space into a plastic arts discourse. At the same time, Futurist sound poets talked about thickness, opaqueness, weight, and palpability, introducing these features of painting and sculpture into their poetry creation and performance. The process was mutually enriching. Thus, painters Boccioni, Russolo, Carrà, Balla, Francesco Cangiullo, and Gino Severini, together with poets, actors, and musicians, created boisterous multimedia events of serate that informed the theatricality of Futurist synthetic pieces, again written and performed by artists of diverse profiles. Painter Russolo's daring tractate "The Art of Noises" was equally inspired by poet Marinetti's liberation of words and composer Balilla Prattela's enharmonic music. The first Russian Futurist opera, Kruchenykh's *Victory over the Sun*, was a theatrical extension of zaum poetry by painter Kazimir Malevich and composer Mikhail Matyushin. Khlebnikov's supersaga *Zangezi* reached its stage form designed and performed by Constructivist painter and sculptor Vladimir Tatlin. The list of interdisciplinary contributions by poets, painters, and musicians could easily go on, including Kandinsky, Kublin, Elena Guro, Natalia Gonchareva, Mikhail Larionov, and many others.

SOUND AND MEANING: PERFORMATIVE IDIOM VERSUS DISCURSIVE LANGUAGE

The focal point of the avant-garde's struggle against the existing art practice was the rejection of logocentrism and discursive language employed in fiction, poetry, drama, and the entirety of Western cultural production. The main target of "A Slap in the Face of Public Taste," a manifesto signed by David Burliuk, Alexei Kruchenykh, Velimir Khlebnikov, and Vladimir Mayakovsky in December 1912 in Moscow, was conventional poetry that uses a fossilized language emptied of life energies and is, as such, useless for art. The document reads: "We *order* that the poets' *rights* be revered: 1. To enlarge the *scope* of the poet's vocabulary with arbitrary and derivative words. 2. To feel an insurmountable hatred for the language existing before their time."[65]

To release language from its enslavement to rational thinking, Kruchenykh and Khlebnikov created zaumny yazyk, an idiom beyond sense. Zaum was a transrational, emotive, and intonational speech consisting of freely combined verbal roots, phonemes, and sounds. It harvested a vocabulary from ancient forgotten languages, vocal practices of schizophrenics, folk incantations, baby talk, glossolalia, and onomatopoeia. Zaum evolved from remnants of an *Ur-sprache* (proto-language) in which sounds and meanings were not yet alienated, kernels of primordial sound, "sound patches" that floated still alive within the language otherwise worn-out by practical use. Preferring the sound of language to its meaning, the poets of zaum relied on the phonemic rather than syntactic or signifying quality of the "word as such" for which Khlebnikov exclaimed: "the word is no tool for thinking anymore but material for art."

In numerous manifestos such as "New Ways of the Word: The Language of the Future, Death to Symbolism," Kruchenykh and Khlebnikov argued:

> before us there was no verbal art
> there were the pathetic attempts of servile thought to present everyday reality, philosophy and psychology … but
> *the art of the word*
> did not exist. …
> In art we have declared:
> THE WORD IS BROADER THAN THE THOUGHT
> the word (and its components, the sounds) is not simply a truncated thought, not simply logic, it is first of all the transrational (irrational parts, mystical, aesthetic).[66]

The two men sought a new art of words – poetry as word/sound art. Khlebnikov's goal was to build a language accessible to all of humanity, based on the internationally shared sound structure of primordial phonemic roots. Kruchenykh, for his part, searched for zaum in primitive chant structures, incantations of archaic cultures, and the glossolalia of religious mystics. He often referred to the practice of the flagellant Varlaam Shishkov, who, when in ecstasy, would chant in a language previously unknown to him: "namos pamos bagos / gerezon drovolmire zdruvul /

dremile cherezondro fordei."[67] Following the same intuitive impulse, Kruchenykh had been able to declare the unintended birth of his exemplary zaum poem.

> On April 27, at 3 o'clock in the afternoon, I instantaneously mastered to perfection all languages Such is the poet of the current era I am here reporting my verses in Japanese, Spanish and Hebrew:
>
> iké mina ni
> sinu ksi
> iamakh alik
> zel
> GO OSNEG KAUD
> M R BATUL'BA
> VINU AE KSEL
> VER TUM DAKH
> GIZ
> SHISH[68]

Both Italians and Russians repudiated logocentric, referential, and communicative features of language. Marinetti compared syntax to a boring interpreter or tour guide who confines a poet to language "that is traditional, heavy, restrictive, earth-bound, with neither arms nor wings, because it is merely intelligent."[69] Khlebnikov praised the ability of "primitive" man (along with insane persons or poets) to "express his emotions in novel pronouncements and rhythms far from everyday frozen language with its conventional attachments that link precise meaning with articulation."[70] Their words conform to Artaud's well-argued diatribes against worn-out language, which were adopted by the whole avant-garde. "We must agree words have become fossilized, words, all words are frozen, strait-jacketed by their meanings ... Under these conditions it is no exaggeration to say that in view of their clarity defined by a limited terminology, words are made to stop thought, to surround it, to complete it, in short they are only a conclusion."[71]

Obviously, the production of meaning that depends on linguistic encoding already inscribed in the arbitrary pairing of signifier and signified, was inappropriate for the expression of avant-garde revolt against the cultural and artistic status quo. Avant-garde artists rejected the normative language that functions within the closure of teleological schemes of representation as a weak and unsuitable device for an art that wanted to change the world. They felt trapped between *langage* and parole (language as a cultural denominating system and speech as an act of individual expression), between a representational and a presentational mode of speech, or between "enunciated discourse" and "enunciating gesture," as Patrice Pavis words this dichotomy. Futurists looked for a way out of this trap by insisting on authentic vocal enunciation. They eschewed conventional verbal content, radically shifting focus from the word's meaning to its vocalization/sounding so that voice/sound in their performance poetry ceased to be a mere vehicle for communicating the "enunciated discourse" and acquired characteristics of a self-realizing vocal gesture.

Steve McCaffery sees this tendency as an essential tenet of the avant-garde, which executed "a full scale revision of the word as a desired destination when purified of its cultural bondage to meaning. As part of this complex transformation of the semantic paradigm, the materiality of the sign emerged as a central, almost primitivistic preoccupation."[72] By recognizing the materiality of voice/sound and reaching for the intrinsic performativity of words locked in their oral/aural potential, avant-garde sound poets paved the way for the "performative generation of materiality," a tenet of the historical "performative turn" of theatre described by Fischer-Lichte. As this extends further toward the understanding of sound's ability to materialize onstage and participate in "moto-rumorist" structural scenography, it becomes clear that a new theatrical idiom – evolved from the avant-garde and Futurist initial probes into sonority of performance – prefigured the "acoustic turn" in the arts and the aurality of the postdramatic stage.

SEMIOTICS AND THE POSTMODERN RENEWAL OF AURALITY

Human culture forever lives in between the non-rational, destabilizing power of sound and the clarifying, analytic predisposition of vision. While the indigenous oral cultures continue to provide human connection with the world through ritual practices of chant and dance, a "sound alignment" of language with nature, as well as the sound symbolism of ideophone words,[73] the Apollonian dream of clarity and vision came to dominate Western civilization in opposition to the Dionysian inebriation with music. Our culture of work, trade, clear-cut communication, and state authority relies almost exclusively on visual certainty and the graphic encoding of words and signs. However, in the works of contemporaries hungry for the authenticity and identity that are no more in the age of simulacra, we witness "the postmodern renewal of aurality." This is how Martin Jay terms a contemporary philosophical trend described in his study *Downcast Eyes: The Denigration of Vision in Twentieth-Century French Thought*. The book scrutinizes critiques, by a number of influential French thinkers, of vision's allegedly superior capacity to provide access to knowledge. In such works Jay discovers the focus on aurality as a critical probe into metaphysical schemes of discursive language and big narratives of dominant culture that, relying on sight – which is intrinsically less temporal than hearing – "tend to elevate static Being over dynamic Becoming." Henri Bergson's discussion of Zeno's paradox of Achilles and the tortoise, and his ensuing concept of spatio-temporal continuity, make the initial link here. Besides Bergson, among the main proponents of this train of thought are Maurice Merleau-Ponty, Jacques Lacan, Luce Irigaray, and Emmanuel Levinas. For my purposes Roland Barthes, Jacques Derrida, and Jean-François Lyotard, whose writings on voice, language, and theatre have greatly informed my study of the avant-garde and the postdramatic dramaturgy of sound, are even more important. Jay's diagnosis of the "postmodern renewal of aurality" in contemporary philosophy points to the interconnectedness of ideological development (in cultural studies of the postmodern condition) and artistic methods (in postdramatic theatrical practice). His argument encourages an aesthetic analysis of the aural aspect of postdramatic theatre as a part of fundamental inquiry into the overall cultural change.

Steven Connor, in his essay "The Modern Auditory I," adds to the argument for the artistic sway towards aurality on the premise of the postmodern disregard of the Cartesian perspective, with its fixed point of view. "For, perhaps because of the very dominance of the visual paradigm in conceptions of the self, the auditory or acoustic has often been experienced and represented, not as a principle of strength, but as a disintegrative principle. Indeed, it was precisely this aspect of the aural which may have recommended it to the arts of dissolution practiced by Futurism and Dadaism."[74] This conscious dissolution, exemplified by the historical avant-garde's penchant for the sound of performance, shifted the artist's orientation from the static, figurative reassurance of the cognitive eye to the uncertain temporality and flux of the sensitive ear. Consequently, the postdramatic actor/poet voices, performs in the domain of aurality, or physically presents on the stage, his or her self – however unstable – to the listener's ear.

The postmodern mistrust of the signifying process can be traced clearly back to the Futurist and Dadaist subversion of an authoritative visual paradigm by a destabilizing aural paradigm that extends beyond the limits of artistic creation. Thus, Thomas Docherty describes the subversive cultural impact of the aural paradigm of thought on contemporary philosophy, gracefully playing with the French word *entendre*, which denotes both "to hear" and "to understand." He stresses that the "prioritization of the aural over the visual" has introduced into postmodern thought "a mode of hearing, of *entendre,* which will not allow for an easy slippage into 'understanding.'"[75]

In the same vein, the antitextual gesture that caused a shift in avant-garde artistic focus from the verbal meaning to the vocal sound meant both expressive and cultural disruption in theatre practice. Erika Fischer-Lichte underlines: "The revolution of the theatre can only occur as cultural revolution if it succeeds in developing a 'language of the theatre' with which no messages are formulated but rather reactions evoked and provoked – in other words in which not the semantic but rather the pragmatic dimension dominates."[76] The avant-garde theatre's switch between the semantic and the pragmatic, between the language of literary drama and the idiom of theatre performance, is clearly concurrent with its turn toward an orality/aurality of performance and a materiality of sound. For this reason, Pavis regards the increasing concern for voice/sound in theatre as a cultural necessity. "At a time when technology and Western civilization have attained a perfection in writing and in space conquered by the gaze and by signs, there no longer remains but the invisible refuse, difficult to locate and to notate, of the voice, of which we are incapable of grasping visually, thus systematically, the 'grain' (Roland Barthes) or the pulsion. By insisting on the vocal signifier, on the orality dimension in theatrical practice, theatre is less interested in the utterances (visible, comprehensible and made concrete in a scenic space) than in the enunciation (place of the enunciating subjects, noises and failures of their production). Theatre thus has *a voice at court.*"[77]

However, most theatre scholars have not addressed the unique role of voice (oral expression) and sound (aural structuring) in the field of stage performance incited by the historical avant-garde. Up to now, only theoreticians and practitioners of sound poetry and acoustic art have paid close attention to it. Investigating the path from "phonic to sonic" in the development of contemporary poetry that extended vocal gestures into acoustic ones, McCaffery alleges that avant-garde sound poets and performers "freed the word from semantic mandates, redirecting a sensed energy from themes and message into matter and force."[78] His definition of sound as the "matter and force" of performance poetry easily translates into Lyotard's notion of theatre performance as the confluence of a libidinal traffic of energies or "pulsional displacements," which function as alternatives to the production of representative replacements.

"The radical redefinition of the theatre, which the avant-garde began at the turn of the century, fundamentally transformed the two categories 'text' and 'performance' and thereby produced a new, highly charged dynamic between them," maintains Fischer-Lichte. "The history of European theatre can be understood as a record of shifting dominance between these two competing dramatic categories."[79] Concurrently, Christopher Innes wonders whether "the central issue in studying drama today is how we evaluate physical aspects of performance: theatre as bodily expression, as opposed to the presentation of written words."[80] Extremely defiant toward the written word, the Futurists transformed their vocal performance into bodily expression, a vocal gesture that questioned the limits of the performer's physicality. Marinetti's onomatopoetic mimesis of the noise of exploding shells, whistling shrapnel, or heavy engine roar replaced the verbal description of the events. The ensuing non-verbal idiom of Futurist performance adhered to Artaud's proposition for a sign language that consists of noises, cries, gestures, poses, and signs: "Abandoning Occidental usages of speech, it turns words into incantations. It extends the voice. It wildly tramples rhythms underfoot. It pile-drives sounds … It liberates a new lyricism of gesture which, by its precipitation or its amplitude in the air, ends by surpassing the lyricism of words."[81]

Analyzing the avant-garde theatre's return to primal ritual forces, Innes discusses a particular use of incantatory language by Balinese dancers that "gave Artaud a working example of the concrete language, intended for the senses and independent of speech, which has been such an influential concept in avant-garde theatre." In Balinese dance, Artaud saw a theatre that not only "eliminates words but expresses a state prior to language," presenting a sacred physical impulse that is before words. "What little dialogue Balinese spectacle contained was in an archaic tongue that apparently neither performers, nor the Balinese audience (let alone the French spectators), nor even priests understood. It thus became an incantation. The only other vocal communication was on the level of pure sound, so that meaning was transmitted on a physical level through attitudes."[82]

One cannot underestimate the role of switching from a logical and understandable wording to an alogical and incantational voicing in the formation of the new theatre idiom. In his reappraisal of the Italian Futurist theatre R.S. Gordon puts forth a similar argument,[83] suggesting that Derrida's analysis of Artaud's "theatre of cruelty" idiom, in which "gesture and speech have not yet been separated by the logic of representation,"[84] applies to the study of Futurist theatre as well. Gordon points to the significant coincidence of the two theatrical poetics, which is particularly tangible in regards to voice/sound. Derrida finds vocal sound in Artaud as "a speech that is a body, of a body that is a theatre, of a theatre that is a text because it is no longer enslaved to a writing more ancient than itself, an ur-text or an ur-speech."[85] Futurist performance founded on the materiality of sound comes close to such non-representational idiom that resides "in theatrical illegibility, in the night that precedes the book, [where] the sign has not yet been separated from the force. It is not quite yet a sign, in the sense in which we understand sign, but is no longer a thing, which we conceive only as opposed to the sign ... It is neither a book nor a work, but an energy, and in this sense it is the only art of life."[86] Accepting Derrida's interpretation of Artaud's illegible, energetic theatrical idiom as a valid descriptor of Futurist performance, Gordon breaks ground for a further exploration of the relationship between the orality/aurality of postmodern theatre and the principles of Futurist dramaturgy of sound.

Vocal sound brings a pure energy, an energetic field of perpetual becoming, to the Futurist theatricality of presence. It acquires materiality and earns dramaturgical currency exactly by dissociating itself from mere verbal meaning. It succeeds at turning text into performance just to the extent that it succeeds in betraying its denotative function. Furthermore, since a temporal event sound/vocal utterance can never be repeated in the same shape twice, it shapes nothing but an immediate non-representational performance. So far, this conforms to avant-garde theatre theory and practice, but now the question arises of whether or not to consider stage sound as an act of theatrical semiosis or a mere performance device. The semioticians of theatre faced this issue when examining a non-textual idiom based on the synergy of sound, light, movement, objects, and people on the contemporary stage. Since the communication of meaning is here seriously put in question, they came up with the notion that such a theatre idiom was, so to speak, a cloud of "floating signifiers." One should remember that the term "floating signifier" was previously coined by Claude Lévi-Strauss to denote "mana," a magic force known from the pre-religious beliefs of indigenous tribes of the Pacific Islands. In theatre discourse it translates into "neither object nor sign but a force," as Derrida would put it. Whether this cloud was drifting toward any signification was left to the audience to decide.

In his discussion of the relationship between avant-garde and contemporary semiotics, Pavis argues: "the present success of *performances* can be explained by the rediscovery of the temporal 'event' aspect unique to the theatre." In that respect, as the historical avant-garde theatre practitioners discovered, its inner material qualities make sound ideally suited to carry the performance as a temporal and immediate event. Sound is temporal by nature; it lives as long as it sounds and it literally does not point to any meaning outside itself. As poet McCaffery claims: "sound – the event and not the servant of semantics – becomes a possible antidote to the paradox of sign. That a thing need not be *a this* standing for *that* but immediately *a that* ... [makes sound] free of the implications of the metaphysics of linguistic absence."[87] Similarly, the avant-garde performance following an aural paradigm in its eventness and temporality stands in contrast to the visual, textual, and rational concepts. Fleeing the "linguistic absence," it generates the crisis of the sign that remains wavering between the discursive language of the text and the performative idiom of the theatre. However, our understanding of the aural and the temporal, as distinguished from the visual and the spatial, may be liberating, proposes Pavis. "If the concept of language, sign or specificity is thus in a state of crisis, crystallizing, but also blocking avant-garde thought, this is probably because it has linked its fate too closely to the notions of *mise en scène* and spatiality ... A domination of another avant-garde, that of time, rhythm and voice, is seeking to break. Perhaps one should see in this mutation the failure or at least the limits of semiology based solely on a Cartesian examination, measurable, geometric and in a word, *spatial*, of the theatrical performance ... Insistence on stage visuals as opposed to text too hastily dismissed the temporal, continuous and pulsional aspect of the theatrical performance."[88] Pavis admits the failure of our contemporary discourse that, concerned with the avant-garde's shift from text to performance that is apparent in the spatial field of the mise en scène, missed the same shift in the theatricality of rhythm, voice, and sound. He thus opens a possibility of a renewal of an oral/aural approach to theatre that puts, as he says, "a voice at court." Since the Futurist and Dadaist liberation of words, synoptic declamation, simultaneous performance, bruitism, absurdism, and abstractionism first put "a voice at court," exploring its performative potential and independent sonority, the next chapter looks more closely into these formative elements of the dramaturgy of sound.

3

Sound Poetry and *Bruitist* Performance: Words-in-Freedom

ORALITY AS THE THEATRICAL SUBSTANCE OF FUTURIST *SERATE*

With the belief that "only theatrical entertainment is worthy of the true Futurist spirit," Marinetti and friends started an intense campaign of staging their evenings in grand theatres all across Italy in 1910. They spread from Politeama Rossetti di Trieste and Teatro Lirico di Milano to Teatro Costanzi di Roma, Politeama Garibaldi di Palermo, and Galleria Futurista di Napoli. Futurist performers, mixing poetry declamations, conferences, concerts, exhibitions, and performances, toured Europe as well; the eroiche serate stirred audiences in London and Paris in 1912 and in Moscow, St Petersburg, and Berlin in 1914.[1] A typical Futurist serata would begin on a serious note with hymns like "Inno alla vita – sinfonia futurista del maestro Balilla Pratella" or "Inno alla poesia nuova" by Paolo Buzzi. But its celebratory note would not last long; through loud manifesto readings in praise of the self-professed revolutionary art, it would soon deteriorate into the provocative denigration of establishment and passéist art. The evening would then continue with the declamation of chains of incomprehensible words like "clof, clop, cloch, cloppete, cloffete, clocchete, chchch" of Aldo Palazzeschi's poem *La fontana malata*.[2]

The initial seriousness of a serata, already shaken up by declamations of poetry and manifestos, would then inevitably turn into a radical form of variety cabaret, replete with ludic free-word novelties of Buzzi, Luciano Folgore, Auro d'Alba, Francesco Cangiullo, and others. No doubt most irritating for audiences were the absurdist, parodic, and circus-like group recitations, such as *Discussione sul Futurismo di due critici sudanesi* (Discussion between Two Sudanese Critics on Futurism) by Giacomo Balla and *Piedigrotta* and *I funerali di un filosofo passatista* (Funeral of a Passéist

Philosopher) by Cangiullo. Balla's two imaginary Sudanese critics, for example, talked about Futurism in a language that did not make any sense: "Farcionisgnaco gurninfuturo bordubalotaompimagnusa."[3] The culmination would be reached by the cacophony of the most celebrated case of onomatopoeic declamation, the sound poem of the battlefield *Zang Tumb Tumb*, performed by the orchestrator of all the ado, Filippo Tommaso Marinetti: "zang-tumb-tumb ta-ta-ta-ta-ta-ta stop … uuuuuuu-urlaaare degli ammalati nel crrrrrrrrpitare delle palle."[4] This type of nonsense tended to catch audience members off guard and induce stupor, which often caused their belated and angry reaction. Futurists' declamation of coarse words and sound clusters, put in place of conventional literature's appeal to empathy and reason, was a part of their strategy for the renewal of sensibility; it served to jolt audiences from complacent listening. In order to provoke a violent response in the stalls they deliberately shifted focus from benign entertainment and education to subversive ridicule; they welcomed the audience's animosity as a rewarding experience and delighted in the "pleasure of being booed." Besides heating up the atmosphere with noisy declamations, Marinetti would sharpen the antagonistic attitude toward the public by scolding locals for passéist practices, as is known from his addresses to Venice, Florence, and Rome. Naturally, the crowds would erupt with hostility.

Lacerba, 15 December 1913, reported on the *Grande serata futurista* held at the Florentine Teatro Verdi, publishing a poster with the subtitle *Resconto sintetico (fisicale e spirituale) della battaglia* (A Synthetic (Physical and Spiritual) Description of the Battle) on the front page. It presents two antagonistic camps graphically in two parallel columns. On the stage side are two poets (Marinetti and Cangiullo), three painters (Boccioni, Carrà, and Ardengo Soffici), one anti-philosopher (Papini), one immoralist (Italo Tavolato), and one occasional volunteer. On the hall side are 5,000 enemies: clerics, bourgeois, students, liberals, aristocrats, the virtuous, journalists, police officers, and commoners. Two adjacent columns list arms, states of mind, allies, wounded, and the results of the battle on both sides. Symptomatically, the list of enemies is exhaustive. It includes even students and liberals, who could be counted as supporters – but the essence of Futurist performance strategy for an *arte-azione* event was to antagonize everyone, including supporters.

A bellicose attitude obviously became integral to the Futurist theatricalization of the act of reading poetry and manifestos. The unnerving cacophony of the poetry and the aggressiveness of the manifestos, usually inadmissible in bourgeois theatre, marked the oral/aural performance at the serate. Günter Berghaus emphasizes: "The futurist declaimer now served as an object the audience could react *against*. The reading set in motion a mechanism that went far beyond the appreciation of an artistic creation. The text functioned as a score, the reciter as a conductor, and the audience as the orchestra. The main task of the declaimer was to challenge the spectators and to provoke them into reactions of an unpremeditated kind."[5]

The Futurists' choice of performance space was made with the same conflictual attitude. Big theatres were not chosen as venues of the staging of the serate for their functionality; they were singled out as *the* architectural sites of an antagonistic artistic and cultural tradition that needed to be demolished. For the Futurists there was nothing more passéist than a Belle Époque theatre hall and its applauding public. At the same time, aware of the popularity and the tangible social and political impact of Giuseppe Verdi and Gabriele D'Annunzio's theatre, Futurists believed that "the only way to inspire Italy with the warlike spirit today is through the theatre."[6] Consequently, they orchestrated a rebellion by introducing an unconventional form of site-responsive performance. Futurists used the theatre as a topical resource of their disdain, and its physical space (stage and auditorium) as a playing area of their provocative, non-illusionistic, hybrid performance. They played with theatre's institutional character and manipulated spectators into participating in an anti-theatrical environmental event or happening. The serate, therefore, can be considered an embryonic form of avant-garde environmental theatre stretching toward more recent site-specific performances of the Theatregroep Hollandia, for example.

The antagonistic tone of manifesto readings, according to Michael Webster, is a sign of the intrinsic orality of Futurist performance: "In this [oral] context 'stirring the audience up' by direct address, pathetic exhortations, and emotional and humorous exaggeration is not at all uncommon. Such a practice has the immediate character of an event, is descriptive and propagandistic rather than narrative, and leads naturally to the theatricality of the futurist manifestos and the deliberate audience-baiting at the *serate futuriste*."[7] His argument derives from the distinction between orality and literacy established by Walter Ong, who claims that while orality retains a confrontational attitude as its genuine characteristic, "writing fosters abstraction that disengages knowledge from the arena where human beings struggle with one another."[8] Hence, oral cultures situate knowledge within a context of struggle, where language is a mode of action rather than a countersign of speculative thought. Ong provides a substantial number of illustrations of such verbal practice in folk riddles, counting exercises, tongue twisters, and exhorted confrontations found in ancient rhetoric and classic literature such as the *Iliad*, *Beowulf*, the *Old Testament*, and medieval European romance. In all of these, words are taken as actions or oral events whose truth has to be tested through antagonistic performance acts. Ancient orators, poets, and minstrels often competed publically in angry but eloquent exchanges of insults called flyting. The same kind of oral practices are panegyrical exultations, victory odes, or funeral speeches, but, in this case, the orator exaggerates the positive side of its subject. The use of the psychodynamics of orality, as Webster posits, places Futurist manifestos in the wider genre of oral literature.

Marinetti considered manifesto writing a special verbo-vocal art form, as his letter to Gino Severini indicates: "I have read your manuscript [...] it has nothing of *manifesto* in it ... I advise you to ... rework it ... recasting the whole new part in the form of *manifesto* ... I think I shall persuade you by all that I know about *the art of making manifestos*, which I possess, and by my desire to place in *full* light, not in *half* light, your own remarkable genius as a futurist."[9] When advocating "the art of making manifestos," Marinetti had in mind his own uncompromisingly emphatic style: "We make use of every ugly sound, every expressive cry from the violent life that surrounds us ... We bravely create 'ugly' literature ... Each day we must spit on the *Altar of Art*."[10] Continuing to promote the manifesto's succinct style, Marinetti did not mince words: "It is stupid to write one hundred pages where one would do."[11] His arrogant manifestos surely provoked the unassuming public into open hostility. No less provocative, his sound poetry often constituted a functional part of those manifestos. "Technical Manifesto of Futurist Literature, 1910," for instance, contained an early example of "words-in-freedom," an extract from the poem *BATTLE (WEIGHT + STINK)*. Full of tactile analogies and onomatopoeic words bursting with mimed sound, it reads/sounds: "**tuumbtuumb** alarms Gargaresch bursting crackling pus Tinkling knapsacks rifles clogs [...] filth whirlwind orange blossoms filigree misery nuts squares maps jasmine + nutmeg + rose arabesque mosaic carrion stings bungling ... **tatatata** rifle-fire **peec pac puun pan pan** mandarin tawny wool machine-guns rattles leper's hovels sores forward."[12]

In his "The Painting of Sounds, Noises and Smells," Carlo Carrà masterly applied the art of writing manifestos. Relying on the use of onomatopoetic sound adopted from Futurist declamation practice, Carrà enhanced his theoretical elaboration of colour-sound synaesthesia by the multiplication of letters in the manner of sound poetry. A crescendo of vocal sounds of vowels and consonants in his manifesto suggested an intensification of colour tone and thickness:

I rossi, rooooosssssi roooooosssissssimi che griiiiiidano.
I verdi i non mai abbastanza verdi, veeeeeerdiiiiiissssssimi, che striiiiiidono;
i gialli non mai abbastanza scoppianti; i gialloni-polenta; i gialli-zafferano; i gialli-ottoni.

Reds, rrrrreds, the rrrrreddest rrrrrrreds that shouuuuuuuut.
Greens, that can never be greener, greeeeeeeens, that screeeeeeem;
yellows, as violent as can be; polenta yellows, saffron yellows, brass yellows.[13]

Presupposing an emphatic rendition, these lines of words-in-freedom represented a palpable support for the theoretical content of the manifesto. The uneven verbalization of the hybrid script (sound-poem/manifesto) and its loud vocal performance exposed audience members to the interpenetration of sensual attractions aimed at the total renewal of sensibility. Carrà thus pragmatically proved his conviction that "the systematic use of onomatopoeia, antigraceful music without rhythmic quadrature, and the art of noises were created by the same Futurist sensibility that has given birth to the painting of sounds, noises and smells."[14]

SOUND AND THE SANE IN DADAIST FOLLY, PRIMITIVISM, AND ABSTRACTION

The formation of a distinct literary genre that includes text-sound art, concrete poetry, *lettrisme,* simultaneism, l-a-n-g-u-a-g-e, and verbo-voco-visual art, which together represent a class of sound poetry, has a long history spreading from Aristophanes and François Rabelais to Christian Morgenstern, Lewis Carroll, and many unconventional modern writers. Sound patterning is characteristic of indigenous oral cultures that are concerned more with the "sound alignment" of their idioms with the phenomenal world than with the cognitive, logical structuring of perceptions known in the developed languages.[15] It marks the "primitive" creation of euphonic structures, incantations, chants, syllabic mouthing, and lexical distortions in their sacred and profane languages. One can find unintended sound poetry in popular white magic, nonsensical children's rhymes and word games, ludic noisemaking at carnivals, mnemonic counting aids, and rhythmic vocal practices that accompany language acquisition, work processes, and shamanic rituals. Futurist, Dadaist, and Surrealist poets revisited all these forms in their experiments with sound that broke ground for contemporary poetry making. Unlike the standard poetry that concentrates on versification, rhythm, rhyme, euphony, assonance, alliteration, and other literary tropes, their poems explored the way in which sound can be extended beyond its use as a prosodic device.

As Steve McCaffery asserts, "sound poetry manifested itself in several diverse and revolutionary investigations into language's non-semantic, acoustic properties."[16] Luigi Russolo, for instance, envisioned a broad potential of vocal "noise" in poetic expression. "Language has a richness of timbre unknown to the orchestra, which should prove that nature itself had recourse to the timbres of noise, when it wished to increase and enrich the timbres of the magnificent instrument of the human voice ... For centuries, poets did not know how to derive from this very effective source of expression in language ... Only the futurist poets, with their *free words*, were able to hear the entire value of noise in poetry."[17] Only when vocal sound dissociates itself from verbal meaning and, by its sensorial-perceptive materiality, becomes an aesthetic object *per se*, only then will the vocal utterance become capable of giving its message a human resonance, argued Russolo.

Another type of incision into the non-semantic, acoustic tissue of poetry comes from the revelation of "a denial of signification toward an ideal of the unification of expression and indication"[18] in the avant-garde performance idiom, suggests Jon Erickson. Breaking away from the logocentric orientation of language, the performance poetry of the historical avant-garde literally brought out the sensory essence of the word – a sound gesture in which "expression and indication" amalgamate. The idiom of performance thus escaped the confines of the text and survived as a vocal action aimed at the co-presence of the performer and the audience. Following Artaud's idea of a theatre of presence, Erickson calls the idiom of sound poetry "*emotive language* or *language of presence*, as opposed to a language of *signification* – language of absence ... This language should be incantatory, summoning forth the power of presence within every fiber and organ and nerve of the human being, uniting the spiritual with the physical, tapping into dormant and primal creative energies, and emanating outward to connect with the listener."[19]

To achieve such immediacy, painters, poets, musicians, and theatre artists of the historical avant-garde returned to the "primitive" idioms of non-Western cultures. Called "barbarians of the twentieth century," they turned inward for the liberation of powers of the collective unconscious and "backward" to primitive/aboriginal art and culture, looking for a remedy for the sickness of culture in the age of secular progress. While Pablo Picasso's *Demoiselles d'Avignon* (1907) and Béla Bartok's *Allegro Barbaro* (1911) paid tribute to primitivism in visual art and music, Kandinsky's almanac *Der Blaue Reiter* "included, besides Cézanne, Matisse, Gauguin, and Delaunay ... naïve Rousseau, Russian and German folk art, woodcuts, children's drawings, masks, carvings, and votive paintings."[20] Expressionist Franz Marc, a co-editor of the almanac, wrote "our ideas and ideals must be clad in hair-shirts ... They must be fed on locusts and wild honey, not on history, if we are ever to escape the exhaustion of our European bad taste."[21] Following Nietzsche, who already challenged "the visually oriented rationalist tradition in sensory terms as the 'Apollonian dream world of the scene' that irrationally seeks to suppress the acoustically oriented 'Dionysian poetry of the chorus,'"[22] writes Andrew M. Kimbrough, "Artaud demanded a rejection of text-based theatre and, in its place, proposed performance milieu that captured the oral sensibilities of the primitive tribe."[23] In a similarly Nietzschean gesture, thirsting for the authentic, the avant-gardes began to liberate words from the burden of historical and teleological discourse. Thus, in the Dadaist Cabaret Voltaire, one could hear Tristan Tzara's *Negro Chants*, Hugo Ball's *Elefantenkarawane*, and Richard Huelsenbeck's wild drumming. Huelsenbeck remembers: "With Nietzsche we had learned the relativity of things and the value of being unscrupulous ... we understood the meaning of primitivity – Dada, the babblings of children, Hottentottery – primitivity, of which the age seemed to be giving signs."[24] Since the avant-garde artists recognized a welcome reminder of humankind's infancy in the indigenous cultures, they produced numerous replications of naïve tribal art and children's spontaneous creations as an antithesis of the desiccated art of academies and museums. Relatedly, Richard Kostelanetz, an American avant-gardist of the 1960s, uses a children's tongue twister to explain the principle of text-sound art in which sounds create their own coherence apart from the meaning of words:

> If a Hottentot taught a Hottentot tot
> to talk 'ere the tot could totter,
> ought the Hottentot tot be taught to say
> ought or naught or what ought to be taught 'er?

and comments, "The subject of this ditty is clearly neither Hottentots nor pedagogy but the related sounds of 'ot' and 'ought.' What holds this series of words together is not the thought or the syntax but those two repeated sounds. Though superficially playful, text-sound art embodies serious thinking about the possibilities of vocal expression and communication; it represents not a substitute for language but an expansion of our verbal powers."[25]

Such seemingly childish but serious understanding of our verbal powers is found in the playful sound poems of Futurists Elena Guro and Aldo Palazzeschi and in Dadaist Hugo Ball's *Verse ohne Worte* (Verses without Words). In fact, all of Dada owes its historical formation precisely to this kind of infantile, primitivistic denial of adult logic. The anarchic infantile behavior of Dada was the only possible sane reaction against the so-called intelligent and sensitive mass of people "buried beyond recognition" beneath tons of journalistic lexical garbage that day after day kept providing a rationale for the First World War.

As a reaction to this historical nonsense, Dada was born when several young men, mostly draft dodgers, such as Marcel Janko, Hugo Ball, Richard Huelsenbeck, Tristan Tzara, and Hans Arp, formed the first Dadaist group in Zurich's Cabaret Voltaire in 1916. At the time Zurich was an international city of dissent where one could meet disenchanted modernist writers, refugees, and revolutionaries of various backgrounds, from Romain Rolland, Frank Wedekind, and James Joyce to Vladimir Ilyich Lenin and Grigory Zinoviev. Revolted by the slaughterhouse of the Great War and disgusted by bourgeois culture and the social system that had generated it, Dadaists started organizing boisterous artistic soirées at the Cabaret Voltaire and publishing the international review *DADA*. In his Dada diary, Ball writes: "Our cabaret is a gesture. Every word that is spoken and sung here says at least this one thing: that this humiliating age has not succeeded in winning our respect. What could be respectable and impressive about it? Its cannons? Our big drum drowns them."[26] While the childlike syllabic mouthing of "da-da" may have baptized the movement of political dissent, for Ball the non-sensical playfulness of children was serious business: "A child's innocence, I mean, borders on the infantile, on dementia, on paranoia. It stems from the belief in a primeval memory ... Unreached by logic and the social apparatus it emerges in the inconsiderate infantilism and madness, where all inhibitions are removed. This is a world with its own form; it poses new problems and new tasks, just like a newly discovered continent."[27] Poetry should harvest words from the world of the instinctive and not the rational, thought Ball. To destroy language as an ordinary social organ of communication and transform it into an idiom capable of expressing the most profound human experiences, he started writing poetry without words, in which he employed sounds as magical incantations capable of forming a new sentence of an "innately playful, but hidden, irrational character."[28]

Ball is also indebted, in his composition of a non-verbal/non-syntactic sentence that remains impervious to logic, to Marinetti's practical destruction of syntax in poetry. In a dada diary entry for 9 July 1915, he frankly admits: "Marinetti sends me *Parole in Liberta* by himself, Cangiullo, Buzzi and Govoni. They are just letters of the alphabet on a page; you can roll up such a poem like a map. The syntax has come apart ... There is no language any more ... Disintegration right in the innermost process of creation. It is imperative to write invulnerable sentences. Sentences that withstand all irony. The better the sentence the higher the rank. In eliminating vulnerable syntax or association one preserves the sum of the things that constitute the style and the pride of a writer – taste, cadence, rhythm, and melody."[29]

Ball praised the circle of poets around Marinetti because they "nourished the emaciated big-city vocables with light and air and gave them back their warmth, emotion, and their original untroubled freedom,"[30] and he appreciated their taking the word out of the frame of the sentence. However, in his view, Wassily Kandinsky's theory of inner sound was the most important pretext for the art of sound in poetry. Kandinsky's belief in the essence of art as a flow of inner sound energy from object through artist to spectator led many avant-garde artists – Italian Futurists Carlo Carrà and Enrico Prampolini, Russian Rayonists Mikhail Larionov and Natalia Goncharova, and Russian Suprematist Kazimir Malevich among them – to approach painting as a vibrational phenomenon akin to music or sound. Ball followed suit for "the whole secret of Kandinsky is his being the first painter to reject – also more radically than cubists – everything representational as impure, and to go back to the true form, the sound of a thing, its essence, its essential curve."[31] Consequently, he began to seek for a poetry that would do away with language the way the painters had discarded the object, abandoned the figurative, and adopted an anti-representational stance to connect with art's innermost source: "the sound of a thing."

Ball launched his own version of sound poetry inspired by *The Yellow Sound*, a play in which Kandinsky, he claimed, was "the first to discover and apply the most abstract expression of sound in language, consisting of harmonized vowels and consonants."[32] In the oft-quoted journal entry for 23 June 1916, he describes the workings of this new poetry genre and its performance:

> I have invented a new genre of poems, *Verse ohne Worte* [poems without words] or *Lautgedichte* [sound poems], in which the balance of the vowels is weighted and distributed solely according to the values of the beginning sequence. I gave a reading of the first one of these poems this evening. I had made myself a special costume for it. My legs were in a cylinder of shiny blue cardboard, which came up to my hips so that I looked like an obelisk ... I was carried onto the stage in the dark and began slowly and solemnly:
>
> Gadji beri bimba
> Glandridi lauli lonni cadori
> Gadjama bim beri glassala
> Glandridi glassala tuffm i zimbrabim
> Blassa galassasa tuffm i zimbrabim[33]

The poet's account of his historic recitation at the Cabaret Voltaire holds the same awareness and concern for stage effect that Marinetti had expressed in the report about his London appearance with *Zang Tumb Tumb*. In both cases, the poem's aural content dictates the shape of performance. Ball remembers how in his rendition "the emphasis increased as the sound of consonants became sharper," so that he started to worry about how to balance his "method of expression" with "the pomp of staging." Wrapped in an abstract cardboard costume, without plot and character as dramaturgical prompts for interpretation, he had to rely on the dramaturgy of sound, that is, the balancing of vowels and consonants in his sound-text poem. His recital included two more poems whose rhythm and sound equally shaped the performance and determined the stage movement – the "Labadas Gesang die Wolken" (Labada's Song to the Clouds) and the "Elefantenkarawane" (Elephant Caravan). Here is Ball's description of the latter: "I turned back to the middle [...] flapping my wings energetically. The heavy vowel sequences and the plodding rhythm of the elephants had given me one last crescendo. But how was I to get to the end? Then I noticed that my voice had no choice but to take on the ancient cadence of priestly lamentation, that style of liturgical singing that wails in all the Catholic churches of East and West."[34]

The arc of Ball's performance, in terms of its musical shape, starts and finishes on a note of solemnity matching the author's predisposition for Christian mysticism. Still, there was something factual, physical in his performance as well: as he put it, his "voice had no choice." It is hard to know whether Ball's doubt about how to finish came from his struggle with the indeterminacy of acoustic material, or from the fact that the score for his performance was already inscribed in the sound-text poem. Had the poet/performer been taken by a spontaneous realization of the poem's musicality, or had the poem already been designed to determine his performance style? If we take into account Ball's infatuation with Kandinsky's theory of inner sound, as well as his experiences at the Max Reinhardt School of Dramatic Art in Berlin and at the Munich Chamber Theatre, where he worked as a stage director, it seems likely that the poem already contained this note of priestly lamentation. In fact Ball's performances at the Cabaret Voltaire may well have been conscious attempts to build a new style of theatre expression based on sound poetry. Indeed formally, at least, the performances resembled the Expressionist Geist style of acting later developed by Lothar Schreyer, another of Kandinsky's followers. In the *Gadji beri bimba* performance, Ball strived to incorporate a "sound figure" (Schreyer's term for Geist-style acting); he did not care for the portrayal of psychology or emotions. Unlike a dramatic representation or a conventional poetry reading, his recitation of the text-sound poem relied exclusively on phonetic material in which he immersed himself. It was a living example of a Dadaist (indeed simply avant-garde or postdramatic) performance that went beyond uttering lines of an individual dramatic character, sculpting a "sound figure" from its own voice.

The avant-gardes inherited their interest in linguistic ambiguity from the likes of Paul Scheerbart and Christian Morgenstern, whose enigmatic sound poems Ball had more than likely heard in the cabarets of Berlin. Morgenstern's parody of D'Annunzio was included in the opening night program of the cabaret *Überbrettl* (1900), alongside a mixture of short plays, poems, and chansons. His mordant, intriguing, darkly humorous poems in the collection *Galgenlieder* (Songs from the Gallows, 1905–1910) belong to the genre of Dada-like poetry of subversive nonsense and superior sense. As Walter Arndt claims, "Morgenstern turns language inside out, discovers new shapes, and invents meanings. The procedure often undoes metaphors of millennial standing [… and offers] a rare insight into that occult interrelation between signifier and signified that has long preoccupied linguists and philosophers."[35] Some of Morgenstern's nonsense poems clearly resonate in the sound poetry of Ball and Kruchenykh. One of these is *Das Grosse Lalula*, which relies solely on the innovative sound of its vocables.

Kroklokwafzi? Semememi!
Seiokrontro - prafriplo:
Bifzi, bafzi; hulalemi:
quasti basti bo …
Lalu, lalu lalu lalu la![36]

Similarly irreverent toward the semantic value of words was Paul Scheerbart's "phone-poem" *Kikakoku*, composed of sound clusters as one of sixty-six intermezzos in his train stations narrative *Ich liebe dich! Ein Eisenbahnroman* (I Love You! A Railway Novel, 1897):

Kikakoku!
Ekorolaps!
Wîso kollipánda opolôsa.
Ipasatta îh fûo.
Kikakokú proklínthe petêh.
Nikifilí mopa Léxio intipáschi benakáffro – própsa pî! própsa pî![37]

Dadaist experimentation with the sound of words, inspired by entirely incomprehensible verses such as these, stands for more than a mere provocation of bourgeois audiences. In truth, Dada poets tried to undertake a much more responsible task, avows Raymond Federman. They tried to enter "the occult interrelation between signifier and signified," which was possible only, if at all, through "a new poetic language – a true intermedium of words," an idiom that lives in the interstice between pre-verbal sign/gesture or vocal utterance and written text and articulated speech.[38] Historically, there was not much novelty in Dada practice: Russian Futurist zaumny yazyk was already far ahead with its experiments with sound texture and neologisms, while Marinetti's program for the poetry of parole in libertà placed absolute emphasis on sound in order to enter the inner structure of language and break its discursive hold. But furthering their poetics, the Dadaists totally demystified words/vocables, pushed them beyond any possible signifying border, and emptied them of all semantic meaning. Theirs was a poetry that signified nothing, but celebrated human presence in "a true intermedium of words." Absurd and nihilistic at first glance, "Dada poetry was less a negation than an affirmation. In it, a new reality emerged, not that of reason, not that of intelligence, not that of sentiment, but the obscure source of man's authentic self."[39]

This Dadaist entry into the unknown fissures in between words adheres to Artaud's call for an authentic language of incantation, cry, and vocal expression "half-way between gesture and thought." "This naked language of theatre (not virtual but a real language) must permit … the transgression of the ordinary limits of art and speech, in order to realize actively, that is to say magically, *in real terms*, a kind of total creation in which man must reassume his place between dreams and events."[40] According to Derrida, following these difficult undercurrents of language in theatre performance meant descending "in the night that precedes the book, [where] the sign is not yet separated from the force. It is not yet exactly a sign … but it is not any more a thing."[41] That was exactly what the avant-garde sound poets strived to do: attempting to express human authenticity, they reached out to a large scope of poetic material waiting to be unearthed from the intermedium between a thing and a sign.

SYNCRETISM AND SIMULTANEITY

The correspondence between the visual and the aural – notably between the shapes and sounds of letters and words – was at the heart of avant-garde painting and poetry. Kandinsky thus published a book of rough woodcuts and verses called *Klänge* (Sounds, 1912). Guillaume Apollinaire experimented with his *ideogrammes lyriques* in the collection *Calligrammes, poèmes de la paix et de la guerre 1913–1916* (Caligrams: Poems of Peace and War 1913–1916), as verbo-visual compositions based on an amalgamation of graphic art and poetry writing. Symbolist Stéphane Mallarmé also tried to set words free from their descriptive function: the typographical display of his poem "Un coup de dés jamais n'abolira le hasard" (A Throw of the Dice Will Never Abolish Chance, 1892), announced the revolution in typography carried on later by Futurists. In *Un coup de dés*, a verbo-visual flow of words subsumed to a spatial, visual syntax instead of a grammatical one: simultaneous verses, individual words, or lines of different lengths slide up against each other, set in motion by a non-linear typography. This audacious removal of words from their usual position in the verse established a great precedent for Futurist *tavole parolibere* and Dadaist *poèmes simultanés*, which as visual counterparts of avant-garde experiments with sound introduced a verbo-voco-visual form into modern text-sound poetry.

The term *simultanéisme* (simultaneity as an artistic method) was originally coined by Henri-Martin Barzun in "The Aesthetics of Dramatic Poetry," an essay on the musical technique applied to his literary and dramatic work in the book *Voix, rhythmes et chants simultanés* (1913). Barzun's notion of polyrhythmic and simultaneous "chant," which replaces a set of monadic verses in a poem, was integral to his polyphonic poetry that celebrated the dramatic synthesis. His simultaneous poems, or *dramatismes*, as he called them, were composed of different verbal, vocal, and musical elements played one against the other. To highlight the musical character of his poems in print, Barzun typographically aligned some of them as chorus scores. When performed at Parisian soirées, these polyphonic poems on occasion assumed a composite form of declamation and vocal chant, and were enhanced by phonograph music or another sound accompaniment. At about the same time Apollinaire started to use the term "simultaneity" in reference to the visual arts when describing the *Prose du Transsibérian* (1913) by poet Blaise Cendrars and painter Sonia Delaunay-Terk.[42] In Cubist circles, this hybrid composition of text and painting was considered a quintessentially simultaneist work. The picture/poem consists of an almost two meter long sheet of folded cardboard on which the written text and a swirl of vividly coloured forms flow in parallel arrangement, depicting a train ride as an abstract, stream-of-consciousness evocation of travel. Apollinaire praised the work for allowing the spectator to capture its content the way an orchestra conductor captures superimposed notes on a sheet of music, deciphering graphic and written elements at the same time. But while his praise for the simultaneity of the *Prose du Transsibérian*'s graphic chart still allowed for the supremacy of sight, Dadaist simultaneous poetry favoured the aural displacement of any possible chart by chance noise.

The performative implications of Dadaist simultaneous text-sound poetry figure prominently in the 1916 rendition of the poem *L'amiral cherche une maison à louer – Poème simultané par Richard Huelsenbeck, Marcel Janko, Tristan Tzara* at Cabaret Voltaire. Here, three Dadaist poets simultaneously sang, whistled, and declaimed verses in German, French, and English. It was an energetic parallel delivery of the verbal lines, to which poets/performers added vocalizations of non-verbal sounds, coughs, sighs, and grunts in such a way that the clash of surprising utterances created a cacophony of sound and sense. Fulfilling the Dadaist aleatoric credo, the number of possibly different outcomes of such simultaneous recital made each performance a singular, unrepeatable play of chance.

HUELSENBECK Ahoi ahoi Des Admirals gwirkles Beinkleid schnell zerfällt
Teerpappe macht Rawagen
JANKO (chants) Where the honny suckle wine twines itself around the door
a sweethart mine is waiting patiently for me

TZARA Boum Boum Boum Il désabilla sa chair quand les grenuilles humides
comencèrent à bruler j'ai mis le cheval dans l'âme du

HUELSENBECK und der Conciergenbäuche Klapperschlagengrün sind milde ach verzert
in der Natur chrza prrrza chrrrza

JANKO (chants) can hear the weopour will arround arrund the hill
my great room is

TZARA serpent à Bucarest on dépendra mes amis dorénavant et c'est
très intéresent les grilles des morsure équatoriales

HUELSENBECK prrrza chrrrza prrrza Wer suchet dem wird
aufgetan Der Ceylonlöwe ist kein Schwan Wer Waser braucht find

JANKO (chants) mine admirably comfortably Grandmother said I love the ladies
I love the ladies

TZARA Dimanche: deux elephantes
Journal de Geneve au restaurant télégraphist assassiné

HUELSENBECK hihi Yabomm hihi Yabomm hihi hihi hihiiii
TZARA rouge bleu rouge bleu rouge bleu rouge bleu rouge bleu
SIFFLET (Janko) ———. ————. —. —. ———. —. ——.
CLIQUETTE (Tzara) rrrrrrrr rrrrrr rrrrrrrrr rrrrrrrrr rrrrrrrr rrrrrrrr
GROSSE CAISE (Huels.) OOO OOOOO OOOOO OOOO OO [43]

The layout of *L'amiral cherche une maison à louer* undoubtedly shows that it is a script to be performed on the stage rather than a poem to be read from a book. It was originally printed on two pages of an open book with lines running across the whole width to accommodate a spate of words, syllables, or verbalizations of noise. Visually it is reminiscent of a musical score with staved notation; the parallel graphical flow of its word/sound verses determines a sound structure to be conveyed by a simultaneous recitation. The cacophonic tone of the poem comes from the aleatoric combinations of words in three languages arranged in sliding lines with irregular beginnings. The indications for various levels of loudness and tempi added underneath the lines of the noisemakers: a whistle, a *cliquette*, and a "big box," additionally stress the authors' musical approach. The Futurists also used a score-like graphic layout of the page to apply musical principles to poetry making. Such an attempt is evident in Francesco Cangiullo's book *Poesia pentagramata*, where the text of the poems is set out on five-stave sheet paper, while some, like *Canzone pirotecnica*, include actual musical notation.

ZANG TUMB TUMB: PERFORMANCE POTENTIAL OF THE VERBO-VOCO-VISUAL FORM

Zang Tumb Tumb, a famous sound poem by Filippo Tommaso Marinetti, represents one of the boldest experiments in Futurist poetry. The poem was executed in the newly invented writing parole in libertà technique, aimed at the poetic expression of "an intuitive psychology of matter," and represented a major practical probe into his concepts of onomatopoeia, destruction of syntax, imagination without strings, typographic revolution, and free expressive orthography. All means of traditional poetic prosody – including *vers libre*, which Marinetti had practiced earlier in his French-language poetry – seemed insufficient for such an ambitious task. After 1909, when he wrote "The Founding and Manifesto of Futurism," a watershed in his literary output, Marinetti began to write mainly in Italian; aggressively promote Futurist art revolution; and experiment with new means of poetic expression, particularly with onomatopoeic sounds and iconic typography. He rejected the vers libre technique, convinced that it "pushes the poet fatally towards facile sound effects, a banal playing with speech, monotone cadences, [and] foolish rhymes."[44] The words-in-freedom technique, on the other hand, strives for a dynamism, simultaneity, and compenetration[45] unattainable with free verse. This new method of poetry writing, Marinetti professed, would dynamite the chains of logical speech and syntax and, by doing so, bring the poet closer to the raw poetic material (words/sounds) and allow him to challenge the dichotomy of art and life.

Marinetti summarizes the poetics of parole in libertà in a paragraph of his "allegorical" novel *Gli indomabili* (The Untameable, 1922). "Words-in-freedom are an absolutely free expression of the universe beyond prosody and syntax, a new way of seeing the universe, an essential estimate of the universe as the sum of forces in action [motion] that intersect at the threshold of consciousness of our creative *ego*, and are recorded simultaneously with all the expressive means at our disposal … Words-in-freedom orchestrate colors, noises, sounds; they mix the materials of language and dialect, arithmetic and geometric formulas, musical signs, old words, altered or recoined, the cries of animals, wild beasts, and motors."[46] Liberated from prosody and syntax, words-in-freedom stood for the world of phenomena as sound-images, aural icons, or ideograms. They meant an orchestration of colours, noises, and sounds in the synaesthetic oneness of a work of art. Offering an intuitive insight into the world of swift change and constant flux of an always already present future, parole in libertà expressed a Futurist poet/artist/performer's involvement in the world's dynamics rather than his fixed point of view. Undoubtedly, the medium of sound, temporal in its essence, was a proper conduit for the absolute immersion in life forces that Futurists sought.

Zang Tumb Tumb was conceived as an oral/aural report of a month-long siege of the Turkish city of Adrianople by Bulgarian troops in 1912, a bloody conflagration between Balkan nations that served as a prelude to the First World War. Marinetti saw the siege close up, as a war correspondent for the French newspaper *Gil Blas*. "I finished that short synthesizing noise-making poem while witnessing the machine-gunning of three thousand horses ordered by the Turkish general who was the governor before the fortress fell."[47] Returning to Milan, he began to put together the poem using free expressive orthography and synoptic free-word tables, iconic displays of the battle details made of printed words dispersed on oversized, foldable pages. In 1913 Marinetti started publishing poem excerpts in *Lacerba* and performing dynamic declamations of "Bombardamento," its especially noisy fragment that soon became a main attraction of Futurist serate. Finally, in 1914, the 159-page book *Zang Tumb Tumb, Adrianopoli ottobre 1912, parole in libertà* appeared in Milan, published by Marinetti's *Edizioni Futuriste di Poesia*.[48] It is worth noting that during the same period of approximately two years, Marinetti published his three major poetry manifestos: "Technical Manifesto of Futurist Literature," "Destruction of Syntax – Wireless Imagination – Words in Freedom," and "Geometric and Mechanical Splendor and Numerical Sensibility" (the first two were later republished together with *Zang Tumb Tumb* in *Les mots en liberté futuristes*, 1916). The poem and the three manifestos demonstrate the parallel development of Marinetti's poetics and politics.

The book is printed in a dramatic page layout with letters of different typefaces, some designed by hand, increasing or decreasing in size and boldness and surging unevenly along horizontal, vertical, diagonal, and curved lines. The text bursts before the reader's eyes as a rich and diverse visual offering that, at the same time, provided material for vocal performance. Apparently, the poem's graphic layout and typeset, a sound-image of metal and human forms shattered by a huge explosion, indicated a noisy vocal interpretation. Hence, McCaffery describes it as "the earliest successful, conscious attempt to structure a visual code for free kinetic, and voco-phonetic interpretation."[49] This technique provided the score for Marinetti's bruitist declamation of *Zang Tumb Tumb*, a poem with the title borrowed from the noise of howitzer fire, one of the main attractions, or disturbances, of the Futurists' tours throughout Europe. Saved as a recording, "Bombardamento di Adrianopoli" still circulates among poets as an inspirational and influential source of concrete poetry, sound-text art, *lettrisme*, and graphic design.[50]

There is no doubt that *Zang Tumb Tumb*'s non-linear typography and aural richness, expressed by the multitude of new vocables intuited or invented to mime the noises of war – artillery shelling, commands, shouts, destruction, and death – made the poem an absolute novelty. By virtue of its verbo-voco-visual complexity, the fragmented, deformed, exploding sound-picture of *Zang Tumb Tumb* has been acknowledged among text-sound poets as an epochal achievement in much the same way that Picasso's *Guernica* (1937) has been singled out in the history of avant-garde painting. Recognizing the different attitudes of Marinetti and Picasso toward war, I nonetheless dare to compare these two works on formal, innovative, and aesthetic grounds. Challenging the confines of political correctness, my comparison goes to the artistic fields of contemporary sound-text poetry and painting, not to the diametrically opposed ideological content of these two artistic presentations of war theatre. My comparison, unexpected and itself quite Futurist, suggests the need for a re-evaluation of the formal aesthetic merits of Marinetti's art in spite of the stigma he brought to himself by his later Fascist engagement.

Zang Tumb Tumb is an ear-witness's telegraphic account of the battlefield first in history to deploy an air force. Marinetti here observed the theatre of war as a collision of elementary physical forces rather than as a human affair with which the reader-listener might empathize. In order to dissect the battle in the manner of modern physicists who plunge into the domain of the infinitesimal to explain the material nature of things, Marinetti eschewed the passéist burden of humanity, empathy, and psychology. "We systematically destroy the literary 'I' in order to scatter it into the universal vibration and reach the point of expressing the infinitely small and the vibrations of molecules. E.g. lightening movements of molecules in the hole made by a howitzer (last part of the 'Fort Cheittam Tépé' in my *Zang Tumb Tumb*). Thus the poetry of cosmic forces supplants the poetry of the human," explains the poet.[51] Marinetti describes his earlier poem/war-report, *La Bataille de Tripoli* (Battle of Tripoli), in similar terms; he "observed in the battery of Suni, at Sid-Messri, in October 1911, how the shining, aggressive flight of a cannonball, red hot in the sun and speeded by fire, makes the sight of flayed and dying human flesh almost negligible."[52] Clearly, Marinetti's fascination with the speed and shimmer of a cannonball typifies Futurist lyrical intoxication with matter that replaces the sentimental and human compassion of passéist literature. In "The Technical Manifesto of Futurist Literature," he demands:

> To capture the breath, the sensibility, and the instinct of metals, stones, wood, and so on, through the medium of free objects and whimsical motors. To substitute for human psychology, now exhausted, the lyric obsession with matter ...
> Three elements hitherto overlooked in literature must be introduced:
> 1 Sound (manifestation of the dynamism of objects)
> 2 Weight (objects' faculty of flight)
> 3 Smell (objects' faculty of dispersing themselves) ...
> Deep intuitions of life joined to one another, word for word according to their illogical birth, will give us the general lines of *an intuitive psychology of matter*.[53]

Marinetti's intention in *Zang Tumb Tumb* was, he makes clear, to open "attentive ears eyes nostrils" to the piercing notes of the battle by the use of parole in libertà. The poem reaches the apex of onomatopoeia and verbal sonority in "Bombardamento" (Bombardment), a segment most often declaimed by the poet himself. A few lines below, in Italian so that the original sound is maintained, highlight the sound of artillery:

zang-tumb-tumb tata-tatatata stop
uuuuuuuurlaaare degli
ammalati nel **crrrrrrrrpitare** delle **palle** fischi **schianto** di vetri
rottttti sportelli bersagli Adrianopoli interamente accerchiata treno
abbandonato dai meccanicci e dai soldati rabbbbia degli shrapnels bulgari[54]

Here the text verbally denotes and onomatopoetically revives the hiss of the projectiles, the crackling of bullets, and the crash of shattered glass, mixed with the screams of the sick in the train abandoned by mechanics and soldiers under the hail of Bulgarian shrapnel. This kind of brief, onomatopoeic sound score, which reappears with variations several times throughout "Bombardamento," undoubtedly presents an additional physical challenge for the performer. As the onomatopoeias of war noise intensify, and as the poem moves toward the final act of bombardment, the performer's larynx, vocal cords, and entire speaking apparatus must endure extreme stress to produce the mimetic vocalization of inanimate sounds. A Futurist poet, then, intentionally evokes the dynamism of the world through onomatopoeia of its sounds, while the performer, most often a poet himself, turns into a miming sound machine to reproduce this worldly noise.

Marinetti's dynamic declamation of "Bombardamento" at the Doré Gallery in London, 28 April 1914, exemplifies a further step toward theatrical performance:

> Dynamically and synoptically I declaimed several passages from my ZANG TUMB TUMB (The Siege of Adrianople). On the table in front of me I had a telephone, some boards, and matching hammers that permitted me to imitate the Turkish general's orders and the sounds of artillery and machine-gun fire. Blackboards had been set up in three parts of the hall, to which in succession I either ran or walked, to sketch rapidly an analogy with chalk. My listeners, as they turned to follow me in all my evolutions, participated, their entire bodies inflamed with emotion, in the violent effects of the battle described by my words-in-freedom. There were two big drums in a distant room, from which the painter Nevinson, my colleague, produced the boom of cannon, when I told him to do so over the telephone. The swelling interest of the English audience became frantic enthusiasm when I achieved the greatest dynamism by alternating the Bulgarian song "Sciumi Maritza" with the dazzle of my images and the clamor of the onomatopoeic artillery.[55]

Marinetti's description offers a casebook sample of Futurist mise en scène. Here, *Zang Tumb Tumb* acquires qualities of a straightforward performance text for the staging of a dynamic, synoptic declamation. Its elaborate blueprint suggests a stage that spills into the audience space as if it were an act of environmental theatre. The three blackboards, strategically located at specific places in the hall, worked as blocking points for the choreography, which was deliberately aimed to disorient the audience by making them turn and follow the performer's abrupt changes of pace and direction. From the point of view of physical performance, Marinetti's declamation, running, and swift position changes are nothing but fisicoffolia, as discussed in his "Variety Theatre Manifesto." Furthermore, with his simultaneous use of onomatopoeic words-in-freedom and their visual analogies, sketched rapidly on the blackboards, Marinetti transposed the free orthography and the sound content of the poem literally onto the stage. Apparently, the iconicity of the graphic and aural material of the poem provided dramaturgical potential for theatrical performance. One should not forget that, as the poet reminds us, the piece achieved its high point musically by the counterpoint of "the dazzle of … images and the clamor of the onomatopoeic artillery" with the deep and slow refrain of a Bulgarian folk song, "Sciumi Maritza Okrvavljena" (The Maritza River Gurgles with Blood).

The layout of the page amplifies the expressive power of abstract words and phonemes in "Bombardamento," as well. It actually allows for the sounds of the battle to be heard. Marinetti's treatment of the printed text leaves no doubt that his typographical innovations were intended for an oral performance, as we can see in a fragment whose original graphical appearance is transposed here as accurately as possible:

3 Bulgarian battalions in march **croock-craaack** *[SLOW TWO TEMPI]*
Maritza River gurgles with blood **croock craaack** shouting of officers
slamming like brass plates **pan** here **paak** there ching
buuum
ching chaak *[PRESTO]* **chiachiachiachiachiaak**
down there up there all around watch out high up above the head
chiaack beautiful Flames
flames
flames *flames*
flames *flames*
flames destruction of the forts beh-
flames
flames
hind that smoke Shukri Pasha communicates by te-
lephone with 27 forts in turkish in german hallo **Ibrahim Rudolf Hallô Hallô**[56]

"The text activates the acoustic dimension of language with the buzzing of explosives, while the blank spaces represent a pause, a moment of silence for the eye and for the ear,"[57] comments Clara Orban. The white gaps on the page, otherwise saturated with bold letters of different type and size, are not only empty spaces, when read in the visual/spatial mode, but also silences, when read in the aural/temporal mode. The counterpoint of sounds and images makes these conventionally separate sensations vibrate together. Thus, the interplay between a scarcity and a redundancy of signs at the interstice of the temporal and spatial axes of the poem dictates the rhythm and sonority of its declamation. Since a theatrical performance also evolves along these two axes, the structural principles applied in *Zang Tumb Tumb* can be said to convey principles of Futurist theatre still influential in contemporary experimental theatre, happenings, and performance art.

Quoting liberally from *Zang Tumb Tumb* in his book *Vision in Motion*, László Moholy-Nagy illustrates the constant efforts on the part of the avant-garde "to liberate literature from the disparateness of the eye and ear." He claims: "Apollinaire's ideogram and Marinetti's poems served not so much as models, but as tradition-breakers which freed experimenters to create quick, simultaneous communication of several messages."[58] First, he credits Apollinaire with breaking new ground by the superimposition of variously sized words and letters that made them almost audible. "These ideograms … actually dynamited convention. Apollinaire introduced the 'annoyance-use' of words with physiological connotation. He also scoffed at normal syntax, discarded conventional printing with the horizontal-vertical axis ... The eye-ear sensation (about 1913) is only one of his innovations ... he also introduced the poetry of 'simultaneity,' meaning synchronization – happening at the same time – a time coordination of space and action ... cubist collage and film montage."[59]

Marinetti's exploration of a "free expressive orthography" in parole in libertà concurs with Apollinaire's experiments with *calligrammes* and *ideogrammes*. The mutual influence between two poets cannot be ignored, for, although Futurists considered Apollinaire a revered member of the inimical Cubist camp and a mouthpiece of Cubist ideology (participating in frequent public polemics and controversies), Marinetti nevertheless included his *L'antitradizione futurista* in the collection of Futurist manifestos published in 1914 by *Lacerba*. Moholy-Nagy credits Marinetti with the invention of "an acoustic collage (onomatopoeia)" in which he included "a great number of new elements to contemporary poetry; sound effects; verbalization of sound and sight correspondences; sound collage, etc."[60] While Moholy-Nagy's mention of correspondences alludes to the impact of Symbolists' or Kandinsky's synaesthesia on Marinetti's verbalizations, his reference to onomatoeia as an acoustic collage suggests the Futurists' links with Cubists. Clearly, unlike Symbolists, the avant-gardes no longer looked into the mystical or spiritual nature of sound, light, and colour, but rather into their formal and material features. As Futurists juxtaposed concrete/abstract aural and visual elements in a dynamic temporal flux of their poetry, painting, and theatre, they were ushering in common principles of the avant-garde art. Zbigniew Folejewski therefore regards Futurist tavole parolibere as a creation of "a potent, dynamic, multilevel, multi-color, multi-letter expression of what Moholy-Nagy later termed a new vision of the world, a vision in motion."[61] Consequently, Marinetti's dynamic verbalization, free orthography, and typographical revolution may be considered one of the sources of Moholy-Nagy's own concept of a synoptic, synergetic, and synacoustic art form typical of the Bauhaus theatre.

ANALOGY, ONOMATOPOEIA, ICONICITY: FROM SOUND POETRY TO ABSTRACT THEATRE

The principles of parole in libertà laid out in the "Technical Manifesto of Futurist Literature" (1912) required the poet to destroy syntax, scatter words randomly, "just as they are born," and remove the punctuation and linear narrative that stand in the way of spontaneous vocal expression. Analogy was pronounced the main device of a new literature, which was to be written in chains of unexpected analogies. These analogies were supposed to correspond with each other via the most remote associations produced by the unfettered imagination. "Analogy is nothing more than the deep love that assembles distant, seemingly diverse and hostile things. An orchestral style, at once polychromatic, polyphonic, and polymorphous, can embrace the life of matter only by means of most extensive analogies."[62] His is a famous (obviously aural) example of an analogy between a trembling fox terrier and a little Morse code machine. The extensive analogies were made mostly of nouns; adjectives and adverbs were supposed to be abolished (although they still appear in the text of *Zang Tumb Tumb*); and verbs were used sparsely, solely in their infinitive form. Marinetti saved the infinitive mode of the verb from cleansing because of its ability to provide "the elasticity of the intuition that perceives it." Futurist poet Luciano Folgore even suggested that if verbs were abolished altogether, physical sensations would inevitably dominate poetry.

Futurists believed that in the poetic expression of an intuitively perceived reality, driven by physical sensation, there would be no need for a strict substantive or verbal denotation. At this point, onomatopoeia as another major device of Futurist poetry besides analogy comes into play. Onomatopoeia, as a sound-image of physical action, replaces the verb in infinitive and enlivens lyricism with the crude elements of reality. Marinetti held that a sentence with an inflected verb determining a noun's action limited the poetic expression to the mere representational mode. He was convinced that an unmodified noun, with or without a verb in the infinitive, was less restrained. Therefore, he advised Futurists to use chains of bare nouns whose dynamic attributes were to be expressed by their aural shape rather than by their semantic or syntactic determination. In *BATTLE (WEIGHT + STINK)*, for instance, the parole in libertà included nouns whose phonetic structure already contained the onomatopoetic sound of their actions: "Gargaresch bursting crackling pus Tinkling knapsacks rifles clogs nails cannon horses."[63] Similarly, in "Bombardamento," the onomatopoetic mimesis of actions replaced the verbs that would denote them: "wagons pluff-plaff … horses flic flac zing zingshaaack … battalions marching croooc-craaac."[64]

Onomatopoeia became a source of the further disruption of language. "Our lyric intoxication must freely deform, reshape words, cut them, stretch them, reinforce their centers or their extremities, augment or diminish the number of their vowels and consonants ... This instinctive deformation of words corresponds to our natural tendency toward onomatopoeia. It matters little if a deformed word becomes ambiguous. It will marry to the onomatopoetic harmonies, or the summaries of noises, and soon will permit us to reach the 'onomatopoetic psychic' harmony, the sonorous but abstract expression of an emotion or pure thought,"[65] prescribed Marinetti in "Destruction of Syntax – Wireless Imagination – Words Set Free." He proposed words be treated not as fixed grammatical units, morphemes, and lexemes that participate in the linguistic encoding, but as malleable material shaped into "summaries of noises." He did not care for the possible ambiguity of reshaped words; what mattered was the onomatopoetic "sonorous but abstract expression" of the human perception of reality, emotion, or thought. Without a doubt, for Marinetti onomatopoeia stood for a sound mimesis of the world. The idea of onomatopoeia as an aural reference (or sound mime) of the phenomenal world coincides with Ihde's later attempt to establish a phenomenology of sound as a philosophical discipline. Ihde pleads for a phenomenology based on our "desire to hear the voiced character of the world: [since] all sounds are in a broad sense the voices of things." In this way our auditory experience comes from "a listening to the voiced character of the wordless sounds of the world."[66] That is precisely what the Futurist art of onomatopoeia, as an expression of the intuitive relation between the aural world and its mimetic rendition, does. It sets words free by returning them to themselves, that is, to their oral/aural expressiveness as opposed to their enslavement by verbal logic and psychology.

Walter Benjamin had a similar idea of the phenomenal world speaking to us in a wordless language decipherable by onomatopoeia. According to Benjamin, onomatopoeia is a primal source of linguistic meaning formed by a human mimetic alignment with the world. "The context of meaning veiled in the phonetic elements of a sentence," he wrote, "represents the basic resources in which, in a flash-like instant, something mimetic can reveal itself out of a sound."[67] Onomatopoeia, contrary to what the word's ancient Greek root denotes – name making – is not directed at the name of an object or at its signifying referent, but echoes the sound substance of an object or event by a playful or terrifying incantation. Onomatopoeia is a not-yet-coded signifier unmistakably linked to its object by a pure sound that participates in forgotten "primitive" correspondences between man and nature. For Benjamin, modern language, entrapped by Cartesian logocentrism and colonized by the arbitrary coupling of words and objects Ferdinand de Saussure later described, represents "the most accomplished archive of insensible mimesis," that is, one should add, a massive graveyard of "dead" onomatopoeias.

Language studies explore onomatopoeia primarily from the aspect of the relationship between the sound and the meaning of the linguistic sign. For de Saussure, for example, the linguistic sign does not link a thing and its sound but rather a concept and an arbitrary acoustic image used to denote it. He interprets language as a codified nomenclature of terms that signify as many things as they denote. Since the relationship between signifier and signified in such a denotative language is always arbitrary, de Saussure grants verbal/phonetic motivation a limited role and regards onomatopoeia as a marginal case in language practice. In contrast, Raymond Chapman asserts that onomatopoeic words, which imitate the sound of the object or action they denote, represent a powerful expressive means: "There is one area of language where the relationship between the word and the auditory experience is close by nature rather than by conscious artifice. Some words have been formed by an attempt actually to represent the sounds that they describe. They come nearer than other words to being the thing represented, as well as being a referential signal. Sounds here correspond to meaning by imitation and not because of a common agreement within a speech community that they will so correspond. There is a sense of 'cat' in *meow* which is not found in the word *cat* itself."[68]

The aural mime or onomatopoeia reincarnates something essential in the thing, being, or action to which it refers. In this case, that is what the sound 'meow' does to the object 'cat.' In other words, what is communicated here does not require a linguistic loop of codification and decodification to be understood. The onomatopoeic word, in terms of Charles Pierce's logical semiotics, represents an icon referring to its object as something that at once looks/sounds like a thing and is used as a sign for it. The iconicity of the word "meow" comes from the fact that the uttered sound-picture aurally exhibits the referred object, denoting it at the same time. In such an onomatopoeic utterance, there is no name coinage, as the root of the word suggests. Chapman therefore proposes the use of the term "echoic"[69] instead of onomatopoeic for the word formation, based on its aural iconicity.

The iconicity and phonosymbolic organization of poetic language, as Patricia Violi has suggested, "brings us right to the heart of one of the most controversial, yet central, questions for any linguistic and semiotic theory: the arbitrariness of the linguistic sign ... Iconicity seems to be at work any time language is 'reinvented' or 'created,' either consciously, as is the case in poetry and literary texts, or unconsciously, as in children's acquisition, language change, creolisation of pidgins ... Analogy and iconicity appear to be crucial elements for the remotivation of the linguistic sign."[70] Iconicity gains its power to remotivate language as a way of perception that adheres to Pierce's phenomenological category of Firstness, a mode of being that is without reference to any subject or any object. Instead, Firstness is manifested by quality, feeling, freedom, or multiplicity. Pierce's Firstness is the medium of the primordial unity of Dionysian music that survived in Futurist lyrical intoxication and artistic immersion in the swirl of life forces. Futurist onomatopoeia in poetry and fisicoffolia in theatre represent an intuitive "return" to Piercean iconicity and Firstness. It is at that point, as poet and painter Ardengo Soffici envisioned in his "First Principles of a Futurist Aesthetics," that "the word would no longer be a mute symbol of convention, but a live form among live forms, one that becomes one with the material of representation."[71] Italian sound poets of parole in libertà and Russian poets of zaumny yazyk, therefore, strove for words that directly corresponded to things/events as their acoustic icons.

Besides this primitive rejuvenation of language by onomatopoeia, Futurists' dealings with sound bore an optimistic projection of the new expressive means for the new century. In a 1914 manifesto called "Geometric and Mechanical Splendor and the Numerical Sensibility," Marinetti announced: "A new beauty is born today from the chaos of the new contradictory sensibility ... Our growing love for matter, the will to penetrate it and know its vibrations, the physical sympathy that links us to motors, push us to the *use of onomatopoeia*."[72] He went on to define four types of onomatopoeia: (1) direct or imitative, (2) indirect, complex, or analogical, (3) abstract, and (4) composite. These concepts clearly progress from onomatopoeia's primary role of miming natural or mechanical sound, to its detachment from mime and creation of an abstract composition. Miming the "noise of rubbing or striking rapidly moving solids, liquids or gases," a sound poem cracked open a new abstract structure that was, for the Futurists, far more interesting than human psychology. Similarly, scattering letters, numbers, and mathematical symbols like mechanical particles, molecules, and atoms in "synoptic tables of lyric values and graphic analogies," Futurists pulverized the literary "I" that served as the subject of passéist poetry.

At the same time, in the manifesto "Dynamic and Synoptic Declamation," Marinetti demanded: "Metallize, liquefy, vegetalize, petrify, and electrify voice grounding it in the vibrations of matter itself as expressed by words-in-freedom! Gesticulate in a draughtsman-like, topographical manner, synthetically creating in midair cubes, cones, spirals, ellipses, etc."[73] Such poetry performance produced a sonorous noise/music piece, a sound object or sound event *par excellence*. What the audience was left to consider, then, was an abstract performance of "geometrical and mechanical splendor," that is, a poem as an aural, kinetic ideogram, a hieroglyph.

The sound poetry ideas of "geometric and mechanical splendor" and "dynamic and synoptic declamation" reached out toward the poetics of other artistic media. Thus Balla, Cangiullo, and Carrà, inspired by the synoptic tables, created *dipinto parolibero*, a new kind of collage painting consisting of letters, numbers, and graphical symbols. In the performing arts, these ideas gave impetus to the Futurist synthetic theatre and Futurist dance of the shrapnel, of the machine gun, and of the "aviatrix." Finally, following the same path of abstraction, the Futurist scenography of the 1920s adopted the concept of the moto-rumorist complex as a model of multimedial staging.

As Marinetti famously said, "dramatic art without poetry cannot exist, that is, without intoxication and without synthesis."[74] His dictum points to two aspects of the Futurist dramaturgy of sound built on the premise of their sound poetry: the intuitive return to the primal power of sound in onomatopoeia (through intoxication) and the abstract structuring of distant analogies (through synthesis). In his comprehensive study of Futurist theatre, Giovanni Lista describes the dramaturgy of Futurist synthetic plays as an *assemblage*, a process that caries a legacy of the principles of analogy and dispersal of words into independent sound units initiated by Futurist poets. "By replacing the unitary logic and narrative structure of the naturalist drama, the *assemblage* of futurist syntheses followed the same vitalistic intentions. Now, to the word set free the scene set free (*la scène en liberté*) had to correspond, that is, theatrical kernels (*nœuds théâtraux*), the most intimate constitutive elements of the dramatic and theatrical language, had to be presented in their autonomy. The elementarization of stage signs came to abolish all principles of conceptual finality of the play in order to affirm the continual and indiscernible flow of reality."[75]

The atomization of artistic material into a number of elemental *nœuds théâtraux* that Lista detects in Futurist synthetic theatre undoubtedly follows poetics of Futurist sound poetry. In other words, the dramaturgy of la scène en liberté, based on the structural assembly of these fragments, finds its precedent in the poetics of parole in libertà, based on principles of analogy and iconicity. Lista thus establishes a theoretical parallel between liberated words/sounds and the elliptical, brief scenes of Futurist synthetic pieces now connected by the sudden spark of analogy. In addition, if the analogy serves as a principle of the collage of theatrical kernels, their iconicity makes them tangible. Recognizing the materiality and iconicity of sounds/words and the power of onomatopoeia to remotivate signs, Futurist poetry significantly influenced the formation of a concrete language of theatrical performance. More specifically, the fluidity, temporality, and immediacy characteristic of sound poetry induced the "indiscernible flow of reality" in the avant-garde theatre, thereby preventing its closure into a fixed textual representation. As the revitalized word/sound was wrested out from its logocentric matrix and, in the flux of performance, developed its own dramaturgy, it contributed to an idiom of the avant-garde theatre still viable in our postdramatic age. The next chapter elaborates how this line of development, notable in the Russian Futurists' *zaum* poetry, spread to the formation of their music, painting, and theatre.

4

Zaum: From a "Beyonsense" Language to an Idiom of Theatre

THE WORD-AS-SUCH: SOUND VERSUS MEANING AND CONTENT VERSUS FORM

The groundbreaking changes achieved in poetry by Russian Futurists – called literally people of the future (*budetlyanskye*) – such as Velimir Khlebnikov, Alexei Kruchenykh, Vasily Kamensky, and Vladimir Mayakovsky, preceded or ran parallel to revolutions in the painting, music, and theatre of the historical avant-garde. The revival of the sensorial essence of words, sounds, painterly/sculptural masses, or colours was the fuel of that revolution. This change was already in the air when Impressionists, followers of the scientific in art, discovered that fragmenting light into coloured dots allows for a painterly rendition of nature that approximated retinal perception, and when Symbolists, followers of the spiritual in art, started exploring the musicality of verse and its synaesthetic potential to reflect "correspondences" of senses. The main concern of the artists in both movements was the immediate impact of the artistic material – that is, sound and colour – on our senses. The avant-gardes went further. Abandoning the transcendental aspirations of bourgeois poetics and focusing on what we literally hear and see in the work of art, they shifted from figurative and narrative methods to experiments with concrete features and forms. Anna Lawton acknowledges this shift in focus among Cubo-Futurists, Rayonists, Neo-primitives, Suprematists, and Constructivists, whose "search for the essence of things generated a specific concern with form and produced a heightened awareness of the given medium and its potential."[1]

In their very first manifesto, *A Slap in the Face of Public Taste* (1912), the Russian Futurist poets envisioned the glimmer of "the Summer Lightening of the New Coming Beauty of the Self-sufficient Word (*samovitoye slovo*)"[2] and opted for the "word-as-such" as the exclusive material of their art. In their view, only the "word-as-such," liberated from its syntactic and signifying mandates, could provide a literal, concrete, aural link to the essence of things. Sound appeared to be the given medium for that task. Therefore, poets no longer considered the word as a fixed unit of the language's standard vocabulary but rather as a unit of sound that reverberates with all other sounds of nature and culture, from birdcalls to astral talk, and from children's primitive language acquisition, mumbles, and cries to the ecstatic, religious speaking in tongues. Such a word – a vocable, a sequence of sounds and letters (phonemes), a composite of consonants and vowels, syllables and phonetic roots – was now recognized and employed as an aural element of language rather than a signifying one. A Futurist poem was then an oral/aural composition of sound-images meant to replace the Symbolist melodic weaving of verses.

Khlebnikov and Kruchenykh played with the verbal textures and phonetic substance of words, fashioning neologisms from sound clusters and using intentional decomposition of existing words by a morphological and, more often, phonetic shift (*sdvig*, as Russian Futurists called their main poetic device). They adopted a method of sculpting or building their sound poetry and, for that reason, proudly called themselves word makers – *rechetvortsi*. This kind of poetry-making was diametrically opposed to the Symbolists' use of poetic images – made of words that carry a metaphorical charge – favoured by leading Russian philologist Alexandr Afanasievich Potrebnya (1835–1891). A representative of the psychological school of linguistics, Potrebnya theorized poetic language as a special mode of perception and expression attainable via the metaphorical process of "thinking in images." His view was widely accepted by the Symbolists, and continued to prevail in literary theory until the Futurists and their theoretical counterparts, the Formalists, threw it "overboard from the Ship of Modernity." Completely in keeping with the Futurists' line of thought, young linguistic scholar Victor Shklovsky renounced the poetics of Symbolism and promoted the literalness of Futurist zaum poetry and "the palpability of the word" in opposition to Potrebnya's authoritative theory of "thinking in images." On 23 December 1913, at the St Petersburg's Stray Dog Cabaret, which was notorious for Futurists' brawls with the audience, Shklovsky delivered a lecture entitled "The Place of Futurism in the History of Language." His academic text established a "connection of the devices of Futurist poetry with the devices of general linguistic thought-processes"[3] and acknowledged the materiality of the linguistic sign embedded in its aural substance.

Shklovsky's lecture, published a few months later as a pamphlet called *The Resurrection of the Word*, is today considered a fundamental text of Formalist linguistic, literary, and art theory. It justified the Futurist use of difficult, semi-comprehensible language as an artistic effort for the "resurrection of things" and return of the true sensation of the word/world to humanity. In addition, it revealed the diachronic correlatives of zaum poetic practice in the incantations of the old Yakut Turkic or Slavonic languages and the ancient oral production of words that strike the ear. Shklovsky's evidence, extracted from a wide range of historical poetry and language development, proved that the genuine value of words, now eroded by everyday use, still lives in the sensuous quality of their sound. These linguistic findings implied the possibility of the revival of words by their concrete sensory form/content, and made a case for a novel theory of "'artistic' perception in which the form is sensed (perhaps not only form, but form as an essential part)."[4] Shklovsky thus, by acknowledging the emergence of a unique form of Futurist poetry from its aural content, introduced the notion of equivalence between form and content applicable to any work of art, a pivotal concept in the development of Formalism, preceding Structuralism, Post-structuralism, and their derivates in postmodern art theory. Krystyna Pomorska, who sees Russian Futurist poetry as "the creative ambience of Formalist theory," alleges: "The *material* itself plays the expressive role in poetry; consequently, there is no opposition between *material and form*, hence *material is equated with form*. Instead, the opposition which occupies the Futurists in their polemics is that of the pair: mimetic (imitative, 'objectful') as opposed to non-mimetic ('objectless')."[5]

The dichotomies of material versus form and mimetic representation versus formal abstraction were discussed relentlessly in Futurist poetry and plastic arts circles. In their works, both Russian poets and visual artists eschewed figural and representational modes and focused on the materiality of their means. Futurist/Formalist ideas prominently figured in the theories of Rayonism, Suprematism, and abstract art advanced by Mikhail Larionov, Natalia Gonchareva, and Kazimir Malevich. As we shall see later in this chapter, these painterly concepts further influenced the shape of Russian Futurist theatre works, especially *Victory over the Sun* and *Zangezi*, where an "objectless" dramaturgy of independent materials – sound, colour, and sculptural mass – and their kinetic relations replaced an "objectful" dramaturgy of plot and representation.

AURAL RESOURCES OF WORD-MAKING (*RECHETVORSTVO*)

The Cubo-Futurists published their first poems when their Symbolist and Impressionist predecessors, followers of Charles Baudelaire, Rimbaud, and Mallarmé, had already mastered a style that employed the imaginative and creative potential of sound. Crucially important to note, however, was that the Futurists started to create a different, sound-based poetic idiom that would not communicate its content by syntactically ordered phrases but rather by phonetically sculpted words. *The Tangled Wood*, a Khlebnikov poem published in the almanac *Studiya Impresionistov* (*The Studio of Impressionists*, 1910), still retains conventional syntax but, at the same time, timidly turns toward the sensual ties of words with natural sounds:

The tangled wood was full of sound
the forest screamed, the forest groaned
with fear
to see the spear-man beast his spear [6]

Paul Schmidt's congenial English translation, based on the phonetic principles Khlebnikov employed, demonstrates how the sonority of these verses has been built. In the second verse, for example, disquieting onomatopoetic consonant clusters in the words ***forest***, ***scream***, and ***groan*** sound against the traditionally silent backdrop of a mystical forest while the long vowel 'ī' repeatedly echoes in the words *fear*, *see*, *spear*, and *beast*, to intensify the forest's silence. Playing with such pure sound patterns already existing in language, Khlebnikov (Schmidt) made this poem resonate with nature; they literally invoked Symbolist "correspondences" by the affinity between the sounds of human language and the speech of the universe. Similarly, in another of Khlebnikov's early poems whose verses contained no semantically disengaged words, that is, which were not yet transrational, we can hear the predominance of pure sound patterning. Listen!

Kogda umirayut koni, dyushat,
Kogda umirayut travy, sokhnut,
Kogda umirayut solnci, oni gasnut,
Kogda umirayut lyudi, poyet pesni

When horses die, they sigh,
When grasses die, they shrivel

When suns die, they flare and expire
When people die, they sing songs [7]

Here, each of four verses in the original begins with two identical words, the second one (*umirayut*) rhyming on *ut*. Additionally, in the first three verses, this middle rhyme is maintained by a final rhyme on *at/ut*, implemented to lull the reader with its steady, repetitious rhythm. A break comes with the fourth verse, in which two words at the same positions (*lyudi* and *pesni*) rhyme in a completely different tune. The translation follows the same principle when the soft melody of "die, flare, and expire" changes into the ringing sound of "sing songs." This aural shift abruptly erases the poem's initial rhythmic and phonetic scheme and brings a new "meaning" sculpted and communicated in/by sound. It emerges that Khlebnikov probed his material resources to discover a new idiom; he used sound repetition in an almost abstract/concrete manner that later became a marker of his "beyonsense"[8] poetry.

Analyzing the use of repetition in Russian verse, Formalist critic and poet Osip Brik found that "sounds and sound harmonies are not merely a euphonic extra but are the result of an autonomous poetic endeavor."[9] Underneath prosodic devices like assonance and alliteration, masculine and feminine rhyme, rhythmic structure and metric scheme, Brik revealed dominant, independent features of sound composition. His exploration of the phonetic devices used in poetry-making corroborates the idea of autonomous sound material's potential to construct something beyond the poetic image. "However the interrelationship of sound and image may be regarded, one thing is certain: the orchestration of poetic speech is not fully accounted for by a repertoire of overt euphonic devices, but represents in its entirety the complex product of the interaction of the general laws of euphony. Rhythm, alliteration, and so forth are only the obvious manifestations of particular instances of basic euphonic laws,"[10] concludes Brik.

Brik's concept of the autonomy of euphonic devices was amply demonstrated in Futurist poetic practice. Khlebnikov, Kruchenykh, Vasily Kamensky, Elena Guro, Vasilisk Gnedov, and others transgressed the boundaries of versification and rhythm with their aural sculpting. Employing 'arbitrary' and 'derived' words-sounds beyond their prosodic use, they released the energies hidden in their transrational connections with things, nature, and culture. Their genuine form of sound poetry beyond the rational, combined with the interrelated phenomena of avant-garde abstract painting and atonal music, awakened similar tendencies in contemporary theatre, where stage material started to perform its own story and generate its own sense.

The Futurist concept of an independent sound structure of poetic language can be traced back to Symbolist poet Andrei Belyi, who in his 1909 essay "The Magic of Words" claimed that when "the musical force of sound is resurrected in the word, we are once again captivated, not by the meaning, but by the sound of words."[11] Before using words to name things, we utter sounds that convey signs of our human presence in the world, says Belyi. The creative power of sound resides in the "imaginative speech … of words that express the logically inexpressible impression I derive from the objects surrounding me. Living speech is always the music of the inexpressible."[12] Consequently, Belyi conceives of poetic speech as an independent structure whose significance "lies in the fact that it does not actually prove or demonstrate anything with words. In poetry the words are grouped in such a fashion that their totality gives the image. The logical significance of this image is entirely indeterminate."[13]

One of the main Cubo-Futurist programmatic texts, "The Liberation of the Word," discusses indeterminacy as a key feature of poetic language. "Our poetry is free, and for the first time we do not care whether it is realistic, naturalistic or fantastic; except for its starting point, it does not place itself in any relationships with the world and does not coordinate itself with it; all other crossing points of this poetry with the world are *a priori accidental*,"[14] claims Benedikt Livshits. He proposes that the poet's involvement in the materiality of the word is driven "by plastic affinity of verbal expressions, by their plastic valence, by verbal texture, by rhythmic problems and musical orchestration, and by the general requirements of pictorial and musical structure."[15] The multidisciplinary wording of Livshits's manifesto is symptomatic of all Futurist art theory. This kind of cross-referential terminology derives from the fact that the Russian avant-garde scene was a mélange of artists, poets, scientists, and critics who typically transgressed the borders of their disciplines. Their artistic merger was essential to the spread of Futurist poetic principles of the "word-as-such" and their reliance on sound resources into the concepts of other arts.

VERBAL ART: VOWELS, CONSONANTS, AND THE FRAGMENTED WORDS OF *ZAUM*

Poet Aleksei Kruchenykh was first to use the term "transrational" (*zaumnoe*) in the manifesto "Novye puti slova" (New Ways of the Word: The Language of the Future, Death to Symbolism, 1913): "Before us there was no verbal art. There were the pathetic attempts of servile thought to present everyday reality, philosophy and psychology … but *the art of the word* did not exist … The word (and its components, the sounds) is not simply a truncated thought, not simply logic; it is first of all the *transrational* (irrational parts, mystical, aesthetic)."[16]

Zaum poetry should follow the material aesthetic of words/sounds and not the discursive logic of language, proposes Kruchenykh. A rupture with practical language will bring about a new poetic idiom beyond rational concepts, no longer under the yoke of philosophy and psychology. The beyonsense language, although it first appeared in Khlebnikov's verses written in the period from 1906 to 1908, was officially launched as a new poetry idiom a few years later by Kruchenykh's poem "Dyr bul shchyl" (Pomada, 1913). Although the two poets are equally credited for this invention, there is a substantial difference between their approaches to zaum. While Khlebnikov sought a universal language based on phonetic roots beyond the limits of a particular tongue, Kruchenykh fought tirelessly for an innovative sound poetry that often transgressed into proto-Dadaist, alogical, and absurdist word creation. On the other hand, whereas Khlebnikov tended to capture an elevated sense of language in oldest phonetic roots, Kruchenykh tried to release language from the entanglements of signification through irregularity and primitive coarseness.

Their joint theoretical elaboration of the new poetics was published in Moscow in 1913 as the fifteen-page pamphlet titled *Word as Such*. Khlebnikov and Kruchenykh state: "The Futurian painters love to use parts of the body, its cross section, and the Futurian wordwrights use chopped-up words, half-words, and their odd artful combinations (transrational language), thus achieving the very greatest expressiveness, and precisely this distinguishes the swift language of modernity, which has annihilated the previous frozen language." [17] The pamphlet contains several illustrations of *zaum* poetry, the main piece of evidence being Kruchenykh's "Dyr bul shchyl":

dyr bul shchyl
ubeshshchur
skum
vy so bu
r l ez [18]

The poem consists of elementary phonemes, that is, vowel and consonant clusters, irreverent of syntax, versification, or any kind of prosody. Its five verses remain endlessly quoted and analyzed in critical literature, from contemporary Futurist manifestos and Shklovsky's Formalist essays to the literary studies of today. The roughness of sound texture in the poem comes from Kruchenykh's preferred use of consonants. Kruchenykh explains his option: "In art, there may be unresolved dissonances – unpleasant to the ear – because there is dissonance in our soul by which the former are resolved … All this does not narrow art, but rather opens new horizons."[19] It was as if the dissonant sound clusters of "Dyr bul shchyl" answered Marinetti's call to "make use of every ugly sound, every expressive cry from the violent life that surrounds us," and "bravely create the 'ugly' literature."[20] They practically expressed "deep intuitions of life joined to one another, word for word according to their illogical birth, [that] will give us the general lines of *an intuitive psychology of matter*."[21] Certainly, there was an affinity between Russian and Italian Futurists emerging from their use of raw sound in poetry. Nils Åke Nilsson even connects the 1913 mushrooming of zaum poems and word-as-such manifestos with the 1912 appearance of the Russian translation of Marinetti's "Technical Manifesto of Futurist Writers." Nilsson asserts that "the poem ["Dyr bul shchyl"] could be read as an interesting illustration of the ... idea of Marinetti and Soffici: the final goal of art is to lose itself in life, the sounds of poetic language become congruent with sounds of life."[22] Nevertheless, Kruchenykh, in a manifesto published that same year, "The New Ways of the Word," clearly rejects the mechanical use of onomatopoeia associated with his Italian colleagues: "Our goal is simply to point out irregularity as a device, to show the necessity and the importance of irregularity. Our goal is to underscore the great significance for art of all strident elements, discordant sounds (dissonances) and purely primitive roughness ... The Italian 'amateurish' Futurists, with their endless *ra ta ta ra ta ta* ... mechanical tricks – soulless, monotonous – lead to *the death of life and art* ... Our verbal creativity is generated by *a new deepening* of the spirit, and it throws new light on everything."[23] Admittedly, the primitive roughness of "Dyr bul shchyl," dug up from a deep, aural substratum of language, contradicts the direct mimesis of modern, industrial, urban noise prevalent in Marinettian onomatopoeia.

Kruchenykh's poem, textured by its cacophonic consonant instrumentation (containing more Russian spirit than in all of Pushkin, the author boasted), replaced the euphonic beauty and smoothness of Symbolist poetry. Pomorska links the poem's harsh sound with the aesthetics of the "rough surface" and the surprising perspectives of Cubist painting. Pomorska also claims that through the use of the "heavy sounds" of "difficult" consonants like *r*, *sh*, and *shch*, the way Mayakovsky preferred, the "Futurists began to copy the sound patterns of Turkic languages."[24] Believing in the expressive power of the oral idiom of the Central Asian Steppe, in which a tribal, "pagan" sound remained connected with life, Kruchenykh aimed at an Ur-sprache that would tear through the ear like "a formidable chant," as he used to call "Dyr bul shchyl." For Futurist poets, to be authentically Russian meant to embrace the oral poetry practice and harsh melody of the language's pagan, Scythian, Asiatic roots.

PRIMORDIAL INCANTATION AT THE ROOTS OF *ZAUM*

Khlebnikov's poem "Zaklatje smehom" (Incantation by Laughter, 1910) invigorates the Futurist contention that a single word, a word-as-such, can produce yet unknown poetic effects. Here the root of word *smekh* (laugh) explodes into a multitude of expressive forms:

O, razsmeytes', smekhachi!
O, zasmeytes', smekhachi!
Chto smiyutsya smekhami, chto smeyaitvuyut smeyalno,
O, zasmeytes' usmeyalno!
O, rasmeshishch nadsmeyal nykh smekh usmeynykh smekhachey!
O, issmeysya rassmeyalno smekh nadsmeynykh smekhaczey!

Hlaha! Uthlofan, laufIings!
Hlaha! Uflofan, lauflings!
Who lawghen with lafe, who hlaehen lewchly,
Hlaha! Ufhlofan hlouly!
Hlaha! Hloufish lauflings lafe uf beloght lauchalorum!
Hlaha! Loufenish lauflings lafe, hlohan utlaufly![25]

The sound of laughter bursts forth from the newly coined words, which stem from just one phonetic root: smekh/laugh. The poem feels cracked, as if by a fairground jester trying to find ever-funnier derivates of a simple Slavic word – smekh – that are extended by his jolly imaginings of all its possible and impossible prefixes and suffixes. Paul Schmidt describes it as "permutations of the word *laugh* into a weird scenario full of prehistoric chortles."[26] Its unbridled verbal variation goes on and on, like a competitive word game played at an ancient popular carnival. This verbo/vocal technique "mainly alludes to the folk incantation, of which the important property is that language in it becomes both *the tool and the object* – two functions concentrated in one act," finds Pomorska.[27] Her interpretation follows Formalist doctrine that proposes an amalgamation of the prosodic device (the tool) and verbal/aural material (the object), in a union of sign and sound that makes the word palpable. Besides, quite in tune with the avant-garde fight for a new artistic idiom, the restless inflections of the word smekh function as an antidote to its unilateral signification. Such disturbance initiates the carnivalesque "heteroglossia," in place of a literary "monologism" of language, discussed in Mikhail Bakhtin's *Gargantua and Pantagruel*.

Nilsson thoroughly analyzes "Incantation by Laughter" in comparison with its historical counterparts.[28] He rejects its similarity to Marinettian "integral onomatopoeia" or Dadaist aleatoric poetry, suggesting instead that Hugo Ball's *Lautgedichte* (sound poems) are more comparable to Khlebnikov's poems. It is the incantational attitude that allies Ball and Khlebnikov, claims Nilsson. According to Ball's own description, his shamanistic performance of *Gadji beri bimba* at the Cabaret Voltaire aimed to put the audience into a trance; the powerful cadence of words/sounds turned him into "a magic bishop." Certainly, there are similarities between Khlebnikov's incantation and Ball's quasi-ritual chant. Both poets shift sound patterns of words, mischievously flirting on the line between surprise and recognition; they take on the roles of a folk jester or shaman delivering verbal riddles and chanting hypnotic tunes. "Incantation by Laughter" sounds like a shamanistic chant whose power relies on its "primitive" sound and rhythm, regardless of Nilsson's claim that Khlebnikov wrote the poem to encourage the verbal creativity of his friends, the Futurist poets – *smekhachi*.

Khlebnikov's "lauflings" spoke in the tradition of verbal games and the exchange of proverbs and riddles that, according to Walter Ong, "are not used simply to store knowledge but to engage others in verbal and intellectual combat: the utterance of a proverb or riddle challenges the listeners to top it up with an opposite or contradictory one."[29] Challenging the audience was an exquisite weapon of Futurist poetry and theatre on both the Italian and Russian sides. Futurists' aggressive attitude, deeply rooted in so-called '"primitive" oral cultures, has contributed to the ritualistic and participative nature of theatre in the historical avant-garde. Christopher Innes admits: "Perhaps paradoxically, what defines this avant-garde movement is not overtly modern qualities, such as the 1920s romance of technology: George Antheil's '*aeroplane sonata*,' Carlo Govoni's '*poesie elettriche*' or Enrico Prampolini's '*theatre of mechanics*' – but primitivism …

Focus on myth and magic, which in theatre leads to experiments with ritual and ritualistic patterning of performance ... In theatrical terms this is reflected by a reversion to 'original' forms: the Dionysian rituals of ancient Greece, shamanistic performances, the Balinese dance-drama."[30] The incantatory character of Balinese theatre, its semi-comprehensible chant and codified dance movement, incommensurable with ordinary behaviour, inspired Antonin Artaud to search for an idiom that would "consist of noises, cries, gestures, poses and signs which would only include words as incantations."[31] Khlebnikov's poem "My churaemsya i charuemsya" (We Enchant and Recant, 1914) is a perfect case in point of such an idiom:

My churaemsya i charuemsya
Tam charuyas', zdes' churayas',
To churakhar', to charakhar',
Zdes' churil', tam charil'.
Iz churni vzor charny. [32]

The entire poem is based on the sound play between the two juxtaposed, antonymic phonemes *char* (enchantment, allurement, captivation) and *chur* (limiting, warding off, protecting). The repetitive shamanic mantra of these two contrasting, similar-sounding words endows the poem with a particular dramaturgy. The minimal phonetic variation of *char* and *chur* stimulates the reader/performer to exaggerate the pronunciation, pitch, loudness, and rhythm to make their verbal opposition active. Taking on a role of shaman, he/she has to execute a "performative utterance" so that the words become deeds. In J.L. Austin's speech-act theory, "performance utterance" is exemplified by a priest's words that conclude a wedding ceremony making a marriage a deed. But in our case the reader/performer's authority is not embedded in the social hierarchy or symbolic meaning of the word as described by Austin; he/she has to earn it by the specific utterance of the word or the performance of its sound. Thus the sound structure of "My churaemsya i charuemsya", situated halfway between a poem and a score for an aural/theatrical event, reveals its intrinsic performative potential. Reminiscent of a pre-rhetorical oral performance, a shamanic mantra, or a child's game, it relies on a rhythmical, repetitive vocalization that pulsates between redundancy and sparseness of sound signals. Like a "primitive," who through ritualistic sound repetition participates in an eternal cyclical cosmogony, our poet chants and un-chants, charms and un-charms, through the magic of sound.

THE ARTICULATORY ASPECT OF *ZAUM* AND ITS PERFORMANCE POTENTIAL

In his essay "On Poetry and Trans-Sense Language," Shklovski cites German psychologist and physiologist Wilhelm Max Wundt (1832–1920), who examined the links between sounds and words – notably onomatopoeia – that he considered the source of all language. Wundt found that in the development of its cognitive power, humanity encounters things and represents them in iconic pictograms and ideograms, but after the pictorial elements disappear, the meanings of words remain solely linked to their sounds, that is, their "sensual tonality." Adopting Wundt's notion of "sensual tonality," which, he claims, represents the substance of language Futurists were searching for, Shklovsky theoretically assesses *zaumnyi yazyk* as a consequence of general linguistic development. Hence, Futurists' creation of words/sounds beyond logic and syntax no longer represented an eccentric discovery of rebellious poets, but rather an expansion of the linguistic practice already extant in the "sensual tonality" of language. "It appears to us that the closest neighbors to onomatopoetic words are 'words' without concept and content that serve to express pure emotion, that is, words which cannot be said to exhibit any imitative articulation, for there is nothing to imitate, but only a concatenation of sounds and emotion … in which the hearer participates sympathetically by reproducing a certain mute tensing of the speech organs."[33]

Shklovsky's belief that the listener sympathetically participates in the original verbal gesture by his own "mute tensing of speech organs" opens a wide field of explorations into the performativity of the voice and the articulatory aspect of poetic language. Kruchenykh might have had this in mind when providing the phonetic structure of zaum as a locus for a new, vocal play based solely on the physicality of the utterance, that is, the articulation of sounds. Thus, "Dyr bul shchyl"'s articulatory dimension, embedded in the explicit disposition of consonants in the poem, determines a particular pattern of its vocal rendition. Kruchenykh's intentional variation of the vocal energy of individual verses, from the explosive cluster *shchyl* at the beginning to the flattening hiss *ez* at the end, dictates "an oral rendering [that] requires full exploitation of the speech apparatus and a constant changing from one position to another. It reminds one of the 'speech mimic,'[34] concludes Nilsson. In other words, there is a performative potential incorporated in articulatory demands of the very phonetics of the poem. This corroborates Shklovsky's earlier discussion of speech articulation as inherently performative: "In the enjoyment of meaningless trans-sense language the articulatory aspect of speech is undeniably important. It may even be that in general the greater part of the pleasure in poetry is to be found in the articulations in the original dance of the speech organs."[35]

Shklovsky's description of the "dance of the speech organs" concurs with the notion of "the grain of the voice" – a sensual speech that offers the performer's body to the audience – later theorized by Roland Barthes. For Barthes, it is a substance of vocal performance, "a very specific place in which a language encounters a voice ... a double production of language and of music," proving that "every relation to a voice is necessarily erotic."[36] Barthes's thinking has since figured prominently in contemporary theatre studies. Performance art theorists often use his notion of "the grain of the voice" when discussing the bodily and erotic aspect of the performer-audience relationship. According to Barthes, there is always something more than a recited verse or a sung tune in the vocalization of speech or music, "something non-spoken which designates itself: the voice."[37] The voice is always already inscribed in the musicality of the text – one need only "pronounce" it, not "articulate" it as a part of a discursive speech, operatic singing, or dramatic acting. To avoid terminological confusion, we should understand that Barthes, unlike Shklovsky and most theoreticians, uses the term 'pronunciation' for the physical act of vocalization – as opposed to 'articulation,' which strives to appropriate the meaning of speech. He says, "Articulation, in effect, functions abusively as *a pretence of meaning*: claiming to serve meaning, it basically misreads it ... It involves the singer [performer] in a highly ideological art of expressivity ... [while] the *pronunciation* maintains the perfect coalescence of the line of meaning (the phrase) and the line of music."[38] Regardless of terminology, both Barthes and Shklovsky agree that vocal utterance is an act of performance, not an act of verbal representation. As a vocal gesture, a breath, a cry, a physical action of the tongue, and a production of words/sounds, it confirms a carnal presence of the performer here and now, rather than a meaning of words/concepts, which resides elsewhere.

The Futurist idiom of the self-sufficient word, then, recoils from meaning. It is not meant to make a statement; it is meant to exhibit a vocal gesture in the sphere between the lexical and the aural/musical/performative, heavily leaning toward the latter. It was precisely by escaping the pretence of meaning that Futurist poets were able to liberate words. The fresh "pronunciation" of zaum words – phonemes stripped bare of their signifying fetters – made us conceive things anew. Thus, the sound poetry's revival of the word through its sound participated in the process of Shklovsky's *ostranenie* (defamiliarization), a poetic device that seeks fresh insight into the essence of things. It also provided a gateway to new possibilities in the performing arts. Bertolt Brecht, for example, eschewing illusionist and psychological theatrical techniques, used this same method of making things strange to present them in a new light. Even though his primary motivation was scientific and sociopolitical, Brecht's move followed this Formalist shift incited by beyonsense Futurist poetry. In a more formal, structural sense, ostranenie and zaum influenced a multimedial idiom of the first Russian Futurist theatre productions discussed later in this chapter.[39]

AURAL PRINCIPLES OF *ZAUM* IN MUSIC, PAINTING, AND THEATRE

The recognition of the materiality of sound/paint/sign migrated across the borders of avant-garde art disciplines of music, poetry, painting, sculpture, and theatre. As Pomorska has suggested, Russian Futurist poets, under the influence of Cubist painters, celebrated the word from the perspective of sound as the only material and theme of poetry: "The sound is equated to paint, geometrical lines and figures, and it becomes an independent phenomenon to be experienced and enjoyed as the only poetry, real and pure. Thus the Futurists fought for the 'pure word,' not loaded with any referential or symbolic function with respect to the object. 'The word at liberty' was supposed to operate with its own structure, and the associations between sounds should evoke 'new objects,' sometimes called '*zvuko-obrazi*' (sound-images)."[40]

Khlebnikov and Kruchenykh admitted in their initial manifesto that Futurist *rechetvortsi* (word-makers) used chopped-up words in their artful combinations in the wake of Futurist painters who used body parts in their broken perspective. In their 1913 almanac *A Trap for Judges*, eight undersigned Futurist poets further proclaimed: "We have begun to see in letters only *vectors of speech* … We started to endow words with content on the basis of their *graphic* and *phonic characteristics*. We for the first time brought to the fore the role of verbal mass and made it perceivable … We understand vowels as time and space (a characteristic of thrust), and consonants as color, sound, smell."[41]

The terms such as "vectors of speech" and "verbal mass" linked the sound of words with painting material relying on the theoretical scaffolding established in the discussions of plastic dynamism and synaesthesia by Kandinsky, Kublin, and the Burliuk brothers. Inspired by Kandinsky's elaborations of "inner sound" and "stage composition," Kublin and Aleksandr Scriabin extended this interdisciplinary discourse to the domain of music. The leading impresario of the Russian avant-garde, Kublin was also a promoter of important trends of new music: he advocated microtonal music (Pratella), atonal composition (Schönberg), and the art of noise (Russolo), and envisioned a single art that would encompass poetry, music, and the plastic arts. In an essay that appeared in the *Blaue Reiter Almanac* (1912), Kublin called for a music as unencumbered as natural sound, a music liberated from the prescriptions of tonality and metre contained in its conventional notation. He also proposed the use of smaller harmonic intervals in musical composition, such as quarter, eighth, and sixteenth tones, alongside Pratella's and Russolo's endeavours to introduce the enharmonic music. In his manifesto "What Is the Word" (1914), Kublin even devised a synaesthetic alphabet assigning to each vowel its own pitch and to each consonant its own colour. On the synoptic table of these colour-sound correspondences, the phoneme *G* matches a Yellow-Black colour and denotes Selfishness, while *K* matches Black and denotes Hate and so on.[42] Aleksandr Scriabin, the renowned pianist and composer of the turn of the century, devised an even more detailed colour-sound scheme and a notation for audio-visual compositions meant to be played on a specially constructed colour/light organ (*clavier à lumière*). Following Scriabin's code, the musical note C matches the colour Red and represents Human Will, C-sharp is Violet and represents Creative Spirit, D is Yellow and represents Joy, and so on.[43] Kublin's and Scriabin's ideas resound in Matiushin and Malevich's theatrical work on the score, sets, and lighting for Kruchenykh's *zaum* opera *Victory over the Sun*.

The mutual reflection of sound and colour was fundamental to Mikhail Larionov's and Natalia Goncharova's Rayonism, as well. Their theory of painting can be considered typically Futurist, especially when compared to Umberto Boccioni's ideas about plastic dynamism and fluidity of atmosphere reflected by a simultaneous exertion of centrifugal and centripetal forces on a canvas. Rayonist paintings showed objects reverberating in the environment, emanating and reflecting rays back and forth in a dynamic interplay of light, colour, saturation, mass, depth, and texture. As Larionov described, "Obviously, a blue spread evenly over the canvas vibrates with less intensity than the same blue put on more thickly. Hitherto this law has been applicable only to music, but it is incontestable also with regard to painting: *colors have a timbre* that changes according to the quality of their vibrations, i.e., of density and loudness. In this way, painting becomes as free as music and becomes self-sufficient outside imagery."[44] Thus, liberated from any signifying and figural baggage, and in this way similar to words in poetry or sounds in music, objects in the plastic arts reacquired their sensorial potential and tactility. Larionov's painterly concepts clearly reflect ideas hatched in zaum poetry. They correspond to the Burliuk brothers' proposal for "roughing up the texture of the text to make it 'palpable' through an unorthodox use of the verbal material,"[45] or Kruchenykh's effort to reclaim the tactile quality of words through the orchestration of the "various textures of words (*faktura slova*) – tender, heavy, coarse, dry, and moist [...] by rhythm, semantics, syntax, and graphics."[46] Such cross-fertilization of poetry, music, and plastic arts theories certainly stood behind the Futurists' big theatrical endeavour of 1913, the staging of their first opera.

VICTORY OVER THE SUN: A CASE STUDY OF THE THEATRICALIZATION OF *ZAUM*

Victory over the Sun, an opera written and staged by Alexei Kruchenykh with music by Mikhail Matiushin, prologue by Viktor Khlebnikov, and sets, costumes, and lighting design by Kazimir Malevich, was originally performed only twice, on alternate evenings with *Vladimir Mayakovsky: A Tragedy*. Ambitiously announced as the "First Ever Staging of Futurist Theatre, December 2–5, 1913," the event came at the peak of the richest and most tumultuous season of Futurist experimentation in Russia. It followed an exciting autumn on the St Petersburg art scene. In October, almost all of the zaum poets (the brothers Burliuk, Kruchenykh, Livshits, Mayakovsky, Khlebnikov, and Malevich) participated in "An Evening of Speech-Creators" (*Rechetvortsev*); in November, David Burliuk gave a lecture, "On the Futurists," containing his critical observations on Marinetti; and in November and December, the Union of Youth mounted its last art exhibition.

Robert Benedetti, who staged the 1980 reconstruction of *Victory over the Sun* in Los Angeles, describes the 1913 *Zeitgeist* this way: "These were times when traditional boundaries and conventions in art were being destroyed and new forms being developed. *Victory over the Sun*, in fact, may have been the first example of what we now call Performance Art. It was certainly one of the earliest instances of serious multidisciplinary collaboration."[47] To put it bluntly, the contemporary press hated it, as is evident in the acerbic comment in St Petersburg's *New Time*, 3 December 1913: "FUTURIST PERFORMANCE. IN – brr! ... SOL! – brr ... ENCE! – brrrr. This is futurist language. They will understand me. The public also. [Undersigned:] P.K-di."[48] But, regardless of its initial failure or success, it holds true that the production premiered "three and half years before Satie and Picasso's *Parade* ... [and] was one of the first totally modern pieces of twentieth-century performance art ... [where] performers in stylized geometric costumes danced and sang absurdly before proto-abstract backdrops."[49]

The plot of the opera depicts a rebellion against the sun – the capture, killing, and burial of the sun by the Strong Men of the Future – and exhibits ideas parallel to zaum poetry's divorce from the rational and signifying language. The work denies Apollonian clarity and the practical rationality of the Cartesian world, and calls for a return to Dionysian primordial chaos and darkness. The protagonists of the play, the Strong Men of the Future, sing disrespectfully: "We pulled the sun out with its fresh roots; they're fatty, smelled of arithmetic,"[50] echoing Kruchenykh's declaration in a manifesto of zaum: "We do not serve as the reflection of some sun."[51]

In an interview for the St Petersburg newspaper *Day*, 1 December 1913, Malevich and Matiushin frankly stated the subversive intention of the play: "Its meaning is to overthrow one of the greatest artistic values – the sun, in the present instance ... Futurists want to break free of this regulated world ... to transform the world into chaos ... to smash established values into fragments ... to create new values out of these fragments ... discovering new, unexpected and unseen links. So then, the sun – that former value – cramps their style and they feel like overthrowing it ... It is, in fact, the plot of the opera. The cast of the opera should express this in both language and sound."[52]

Kruchenykh's mise en scène centred on the interplay and actions of symbolic figures, rather than dramatic characters, who recited, sang, and moved encased in their Cubist costumes speaking an alogical, often semi-comprehensible dialogue. Even more, it could be described as a staging of the kinetic clash between sculptural and painterly masses, exaggerated light changes, and weird musical punctuations. It looked as if Edward Gordon Craig's *übermarionetten* moved and uttered sounds in Kandinsky's abstract audio-visual ambience, where moving screens reflected the chromatic changes of light and music. The staging demonstrated the authors' predilection for a non-mimetic (objectless) rather than a mimetic (objectful) art method, an attitude that figures in the whole spectrum of Futurist art from zaum poetry to Rayonist, Suprematist, and abstract painting. The same rejection of the representational mode in favour of immediacy, iconicity, literalness, and abstraction determined the theatricality of *Victory over the Sun*. Designer Malevich and composer Matiushin confess: "We have come as far as the rejection of reason because another reason has grown in us which can be called 'beyond reason' and which also has law, construction, and sense."[53] Writer and director Kruchenykh discloses: "The stage was set up the way I expected and wanted it to be. The blinding spotlights. Malevich's sets consisted of large planes – triangles, circles, and parts of machines. The cast was in masks resembling gas masks of the period. '*Likari*' (actors) were like moving machines. The costumes, designed by Malevich again, were cubist in construction: cardboard and wire. This altered the anatomy of a person – the performers moved as if tied together and controlled by the rhythm of the artist and director … What shook the audience particularly were the songs of the Coward and the Aviator (in consonants only) ... [and] the chorus of Undertakers, built on unexpected disruptions and dissonances."[54]

Victory over the Sun is both conceptually and pragmatically a multimedia work of art. Its cacophonic vocalizations, disruptive and dissonant choruses, and geometrical movements of performers wearing cubist costumes on a visually fractured stage explore the possibilities of kinetic sculpture and total theatre. Although the better part of the language of the script can hardly be called zaumnyi yazyk – it is used only sporadically, taking place in the two short arias by the Young Man and the Aviator – the piece's philosophy and performance method undoubtedly derives from Futurist zaum poetry.

Matiushin's role in the development of the performance style of *Victory over the Sun* surpasses the significance of the mere twenty-seven bars in his original score. He was unyielding about the zaum character of Futurist theatrical presentation in St Petersburg. As Susan Compton points out, Matiushin even disapproved of Mayakovsky's language in his tragedy because he "never divorces word from its meaning, he does not recognize that the sound of a word is priceless in itself."[55] In the *First Journal of Russian Futurists*, Matiushin wrote enthusiastically: "Russian youth, without any knowledge of the new theatre experiments abroad presented the first performance on a stage in St. Petersburg of the disintegration of concepts and words, of old staging and of musical harmony. They presented a new creation, free of old conventional experiences and complete in itself, using seemingly senseless words – picture-sounds – new indications of the future that leads into eternity and gives a joyful feeling of strength to those who will lend an ear and look at it."[56] Matiushin praised the student-performers who, "according to our decisions, spoke the words without music, pausing for long intervals between each word. In that way, a word, alienated from its meaning, gave the impression of great strength."[57] This attitude had been clear from the beginning when the poster that called for the audition warned: "Professional actors please do not bother to come." The unsuspecting president of the Union of Youth later complained that the actors, instead of playing their roles before the spectator, were addressing the audience directly the way an orator from the rostrum would. Obviously, their performance style was an attempt to enact a goal of Futurist sound poetry, that is, to disintegrate concepts and words and to produce picture-sounds instead.

The zaum concept of picture-sounds was of utmost concern in the anxious correspondence about the coming production between Matiushin and Malevich. The latter wrote about letters that, rather than expressing things, represent sonic notes. "Arriving at the idea of sound, we obtained note-letters expressing sonic masses. Perhaps in a composition of these sound masses (former words) a new path will be found. In this way, we tear the letter from a line, from a single direction, and give it the possibility of free movement ... Consequently, we arrive at a distribution of letter and sonic masses in space similar to painterly Suprematism. These masses will hang in space and will provide the possibility for our consciousness to move farther and farther away from the earth."[58]

For Malevich, new potentials of picture-sounds (letter/phonemes) lay in abandoning the linearity of former words, which would allow for their spatialization. Subverting the temporality of sound into the spatiality of physical objects, Malevich even comes to envision the stage with sonic masses hanging in space like aural sculptures. These masses that stand, hang, move, and flow on the stage are not only masses of sound but also of light, kinetic scenery, objects, and performers. This was the underlining idea of Malevich's approach to the lighting design of *Victory over the Sun*, which was facilitated by a state-of-the-art lighting system – with a sophisticated central console and movable spotlights – installed at the St Petersburg's Luna Park Theatre, the actual venue of the opera's opening night. The theatre was formerly a site of Vera Komissarzhevskaya's Dramatic Theatre, well known for staging of the experiments of Meyerhold and the Symbolists, now thoroughly renovated with the hope of attracting audiences to American-style entertainment. Livshits, one of the organizers of the event, described the show under the "tentacles of the spotlights" as an outgrowth of Malevich's unscrupulous destruction of forms. "Turning [shapes of light and objects] from the square and the circle to the cube and the sphere with the mercilessness of Savanarola, he proceeded to destroy everything that fell outside the axes that he had designated. This was a *zaum* of painting, one that anticipated the ecstatic non-objectivity of Suprematism ... Bodies were broken up by the beams of light, they alternately lost arms, legs, head, because for Malevich they were only geometric bodies yielding not only to decomposition into elements, but also to complete disintegration in the pictorial space."[59]

Malevich was additionally motivated here by the sculptural volume of the stage, as opposed to the painterly surface he usually dealt with. His Rayonist lighting of the performers encased in voluminous Cubist costumes transformed the stage into a kinetic sculpture characterized by the fluidity of light and sound. This was not just a designer's whim but a deliberately executed transposition of the poetics of Kruchenykh's zaumnyi yazyk into the theatricality of his opera. Apparently, the poet, who also directed the piece, required a juxtaposition of sound, colour, and sculptural mass. Therefore, Malevich's lights shifted from sombre blue to fiery red, and then to green and dark, to make montage cuts between independent stage textures in a manner of Cubo-Futurist collage. It becomes clear that all of what has been seen and heard in *Victory over the Sun* grew from the verbal texture of zaum poetry, whereby word-sounds finally became the picture-sounds. Anticipating the Bauhaus theatre of totality and Italian Futurist experiments with the "plastic moto-rumorist complex," the first Russian Futurist opera reinstated the volume of theatrical space that had been flattened, up until then, by word-concepts of the dramatic text. Its kinetic sculptural dramaturgy was an epitome of the dramaturgy of sound, which, after being conceived in the sound poetry of the historical avant-garde, evolved into a dramaturgy of a "sound-image complex that is constantly communicated" (Kostelanetz), revamped in the theatre of mixed-means of the 1960s. As such it reached toward the "scenic dynamics" (Lehman) that uphold the structure of postdramatic theatre.

ZANGEZI: AN ANTI-BABEL SOUND SCULPTURE

Zangezi: A Supersaga in Twenty Planes is Velimir Khlebnikov's most serious elaboration of the links between sound, colour, word, image, and structure. Intended to elucidate human life and history, the supersaga follows the quasi-scientific calculations of time and space presented in his large prophetic prose work *The Tables of Destiny*, published in 1922. It is the author's ambitious probe of zaumnyi yazyk, born from a mixture of his interests in the primordial roots of language and modern scientific speculation. Besides an investigation of a universal idiom, *Zangezi* offers Khlebnikov's vision of the world influenced by current discoveries such as Albert Einstein's general theory of relativity and Nikolai Lobachevski's concept of non-Euclidian geometry. In spite of the fact that Khlebnikov's script exhibits a much richer use of zaum than Kruchenykh's *Victory over the Sun*, its staging was less theatrically and visually attractive and, as a result, was received less enthusiastically.

Premiering in May 1923, just a few months after Khlebnikov's death, *Zangezi* was designed, staged, and performed by his friend Vladimir Tatlin. Tatlin was known for his grandiose, never-executed Constructivist sculpture-building, the *Monument to the Third International*. A central figure of the Russian avant-garde alongside Malevich, Tatlin built a sculpture of variously textured materials and geometrical shapes on the stage that was meant to replicate the structural principles of Khlebnikov's supersaga. The opening performance, at the Museum of Artistic Culture in Petrograd, was a hybrid of a zaum composition (words/sounds, colour, light) and a constructivist set, objects, and costumes. Like Malevich in *Victory over the Sun*, Tatlin was primarily interested in the sculptural aspect of the staging in *Zangezi*. Thus, Khlebnikov's zaum poetry was an inspiration for Tatlin's kinetic sculpting and multimedia production of the piece. It coincides with Paul Schmidt's assessment of Khlebnikov's supersagas as texts "intended, in some sense, as librettos for operas that had yet to be imagined, but can be guessed at today in the work of artists like Robert Wilson or Philip Glass."[60] Indeed, it is the interest of postmodern performance artists in such pieces that has led to several revivals and reconstructions of *Zangezi*. Peter Urban, for instance, adapted *Zangezi* as an acoustic art piece for broadcast directed by Heinz von Cramer for WDR *Studio Akustische Kunst* (1972), while Peter Sellars directed an American version, co-produced by the Brooklyn Academy of Music in New York and the Los Angeles Museum of Modern Art in 1986.

Following the logic of a language constructed of self-sufficient words, the supersaga moves to the next level of composition; it comprises different, self-sufficient narratives, each keeping its own form. In a short introduction to *Zangezi*, Khlebnikov explains: "A story is made of words, the way a building is made of construction units, minute building blocks ... A superstory, or supersaga, is made up of independent sections, each with its own special god, its special faith, and its special rule ... Each is free to confess its own particular faith ... Thus we discover a new kind of operation in the realm of verbal art ... Narrative is architecture composed of words; an architecture composed of narratives is a supersaga."[61] Following this pattern, Khlebnikov juxtaposes various forms of texts, many of them previously written for some other purpose, as building blocks of a new structure. Thus he creates a more intricate counterpart to beyonsense language, a "beyondstory" that stands between drama, poetry, and a theoretical script. The single narratives, blocks of different verbal textures juxtaposed in unexpected, alogical, and abstract ways, together constitute the foundation of the supersaga's unique edifice.

In several of his earlier stage scripts, Khlebnikov had already attempted a zaum subversion of literary drama. His monodrama *Mrs Laneen*[62] thus explores the possibility of the formal fragmentation of artistic language. Its protagonist, Mrs Laneen, is literally divided into a number of voiced, sensual perceptions. Paradoxically, there are thirteen speaking parts in the cast for this monodrama [sic]. They are distributed to portray protagonist's sight, hearing, recollection, terror, etc. Instead of Mrs Laneen's voice, then, we hear a dialogue between her senses speaking for themselves. In another of Khlebnikov's short plays, *The World in Reverse*,[63] the author uses a method similar to mathematical subtraction to retrace the internal path of a man, Olly, who has just been buried. As Olly escapes from his coffin, the timeline of the plot starts flowing in reverse so that the man and his wife, Polly, live backwards from the moment of his funeral to their happy days in baby strollers. *The World in Reverse* epitomizes Khlebnikov's efforts to achieve one of his programmatic goals – the reversal of unidirectional time, which would allow humankind to control its destiny. These two short plays are remarkably similar to Futurist synthetic theatre pieces and indicate the kinship between Russian and Italian artistic endeavours that has so often been denied.

Zangezi was Khlebnikov's test of the universal power of sound in language, a power of the phonetic shift that not only radically changes the word and its meaning but also alters the world and its structure. The poet's principal intention was to construct the supersaga as an anti-Babel Tower grounded on *mudrost jazyka* (the wisdom of language) that would uphold the myth and history of the universe. Throughout the ten acts of the piece, the prophet Zangezi climbs the tower of knowledge constructed on ten planes followed by his people. On Plane Six, the believers ask Zangezi to recite his "self-sounding poems":

> *Believers*: Describe the horrors of our age in the words of Alphabet!
> So that never again will we have to see war between peoples; ...

> instead let us hear the crash of Alphabet's long spears, the fight of the hostile forces *R* and *L*, *K* and *G* … *R* rips and resonates, ravages boundaries, forms rivers and ravines.
> Alphabet is the echo of space.
> Tell us! …
> *Zangezi*: … when *K* resounded in Kolchak. *K* was knotted a whiplash of shackles, decrees, kicks, commands and rocks. [64]

This play of the consonants R, which "**r**ips, **r**esonates, and fo**r**ms **r**ivers," and K, of "sha**ck**les, de**c**rees, and **k**i**ck**s," was meant to reincarnate the sound of historical reality by a phonetic play similar to the ritual invocation of good and determent of evil spirits practiced in oral cultures. By invoking the sound-icon of a phenomenon, tribal people hoped to appease and tame inimical natural forces. This lives in the formation of words based on sound symbolism, like *grrrom* [thunde**rrr**] shaped by the coarse consonant roll (Belyi). The magic spell of onomatopoeic words is what enables Khlebnikov's universal "alphabet of the mind" to reconcile man with nature and history. The poet uses a living language – not a codified communication system – in which word making "allows form to form itself, [while it] moves freely in search of its own sense."[65] For Khlebnikov, the prehistorical verbal roots that correspond with natural laws are neither fully understandable nor arbitrarily codified, but rather await rediscovery by phonetic exploration. The motivated connection between sound and its meaning, albeit lost in human history, will be reestablished when the separate sounds of language are naturally linked with units of thought in an "alphabet of sounds" announcing an "alphabet of the mind" (*azbuka uma*).

The genealogy of the language in *Zangezi* goes through seven levels of idiomatic expression: speeches of birds (1), gods (2), and stars (3), followed by a language beyond sense (4), the decomposition of words and new coinages (5), sound-image idioms (*zvukopis*) (6), and finally, the language of madness (*bezumnyj jazyk*) found in oral folklore, incantations, conjurations, and glossolalia (7). The character Zangezi, the sage, is Khlebnikov's alter ego and is fashioned after Nietzsche's Zarathustra. He understands and speaks all languages, uniting them in a language of the world (*mirovoy jazyk*). The Afro-Asian roots of the prophet's name, coming from a combination of the names of the rivers Zambezi and Ganges, highlight Khlebnikov's interest in the cradles of civilization, known from his supersaga *Asia Unbound*. Zangezi climbs from plane to plane teaching us secrets of language. They span from the onomatopoeia of the birdcalls (like an exact replication of the yellow bunting call, *kree-tee-tee-tee-tee-ee – tsuey-tsuey-tsuey-sssueyee*; our poet was a passionate bird-watcher) to the elevated truths of gods and stars that connect abstract principles of the motion of cosmic bodies with concrete sound of words whose meanings we have forgotten. Zangezi's reading of and listening to the stars is not a simple guessing game; it provides mathematical calculations that interconnect past, current, and future historical events, wars, catastrophes, triumphs, and defeats. Zangezi's prophecies primarily rely on his mastery of language: "He has learned to control not destiny itself, but the sounds of destiny. And to the extent that sound and meaning are in perfect accord, he can control the world."[66]

In a shaman and seer's chant from "Plane Nine: Thought," we find a perfect example of the confluence between meaning and sound. In a Sanskrit-sounding mantra, Zangezi cyclically repeats the syllable OOM, a vocable that in Slavic languages denotes "mind." As he reaches out for the power of thought and universal meaning using the rich tonality of an ancient call to prayer, the message, feeling, or meaning of OOM gets instantly delivered to the senses of the listener through its musical and rhythmic features:

> Sound the alarm; send the sound through the mind! Toll the big bell, the great tocsin of intelligence! All the inflections of the human brain will pass in review before you, all the permutations of *OOM*! Look up and see! Join us now, all of you, in song!
>
> *GO-OOM*
> *OUR-OOM*
> *OOW-OOM*
> *FAR-OOM*
> *WITH-OOM* of me
> And those I don't know
> *OM-OOM*
> *DAL-OOM*
> *CHE-OOM*
> *BOM!*
> *BIM!*
> *BAM!*[67]

In the manner of zaum poetry, a variety of prefixes and suffixes, phonetic roots that reshape the word's sound and shift its meaning, have been added to the dominant one-syllable phoneme OOM – known from the Indian oral tradition of the Upanishads as an expression of the original pre-lingual sonority of divine presence. The recurring musical and rhythmical pattern of this mantra in a proto-language (or, in this case, a repetition of the Russian word *um*) taps directly into the subconscious spheres of the individual human – be it a member of a tribe participating in a ritual or a spectator at an avant-garde theatre event. At the same time, the onomatopoeia BOM / BIM / BAM echoes the bell ringing and causes ripples of air that reach us as aural sensation produced by the spatial thrust of reiterated vowels and consonants. The energy of the sound released by the explosive bilabial consonant B, carried on by long vowels, becomes almost tangible. Additionally, the protracted articulation of the deep vowels O and U titillates our hearing and speech organs, and adds sensual weight to the vocal performance. Anyone who has ever listened to a Russian male choir's rendition of the well-known folk song "Vecherniy zvon" (Evening Bell) will no doubt immediately recognize and feel its spirit in the sound of Khlebnikov's zaum chant of OOM. One should note here that exactly the chant of a Russian church bass inspired Roland Barthes to talk about "the grain of the voice." "Listen … something is there, manifest and persistent (you hear only *that*), which is past (or previous) to the meaning of the words … something from the depths of the body cavities … and from the depths of the Slavonic language, as if a single skin lined the performer's inner flesh and the music he sings."[68]

That same "single skin" lines Kruchenykh's poem "Vysoty" (Heights) and the Russian church singing of "Symvol veri" (Credo) as well. Kruchenykh's soulful poem, included in the *Declaration of the Word as Such* (1913) as an example of the language of the universe (*vselenskii yazyk*), was composed exclusively of vowels that show "the strange wisdom of sounds," as Khlebnikov would put it. Kruchenykh needed no consonants but only the vowels of the Orthodox liturgical chant to revive its sound-spirit:

Veruyu /	e u yu
v yedinogo /	i a o
boga /	o a
otza vsederschitelya /	o a e e i e ya
tvortza /	o a
nebu i zemli /	e u i e
	i i y i e i i y[69]

However, the sonority of these vowels was nothing like the soothing musicality of Symbolist verse. It carried again "the grain of the voice … a very specific place in which a language encounters a voice ... a double production of language and of music"[70] that reveals not only the depth of the human body but also the depth of human language itself. In this case, it also represented a dramatic testimony of the poet's introspection and search for the aural roots of his own poetic idiom in the collective Russian body and spirit.

Kruchenykh and Khlebnikov believed in an idiom of sounds that would voice the truth of the body and the truth of the world, and immediately communicate both the sensory experience of the human body and the deep mysticism embedded in the roots of language and culture. The same holds true for Kruchenykh's vocalization of the Orthodox chant and Khlebnikov's return to the primordial vocal sound of the word *oom* (mind). This conviction made Kruchenykh claim that his "Dyr bul shchyl" had more Russian soul than Pushkin's poetry. He used harsh consonants and affricates not only for the articulation of words that give "the pleasure ... in the original dance of the speech organs" (Shklovsky), but also as a homecoming to language's spiritual roots. This mix of carnality and spiritualism found in zaum poetry is reflected in the inclination of the whole Russian avant-garde toward the pagan and mythical sources of art evident in Larionov's Gonchareva's, and Malevich's return to the visual simplicity of peasant icons and woodcuts (*loubok*) in their neo-primitive phase of painting.

ZAUM: FROM CORPOREAL SOUND TO ABSTRACT THEATRE PERFORMANCE

The last of seven linguistic categories mentioned in *Zangezi* was *bezumnyj jazyk* (language of madness), found in the speech of people who are intoxicated, enraged, or under emotional stress. Used in zaum poetry together with incantations, conjurations, or glossolalia, it represents the most effective performance tool in the Futurist dramaturgy of sound. Kruchenykh, for instance, utilized glossolalia provided by Varlaam Shishkov, an ethnographer, writer, and practising member of the *Khlysty* flagellants' sect, as a model for the zaumnyi yazyk of Futurist poetry.[71] Practicing glossolalia to attain mystical ecstasy, the sect members repeated "verses" in unknown tongues to the point of physical exhaustion. They used a ritual language as a rhythmical, albeit incomprehensible, verbal response to the mystical power of unknown archetypal forces. Aiming at a "practical" re-animation of certain spirits, their shamanic incantation – alongside magic words, onomatopoeia, and glossolalia – contained cries, groans, laughs, or chants articulated in the living body to disarticulate conventional communication. This practice offered a large physical vocabulary for the avant-garde theatre's adoption of vocal, non-referential performance.

Kruchenykh's textbook for students of acting, *Fonetika teatra* (Phonetics of Theatre, 1923), represents its direct application. "In the presence of strong emotions the meaning (concept) of the word is not that important, it is even forgotten; a person in a state of emotion *mixes up words*, forgets them, says others, *distorts*, but the emotional side of them is not *destroyed* (the *zaum* part); on the contrary *the sound image* and *the sound* (phoneme) live as never before, and the more unusual and expressive they are, the better material they are for expressing *intense emotions*!"[72] Here Kruchenykh manages rather ingeniously to compress the poetics of zaum into a practical device of actors' education. He instructs actors on how to liberate the energies of words (and their own energies) and to utter expressive sound images that need not be equated with their textual concepts.

The interconnectedness of states of heightened emotion and inspiration lies at the core of Italian Futurist "lyrical intoxication with matter" in poetry and fisicoffolia, physical madness in variety theatre. Marinetti describes the urgency of speech under stress as a powerful and liberating poetic device in the same way as Kruchenykh: "Suppose a friend of yours endowed with this lyric faculty found himself in an area of intense life (revolution, war, shipwreck, earthquake, etc) … He would begin by brutally destroying the syntax of his speech … The rush of steam-emotion would burst the sentence's pipeline, the valves of punctuation and adjectival clamps … The narrator's only preoccupation is to render all the vibrations of his 'I.'"[73] Malevich follows suit by advocating a wordless dialect of sound poetry in which "demented" words, accessible neither to the mind nor to reason, rush from the poet's mouth. "I weep or I grieve cannot express anything," argues Malevich in his essay "On Poetry" (1913). "Words are merely distinguishing signs and nothing more. But if I hear a groan, I neither see nor sense it in any definite form. I recognize pain, which has its language – a groan – and in the groan I hear no word."[74]

The poetics of zaum and parole in libertà thus join, carrying bodily impulses in the matrix of their sound-text poems inscribed with an emotive, pulsional, and performative potential that unmistakably lends itself to theatrical use. Marinetti, Kruchenykh, and Malevich encouraged the vibrations of an "I" intoxicated with life, and actors who express their own rhythms, sounds, and vocal gestures – in other words, who perform themselves or are themselves on stage. Their ideas are akin to Artaud's vision of the theatre of cruelty that he describes in the shape of a cry. "Intellectual cries," he writes, are "cries born of the *subtlety* of the marrow. This is what I mean by Flesh. I do not separate my thought from my life. With each vibration of my tongue I retrace all the pathways of my thought in my flesh."[75] The performance that comes from the wisdom, pain, and joy of the flesh, lives in a physical or vocal gesture of bezumnyj jazyk spoken by an intoxicated "I." By stretching toward a performance act beyond representation, such vocal gesture "inscribes the occurrence of a sensory now" that, as Lyotard alleges, makes a distinctive mark of the whole of avant-garde theatre.

The wordless expression of sound poetry and objectless painting of Russian avant-garde proved mutually contagious. In his essay "From Cubism and Futurism to Suprematism: The New Painterly Realism" (1915), Malevich wrote: "The most precious things in pictorial creation are color and texture ... Painters should abandon subject matter and objects if they wish to be pure painters ... In the art of Suprematism, forms will live ... Hitherto there has been realism of objects, but not of painterly, colored units ... Any painterly surface is more alive than any face from which a pair of eyes and a smile protrudes."[76] Malevich's "living" painterly surfaces were counterparts of zaum words on the path to the supreme abstraction that revolutionized the arts in the twentieth century. However abstract they were not detached from human life and reality. Explaining why people's faces are painted green and red in pictures, Malevich commented: "Painting is paint and color; it lies within our organism. Its outbursts are great and demanding. My nervous system is colored by them. My brain burns with their color."[77] Here Malevich comes close to Marinetti, who considered the rarest faculty of intoxicating oneself with life the ultimate resource of poetry. Likewise, Malevich regards the poet as an individual "compelled to create poems devoid of natural forms by the storm of pure and naked rhythm rising within him."[78] Hence, he does not care for semantic or syntactic sense of the statement "I groan," but for the sound of a groan that reveals a word *in statu nascendi*, a pre-textual sound/word born from a physical gesture.

The concept of a pre-verbal vocal gesture became significant in the understanding of the physicality of theatre language. Helga Finter, for one, describes the theatricalization of the voice from the historical avant-garde onwards using Artaud's belief that language, and consequently the idiom he wanted to develop in theatre, "springs from the NECESSITY of speech more than from speech already formed. But finding an impasse in speech, it returns spontaneously to gesture."[79] Artaud's departure from the text for the sake of vocal gesture inspired the physical, ritual, and carnal theatre of the 1960s avant-garde, including performances of the New York Living Theatre; Peter Brook's Theatre of Cruelty season under the aegis of the Royal Shakespeare Company; and Richard Schechner's *Dionysus in 69*. Equally important to his call for bodily presence is Artaud's notion of a hieroglyphic sign as a composite of stage sound, image, space, and action: "It can be said that the spirit of the most ancient hieroglyphics will preside at the creation of this pure theatrical language … The overlapping of images and movements will culminate, through the collusion of objects, silences, shouts and rhythms or in a genuine physical language with signs, not words, as its root."[80]

The abstract, mixed-media theatre of Richard Foreman, Meredith Monk, and Robert Wilson, Finter claims, "disarticulates the logocentric domination which governs the relation between the different signifying systems (verbal/visual/auditory) in our culture and thus brings the *signifying process* to light at the expense of our fixation on meaning."[81] Instead of instituting a hierarchy of sign systems that guarantee textual/dramatic representation, the verbal, visual, and auditory elements of postdramatic performance slip against each other, creating a fluctuating and immediate theatrical event, a happening in-between the media. "Experimental theatre begins with another distribution of the two audio-visual unities of the sign: it centers its preoccupation not on the text, but on the orality, which, on the one hand, takes the written (the seen) as spoken sounds and transforms sight into hearing and kinesthesia and, on the other hand, takes tone and sound as spatially written, thus transforming hearing to sight."[82]

In postdramatic theatre that operates with this understanding of orality, vocal and non-vocal sounds acquire their own theatricality that replaces a habitual transliteration of textual meanings into dramatic representation. These sounds shape an intermedial sign structure, providing for a hieroglyphic stage performance Artaud proposed long ago; they also transform drama into an audio-visual form of theatre that, as Cubo-Futurists would put it, does not mime anything outside itself but assumes an "*a priori* accidental relation to reality." Thus the performance-oriented, anti-textual, and hybrid theatre of today comes into view as a continuum of the battle, fought by the historical avant-garde, against logocentric language, dramatic literature, and figurative painting. In the following chapter, we will look in more detail at how the Italian Futurists' oral approach to performance in their serate futuriste helped put sound to work in their abstract *sintesi teatrale*.

5

The Dramaturgy of Sound: From Futurist *Serate* to *Sintesi*

PIEDIGROTTA AND GALLERY PERFORMANCES: VARIETY THEATRE GOES SYNTHETIC

Francesco Cangiullo's *Piedigrotta*, which premiered on 29 March 1914, at Gallery Sprovieri in Rome and, in the next two months, repeated once in Rome and three times in Naples, came as a sign of significant change in Futurist aesthetics and theatre practice. It coincided with a strategic move from *arte-azione* events for general audiences at theatre halls, called serate futuriste (Futurist evenings), to performances for more sophisticated audiences at exhibition galleries, called *pomeriggi spettacolari* (theatrical afternoons). The history of *Piedigrotta* as an exemplary verbo-voco-visual poem leads from its first appearance as a tiny book of lyrics called *Piedigrotta Cangiullo* (Napoli: Tipolitografia Elia, 1906), through its famous bruitist performances at the site of the permanent Futurist art exposition, to its final publication in 1916 laid out by the revolutionized Futurist typography.

The poem bears the name of an ancient Neapolitan carnival that traditionally takes place each year in September. On these festive days, the entire city of Naples erupts with exuberance; throngs of people sing and dance on the cobblestone streets and in the piazzas, accompanied by noisy tarantella tunes played on primitive folk instruments. Futurists embraced the chance to celebrate this upsurge of folly and absolute reversal of taboos. As a carnivalesque rebellion against the bourgeois order, it was ideal material for the Futurist subversion of passéist literary and artistic rules. Giuseppe Sprovieri, a gallery owner, impresario, and participant in the 1914 event, describes Piedigrotta as "a navy bugle drowning the voice of the individual in the roaring and shouting of the masses ... a primordial expression of an innate musicality brought back to life each year and refined into a 'song.'"[1]

Piedigrotta, which earned fame as a popular number in the repertoire of Neapolitan *café-chantants*, and was known for its explosive mixture of onomatopoetic noise, free words, and strains of folk music, was no doubt proto-Futurist. Cangiullo, who before entering Futurist circles worked as a musician, composer, and orchestra conductor of variety shows in the provincial towns of Italy and southern France, had certainly had a chance to perform in different versions of the Piedigrotta scenario. Armed with this experience and encouraged by his Futurist friends, he seized the opportunity to show off and mock the bourgeois audience in the Italian capital. There were seven performers in Rome: Marinetti and Cangiullo declaimed the poem, accompanied by the chords of an out-of-tune piano, while a troupe of "very famous dwarf artists, *Miss Tofa* (Sprovieri), *Mr. Putipù* (Balla), *Mr. Triccabballacche* (Radiante), *Mr. Scetavajasse* (Depero), and *Mr. Fischiatore* (Sironi)," as the poster reads, played music, danced, and chanted in the crowd. The dwarfs took their names from the instruments they were playing. For the young Fortunato Depero, it was a Futurist initiation in front of grotesque, abstract backdrops, painted by his teacher, Giacomo Balla, and accentuated by the light of red lanterns.

Making the performance out of bruitist poetry, the procession of dwarfs, in grotesque costumes and hats, with hair made of tissue paper, roamed through the gallery gesticulating provocatively, chanting, yelling, and playing rough tunes *à la tarantella* on their bizarre instruments. Sprovieri, whose role included blowing into a big conch shell (*tofa*), remembers that they also intended to carry pizzas on their heads, the way local pizza-bakers did, to add smell to the show's array of sensory attractions. "The greatest surprise," he wrote, "came with the explosions [and smoke] of *tricchetracche* [firecrackers] between the legs of the audience."[2] Marinetti recounted that the audience responded with fireworks of their own: shouts, cheers, cries, and a whole spectrum of unbridled vocalizations in an onomatopoetic fusion with the boisterous interjections of the Futurist troupe. "And the chaotic orchestra of sounds, colours, forms, smells, tastes, touches, convulsions, laughter, joy in explosion, boiling, flames, eruptions, grows, grows, grows, until the demoiselles *Tofa, Putipù, Triccabballacche* and *Scetavajasse* come out from their infernal circle and give by means of their sound the sensation of their triumphant, foolishly entertaining, intoxicating, blinding, suffocating, noisy and deafening festival of *Piedigrotta*."[3] Undeniably, the "demoiselles" achieved the ideal compenetration with the audience. While the audience became the equivalent of their orchestra, they became the orchestrators of the cacophony of onstage and offstage sounds and actions, mixed with the booing from the gallery. Additionally, the performers left the stage to roam around physically intruding the audience space: the orchestrators mixed with the orchestra, creating an environmental theatre event.

At the beginning of the *pomeriggio*, Marinetti introduced *Piedigrotta* and its four obscene and vulgar-sounding instruments to the public adding an ironic reading to the details of their legendary provenance. "A *tofa*: a big shell from which the kids draw a tragi-comic monotonous chant ... a ferocious satire of mythology and all the sirens, tritons and sea shells inhabiting the *passéist* gulf of Naples ... A *scetavajasse*: a genial parody of the violin as an expression of inner life and sentimental anxiety ... A *putipù*: a violent irony with which a young and sane race correct and fight all nostalgic venoms of the moonshine ... A *triccabballacche*: a satire of sacrosanct Greco-Roman processions."[4] Besides depicting their mythological roots, Marinetti ascribed to every instrument its colour: the *tofa* emits a deep blue sound, the *putipù* orange, the *scetavajasse* pink and green, and the *triccabballacche* red. This sound-colour analogy, emphasized in both Roman performance and, later, in Cangiullo's print of the synoptic score, shows the Futurist tendency toward synaesthesia, whose literal application would reach its apex in Depero's synthetic piece *Colori*, which turned into a pure moto-rumorist sculpture.

Noisemakers *tofa, putipù, triccabballacche*, and *scetavajasse* – the primitive contraptions of wood, clay, tin rattles, cans, and shells – were actually idiophone-style musical instruments. Idiophones are, by definition, self-sounded musical bodies unable to produce refined and clear harmonic tunes; they create sound by the vibration of their own bodies, without the help of strings or membranes. Their non-harmonic sound and impure rhythms and cadences made them appropriate for both Futurist noise music and the rustic tarantellas of the Neapolitan festival. Played on these primitive *intonarumori* (noise intoners), Futurist tarantellas sounded like onomatopoetic mimes of "real" tunes; their unrefined sonority was close to Russolo's noise music, which benefited from the instrument's timbre rather than its tonality.

The 1916 publication of *Piedigrotta* displayed a masterful graphic design in the manner of the legendary *Zang Tumb Tumb*. After being developed on the pages of Futurist journals in a series of synoptic free-word tables (tavole parolibere), and revitalized through several energetic gallery performances, the poem now reentered the page in a sophisticated and vivid verbo-voco-visual form. Its revolutionized typography made the rich iconography of onomatopoetic effects palpable. Already on its first page we can enjoy a firework of newly designed, different-sized letters aiming to depict a celebration of noise at a Naples carnival as

> PIEDIGgRrOoTtTtAesco

in which all kinds of

> TROOOMBE, trooombetoooni, trooombeteeeellle and trooombettiiiinne

sound. On the second, from a huge cone of letters rising in size:

> CONOSSUOOOOOOONO

springs a chain of deminutives for stars:

> stelline, stellette, *stellucce*

whose delicate sound ends with a harsh consonant cluster,

> KAISERKAZZ.

Underneath, "**TARANTELLA**," a word reiterated in various forms throughout the text, stands as an extension of

> TUTTA ITALIA.

Many lines are written in the manner of the *poesia pentagramata*, another of Cangiullo's inventions, in which musical signs were applied to poetry:

> (*prestissimo*) ujsciujsciujsciujsci~~~~~~~ Ò scelto un nome eccentrico… éppà >>> (LOIE FULLER **VIOLA**).[5]

Loie Fuller's name appears several times in the fireworks of the *Piedigrotta*, each time printed in different colour, from violet to orange. Fuller, a cabaret diva and pioneer of modern free dance, was the one who introduced Isadora Duncan to European audiences. Already known as an American ballet and cabaret artist, she had set Paris ablaze dancing draped in huge, flying silk sails that under an array of lights of different colour produced incredible forms. Instead of portraying the joy or suffering of an individual character, Fuller exposed on stage brave dance figures/abstract kinetic sculptures. Her performance style showed an affinity with Futurists who wanted to remove all intricacies of personal human psychology and emotion from the stage. It was as if the dancer disappeared in the virtual, or – as Futurists would call it – "moto-rumorist complex" of her robe, propelled by her movement. Her appearance was enthusiastically received in Futurist circles and significantly influenced their dance and stage design, especially Prampolini's luminous scenography. Cangiullo's repetition of Fuller's name in different colours throughout the print of *Piedigrotta* suggests that the locus of Futurist performance moved from the body madness of variety theatre to the synergy of sound, movement, and colour of synthetic theatre. It signalled the change of the Futurist performance style and production technique, which earlier was marked largely by body madness or synaesthesia, into a synthetic one.

It is worth noting here that the manifesto "La declamazione dinamica e sinottica" (Dynamic and Synoptic Declamation) was published as a preface to Cangiullo's *Piedigrotta* rather than to Marinetti's *Zang Tumb Tumb*, as one would suppose. Evidently, it was devised to announce the next stage of performance development, leading from parole in libertà toward synthetic theatre. Ever aware of practicalities, Marinetti ordered: "Gesticulate in a draughtsman like, topographical manner, synthetically creating in midair cubes, cones, spirals, ellipses, etc! … Make use of a certain number of elementary instruments such as hammers, little wooden tables, automobile horns, drums, tambourines, saws, and electric bells, to produce precisely and effortlessly the different simple or abstract onomatopoetic harmonies!"[6] Following these directions, the small group of Futurists enacting *Piedigrotta* ushered in the more abstract style of Balla's *Machina tipografica* and Depero's *Colori*. "Attempting to give the audience the sound and visual emotion of the Neapolitan crowd that fills streets and alleys and saturates the environment with its obsessive, rampant presence," they physicalized a "synoptic table" of free words set in "a pyrotechnic explosion of flashing images and bits of sounds, voices and onomatopoeia."[7]

The next few pieces performed at Futurist gallery afternoons in 1914 also relied on the dramaturgy of sound derived from bruitist performance of parole in libertà. Thus, Marinetti and Cangiullo, accompanied by the author's guitar, performed Balla's *Discussione di due critici sudannesi sul Futurismo* (A Discussion between Two Sudanese Critics on Futurism) using their oral mimicry skills to produce a grotesque speech meant to sound African:

Farcionisgnaco gurninfuturo
bordubalotaompimagnusa
sfacataca snimitirichita
plucu sbumu farufutusmaca
sgacgnacgnac chr chr chr
stechestechetechetetere
maumauzizitititititititi[8]

Discussione was not meant to show disrespect for "primitives": it would be misleading to connect it with the Eurocentric exploitation of exotic topics and white men's fantasy of power that fuelled later colonial invasions of North African countries by Fascist Italy. On the contrary, Balla's invention of a gibberish idiom of Sudanese critics was intended as a jab at critics and the contemporary Italian public. His complex vocalizations produced not a mockery but a surprising, cacophonous cantata. This performance falls in line with attempts at the rejuvenation of pre-logical, savage, primitive, and naïve art forms that spread in avant-garde circles, such as Tzara's and Ball's recitations of "Negro Chants" and "Elefantenkarawane" in the Dadaist Cabaret Voltaire.

Balla, the eldest among the Futurist painters and actually, for many in the group, their former teacher, was known for his inventiveness, bold abstractionism, and encouragement of radically innovative ideas among the younger members of the movement. In his own formative years, Balla studied music and became a proficient guitar player. Regardless, Balla often preferred to use his instrument in the manner of a noise intoner (*intonarumore*). Bruno Corra remembers: "From the guitar he draws forth landscapes, burlesque scenes, protesting crowds, rains, hail storms, battles, etc. Mixing dialogue with sound and with noises of the mouth, he has created such prodigious fantasies as the *Lezione di equitazione* (Riding Lesson) and the *Vignaiolo dopo il temporale* (Winegrower after the Storm)."[9]

Cangiullo's short pieces *Serata in onore di Yvonne* (An Evening in Honour of Yvonne) and *I funerali di un filosofo passatista* (Funeral of a *Passéist* Philosopher), exhibit similar sonic qualities. The first was a musical/recitative performance in which the author and Sprovieri declaimed nonsensical parole in libertà accompanied by an onomatopoetic orchestra – two professional singers who produced vocalizations of orchestral instruments conducted by Balla. The second was part of the Free International Futurist Exhibition in April 1914 at the Sprovieri Gallery in Rome. It was a Grand Guignol performance, with which Futurists launched a mordant attack on Benedetto Croce, the illustrious philosopher and aesthetician emblematic of Italian classical idealism. An enormous clay model of the philosopher's head was carried in procession and placed on a catafalque by poet Radiante [Revillo Cappari] and painter Depero, who marched to the tune of a "heartbreaking" funeral march Cangiullo played on an out-of-tune piano. Marinetti, who chaired the solemn ceremony, delivered a eulogy about the putrid potatoes, onions, and feathers that crowned the philosopher's head. He ended the speech by reciting Luciano Folgore's incomprehensible free-word poetry. Balla, who walked in front of the stretcher, provided the appropriate background by murmuring mournfully, hitting a huge cowbell with a painting brush, and repeatedly chanting the Russian word no: *nieeet-nieeeet-nieeeet-nieeet*. The Futurists' gallery protest against "the solemn, the sacred, the serious, and the sublime in art" thus turned into a full-fledged variety performance.

Cangiullo's and Balla's proto-theatrical works, performed at theatrical afternoons (*pomeriggi spettacolari*), combined onomatopoetic declamation (*rumorismo*) and body madness with the use of independent aural and visual structures in staging. In so doing, they further hybridized performance styles of serate and variety theatre, and heralded the abstract forms of synthetic theatre.

L'ARTE DEI RUMORI: A NEW MUSICAL REALITY

Luigi Russolo's subversion of tonal music by the art of noise was one of the consequences of a chain reaction in artistic practice sparked by Marinetti's liberation of words. Following Marinetti's impassioned call to replace the revered *Winged Victory of Samothrace* with the race car, in his 1913 manifesto Russolo issued a similarly urgent appeal: "We must break out of this limited circle of sounds and conquer the infinite variety of noise-sounds ... We delight much more in combining in our thoughts the noises of trams, of automobile engines, of carriages and brawling crowds, than in hearing again the *Eroica* or the *Pastorale*."[10] He believed that the music of the conventional orchestra left the sea of sound that surrounds us unexpressed. Reduced to tonality and harmonics, conventional music robbed artistic sound of its ability to reflect life in its entirety and to arouse true emotions. For Russolo the time was ripe for "a new musical reality with a generous distribution of resonant slaps in the face, discarding violins, pianos, double basses and plaintive organs."[11]

Unhappy with the limited variety of timbres that a music orchestra – with its groups of bowed instruments, metal winds, woodwinds, and percussion – offers, Russolo proposed an art of noises based on microtonal and improvisational sound structures, composed and performed with the help of special instruments called noise intoners (*intonarumori*). He also developed a new graphic notation for this noise music that freed composition from its traditional harmonic patterning. Although viewed in his time as an eccentric, Russolo has since been credited with the introduction of new aesthetic concepts that are still relevant for avant-garde music and the art of sound. These include atonal and microtonal (enharmonic) structure, musique concrète, sound environments, and the soundscape. Russolo's endeavours were poised to solve Ferruccio Busoni's dilemma expressed in his 1907 *Sketch for a New Aesthetic of Music*: "In what direction shall the next step lead: to abstract sound, to unhampered technique, to unlimited tonal material?" While Arnold Schönberg's atonal works from 1909 offered one possible answer, Russolo – thinking out of the professional musician's box – reached for an expansive array of noise, sound, and silence, which would allow for a full reflection of the din of the modern world. "The great drive of the musical avant-garde in the twentieth century has been towards the liberation and autonomization of noise from the formalizations of musical sound," asserts Steve Connor. "Perhaps the great initiator of this tradition, which runs through the work of Edgard Varèse, Pierre Schaeffer, Pierre Boulez and John Cage, was the Italian futurist Luigi Russolo, who called … for an art of noises which would liberate the musical possibilities of noise in general, especially the diverse and unsynthesizable complexity of sound in the city."[12]

Luigi Russolo's 1913 manifesto "L'Arte dei rumori" (The Art of Noises) proposes the liberation of artistic sound from the realm of harmonic music as a natural continuation of Marinetti's phonic liberation of words from the fetters of syntax in poetry. The manifesto calls for the inclusion of all noises of the environment – mechanical, electrical, industrial, and natural – in the new Futurist music. Russolo argues: "Life in antiquity was mere silence. Only with the discovery of the machine in the 19th Century was noise born. Today noise lays sovereign claim to the sensibilities of mankind … Music today strives towards an amalgamation of the most dissonant, strange and strident sounds. We are approaching a music of noises … Musical sound, alien to our life, always musical and a thing unto itself … has become to our ears what a familiar face is to our eyes. Noise, however, reaching us in a confused and irregular way from the irregular confusion of our life … keeps innumerable surprises in reserve. We are therefore certain that by selecting, coordinating, and dominating all noises we can enrich men with a new and unsuspected sensual pleasure."[13] On his call, everything in Futurist performance practice favouring the impure, blurred but highly expressive sound, from vocal onomatopoeia to the deliberate production of noise, became a powerful artistic/theatrical device.

Promoting noise as quintessential to artistic expression, Russolo followed Marinetti's anti-sentimentalist, brutal lyricism of the most cacophonous onomatopoeias, which replaced a passéist longing for beauty in literature, music, and drama. His inroduction of raw sound in place of tonal music took part in Marinetti's search for an art able "to capture the breath, the sensibility, and the instinct of metals, stones, wood, and so on, through the medium of free objects and whimsical motors ... to substitute for human psychology, now exhausted, the lyric obsession with matter."[14] In "L'Arte dei rumori," Russolo therefore liberally quotes Marinetti's theories, praises his onomatopoetic declamation of *Zang Tumb Tumb*, and acknowledges that his own experiments with noise were nothing more than "the logical consequence of your [Marinetti's, Boccioni's, and Balla's] marvellous innovations."[15] Michael Kirby rightly concludes: "certainly there is literalness about Russolo's desire to incorporate everyday sounds into music. This literal approach stems most directly from Marinetti's *parole in libertà*."[16]

Writing specifically about onomatopoetic poetry, Russolo describes consonants as bearers of noise and vowels as bearers of sound/music. "No noise exists in nature or life (however bizarre and strange in timbre) that cannot adequately, or even exactly, be imitated through the consonants ... Only the Futurist poets, with their *free words*, were able to hear the entire value of noise in poetry ... This element of language, which had previously remained the slave of vowels – the consonant representing noise – is finally adopted for its own sake; and like music, it serves to multiply the elements of expression and emotion."[17] On that same premise, Russian zaum poets roughed up their poems by amassing noisy consonant clusters as a counterweight to the musicality of Symbolist verses, which were based on the sound of vowels. Theirs was another kind of musicality; emerging from a phonetic interplay of consonants and vowels, it favoured noisy dissonance over tonal consonance. In Kruchenykh's and Khlebnikov's poetry, a naked consonant became the spine of the sound poem that gets its flesh from the resonating vowel; the whole endeavour falls more on the side of acoustic art than literature. By praising the Futurist poets' preference for consonants, carriers of noise for its own sake, Russolo was actually promoting his own program: "The art of noise must not limit itself to imitative reproduction ... A tendency toward most complicated dissonances ... can be satisfied only *with the addition and substitution of noises for sound*."[18] Unlike music, he affirmed, noise does not illustrate human sentiment or serve as an accidental embellishment of an action, thought, or emotion in literature or drama. Instead it "must become a prime element to mould into the work of art. That is, it has to lose its accidental character in order to become an element sufficiently abstract to achieve the necessary transformation of any prime element into an abstract element of art."[19] By recognizing the materiality of noise and making it an abstract element of art, Russolo conceives ideas of a dramaturgy of sound that subsequently helped shape Futurist, avant-garde, and postdramatic stage performance. John J. White suggests that "The interaction between the musicians' art of noises, on the one hand ... and the large-scale exploration of the word's materiality by the futurist poets, on the other, is certainly not a matter of a one-way influence but a complex of reciprocal cross-fertilizations. Marinetti's importance for Russolo is matched by Russolo's subsequent influence on Depero and *sintesi* playwrights and creators of futurist ballet."[20] Indeed, the Futurist abstract sintesi, as we shall see later in the book, contained more onomatopoeias or noise than words of dialogue or illustrative music. Their oral/aural forms provided a bulk of concrete material for the subsequent Futurist stage experiments with the moto-rumoristic complex.

Russolo wrote "L'Arte dei rumori" in the form of an epistle to maestro Francesco Balilla Pratella, the Futurist utmost authority in the field of music, who had already been advocating a move away from the principles of traditional composition based on consonance, dissonance, and their resolution. In his 1911 "Technical Manifesto of Futurist Music," Pratella demanded that traditional composition be replaced by the creation of enharmonic music based on micro-intervals in pitch and continuous sequential changes in rhythm. Only that, claimed Pratella, would enable music to adequately express the sounds of nature and the labour of people and machines participating in the complex din of the modern industrial city. The radical switch to noise as primary musical material, however, must be credited to Russolo. Russolo authored first compositions for noise intoners believing that "sounds and noises produced in nature change pitch *by enharmonic graduations and never by leaps in pitch*. For example, the howling of the wind produces complete scales in rising and falling. These scales are neither diatonic nor chromatic, they are *enchromatic*."[21] For Russolo, the standard orchestral instruments traditionally used to represent a windy or rainy afternoon were unable to produce such sound. His standing is reinforced by Kandinsky's criticism of Richard Wagner for using musical motifs incapable of expressing concrete noise.

In *Das Rheingold*, for example, alleges Kandinsky, "the hissing of red-hot iron in water, the sound of the smith's hammer, etc., were still represented musically."[22]

The art of noises came to life when Russolo, together with Ugo Piatti, constructed a number of intonarumori. On 2 June 1913, at a serata in Teatro Strochi in Modena, Russolo and Piatti presented: "a burster (*scoppiatore*) [making] an automobile engine sound with changeable pitch over ten whole tones, a crackler (*crepitatore*) [making] a sparkling sound, a hummer (*ronzatore*) [making] an electric motor sound, and a rubber (*stropicciatore*) [making] a metallic scraping sound."[23] Marinetti clearly supported Russolo's ambitious orchestrations of noise, which, as he wrote, "are not simple impressionistic reproductions of the life that surrounds us but moving hypotheses of noise music. By a knowledgeable variation of the whole, the noises lose their episodic, accidental, and imitative character to achieve the abstract elements of art."[24] He also kept encouraging Pratella to apply principles of the Futurist revolution to his theory of music and asked the maestro to enrich the orchestration of his opera *Aviatore Dro* (1914) by incorporating a few intonarumori within the symphonic ensemble.[25] Pratella acknowledged noise music of Russolo's instruments as a departure from an objective reality they seemingly imitate. He praised intonarumori in view of the fact that by creating "an *expressive abstract* element of state of mind," they become essentially musical. In spite of his verbal support, Pratella used noise intoners in only two of his compositions. At the same time, composers Maurice Ravel, Sergei Prokofiev, Igor Stravinsky, and Ballets Russes impresario Serge Diaghilev showed a vivid interest in Russolo's noise intoners[26] but never actually used them. All of the instruments had been completety destroyed in a bombardment at the end of the Second World War, but their music survived in bits and pieces composed by Futurists Franco Casavola, Nuccio Fiorda, Aldo Giuntini, Luigi Grandi, and Silvio Mix. However, interest in noise music never died, so that today we have several accurate reconstructions of intonarumori built by contemporary experimental composers and noise music enthusiasts.

Physically, an intonarumore looked like a sound box with a large funnel that amplified the sound, which was produced mechanically as the performer cranked the instrument. The cranked wheel would rub a string attached to a single diaphragm, stretched on a cylindrical resonator sending sound out through the funnel. This created a wide array of sounds, which could be tuned and rhythmically regulated by means of mechanical manipulation. The pitch was regulated by a lever on top of the box that continually increased or reduced the tension and length of a vibrating string, allowing for an infinite number of musical intervals divided into semitones, quartertones, and smaller fractions of the enharmonic scale. Different rhythms and timbres were obtained by the physical or chemical preparation of parts of the instrument. The wheel that rubbed the string, as in a traditional hurdy-gurdy, was sometimes notched with small teeth, while the diaphragm was impregnated with special chemicals.

In his manifesto Russolo defined six families of noises, all of which were to be produced by noise intoners. They included *rombi* (rumbles) – roaring, thundering, and explosions; *fischi* (whistles) – the sounds of whistling, hissing, and puffing; *bisbigli* (whispers) – murmurs, mumbling, and gurgling; *stridori* (screeches) – creaking, squealing, rustling, humming, crackling, and rubbing sounds; and noises obtained by percussion on metal, wood, skin, stone, pottery, and so on. The list is rounded out by noises produced by animals and humans – animate sounds like screams, shrieks, wails, death rattles, and sobs. Russolo boasted that he was able to produce thirty thousand different noises of diverse rhythm and pitch "not simply by imitation but by combining [them] according to our fancy."[27] Cangiullo, who attended his demonstration organized in Marinetti's house for Diaghilev, Stravinsky, and Prokofiev, remembered that a *Crepitatore* "crackles with a thousand sparks, like a fiery torrent," while a *Frusciatore* "rustles like gowns of winter silk, like new leaves in April, like the sea rent by summer."[28] In addition, one should acknowledge that intonarumori, appearing more than ten years before musicians started to use electrical amplifiers and loudspeakers, were built in a way that qualifies them as precursors of today's electronic synthesizers and samplers.

Russolo's composition for intonarumori, *Risveglio di una città* (Awakening of a City), was first performed at a *serata* at *Teatro dal Verme* in Milan, 21 April 1914, together with *Colazione sulla terrazza del Kursaal Diana* (Breakfast on the Terrace of the Spa Diana) and *Convegno di automobili e di aeroplani* (A Meeting of Automobiles and Airplanes). The event ended, in the best tradition of Futurist serate, with a physical brawl between the artists and the public, including extremely irritated professors of the Royal Conservatory. As the newspaper *Il Secolo* reported, emergency vehicles of *Guardia Medica* had to take eleven wounded spectators away.[29] This did not discourage Russolo from presenting his noise orchestra at two subsequent concerts in Genoa and starting a European tour with a dozen performances at the London Coliseum in June 1914, which impressed Prokofiev and Stravinsky among others. Unfortunately, the outbreak of the First World War interrupted his exhibition tour, which was supposed to visit Liverpool, Dublin, Glasgow, Edinburgh, Vienna, Moscow, St Petersburg, Berlin, and Paris.

Risveglio di una città sounded like a musique concrète composition. Its specificity was that a conglomeration of noises that brought to life the soundscape of a morning rush in an industrial city was produced by intonarumori. A striking similarity between the montage of environmental sounds and the concert performance of *Awakening of a City* is evident in a London *Pall Mall Gazette* correspondent's description of the event: "At first a quiet even murmur was heard. The great city was asleep. Now and again some giant hidden in one of those queer boxes snored pretentiously; and a new born child cried … a far-away noise grew into a mighty roar … [of] the huge printing machines … hundreds of vans and motor lorries … the shrill whistling of the locomotives … A multitude of doors was next heard to open and shut with a bang, and a procession of receding footsteps intimated that the great army of breadwinners was going to work. Finally, all the noises of the street and the factory merged into a gigantic roar, and the music ceased … I awoke as though from a dream and applauded."[30]

Risveglio was a concretization of Russolo's dream of a music that would include "the muttering of motors that breathe and pulse with an undeniable animalism, the throbbing of valves, the bustle of pistons, the shrieks of power saws, the starting of a streetcar on the tracks, the cracking of whips, the flapping of awnings and flags."[31] Most of the attributes Russolo used here to describe modern noises are of anthropomorphic or zoomorphic origin. As he equates the cacophony of an industrialized city with the convulsive breathing of a mythical Moloch-like creature that devours people, his sound-image calls to mind a scene of the German expressionist film *Metropolis* (1927) by Fritz Lang in which columns of anonymous workers descend into the bowels of such an industrial, mechanical monster – the underground factory.

Walter Ruttmann, a well-known Expressionist filmmaker, produced a similar collage of everyday sounds for radio broadcast, called *Weekend*, in 1929.[32] The basis of Ruttmann's sound piece was his earlier documentary *Berlin – Symphony of a Great City* (1927), a seminal work in the aesthetics of film montage. Here, different details of the daily cycle of metropolitan life were captured by sound camera and put together in an audio-visual montage composition growing from the first, early-morning stirrings of Berlin awakening to the mounting noises and rhythms of the industrial, mechanized city and its inhabitants as the day progresses. The film represents a feast of jump cuts, dissolves, and cross fades. The result of this non-narrative collage of juxtaposed moving images was remarkably similar to Russolo's sound composition *Awakening of a City*. Aware of the aural potential of his material, Ruttman saved the optical filmstrip and returned to it later to create *Weekend*, a purely acoustic work for radio. It is important to note that, unlike the radio artists who followed him, Ruttmann assembled *Weekend* working with film stock rather than the magnetic tape used a few years down the road. In his radio work, Ruttmann employed the same montage principles he had used in the film, and thus introduced a technique that became common among future radio dramatists, directors, and producers of so-called "acoustic film," a form that represents a hallmark of German radio drama in the Weimar period. Thus, the filmmaker contributed directly to German radio-acoustic art and pioneered a method of parallel acoustic and visual montage that is still employed in today's audio-visual art.

A stylistic parallel between Russolo's *Risveglio* and Ruttman's *Weekend* is visible in the only two surviving sheets of enharmonic notation for noise intoners that Russolo published alongside his manifesto. They look like a blueprint for a montage and juxtaposition used in Ruttmann's film, but this time in the sphere of sound/noise. Instead of musical notes, they show several continuous thick lines placed on staves of music paper to indicate microtonal changes of pitch. Such notation with lines runining in parallel, converging, or diverging across six-staff music sheets was meant to facilitate composition of a simultaneous score for intonarumori of different timbres. Indications for "forte" and "fortissimo" written above the lines mark intensity while abrupt line endings indicate the montage cuts of the sound material. These formal features of his score writing point to Russolo's position halfway between the compositional (albeit microtonal) and the organizational treatment of sound.

The principles of sound/image montage shared by Russolo and Ruttmann have remained vital throughout the history of film and theatre. Thus, in the 1928 "Statement on Sound," Soviet film directors Sergei Eisenstein, Alexander Pudovkin, and Grigori Alexandrov "lamented [the] encroaching 'bargain basement realism' of synchronous sound and image [characteristic of narrative film] ... [which they felt was] reducing cinema to little more than canned theater, and derailing the inroads made in montage. They advocated asynchronous sound, which would maintain the independence between sound and image."[33] On similar precepts, Merce Cunningham's collaborations with John Cage and Wilson's with Philip Glass, later in the century, used asynchronous sound and image in a live performance situation.

This method reappeared in *Koyaanisqatsi*, a 1982 film produced by Francis Ford Coppola and directed by Godfrey Reggio, with music by Philip Glass and cinematography by Ron Fricke.[34] *Life out of Balance* (a loose translation of the Hopi-language title) depicts the apocalyptic collision of two vastly different worlds: one urban, usurped by technology, and the other natural, at peace with the environment. A montage of sound and moving images expresses this dramatic clash. They run parallel, meet, twist together, and separate in a continual flux of aural and visual forms. After six years in the making – the first three spent on shooting documentary material and the next three on the musical score and the fusion of sound and image – the film achieved cult status. It has neither dialogue nor narrative but relies solely on the rhythmic pulsation of its aural and visual material. It opens with an oral introduction, a repetitive mantra of the word *koyaanisqatsi*, sung in *basso profundo* against the visual background of a slow pan over the deep shadows of the Grand Canyon. Later in the film, the choral chant of a Hopi prophecy, "If we dig precious things from the land, we will invite disaster," transports the audience onto today's all-too-familiar ground.

Reggio describes *Koyaanisqatsi* as "an animated object, an object in moving time, the meaning of which is up to the viewer."[35] Its pictures literally move in an uneven tempo, with slow-downs, speed-ups, time lapses, and cuts emphasizing their structural, rhythmic, and musical value rather than their narrative content. The pictures thus become musical elements and the film becomes a poem made by an art of noise composition. Philip Glass's soundtrack, fashioned in the composer's recognizable repetitive and augmentative style was also, at many places, derived from the musicalization of concrete noise captured on film. The authors worked in different media but in parallel throughout their long-lasting collaborative production process. They would literally put score against film sequences and, vice versa, film against score to create a non-narrative "object moving in time." This reminds us of how Glass used to compose his minimalist music counterpointing Robert Wilson's slow-paced theatre images. Reggio and Wilson, a filmmaker and a theatre artist at the forefront of the liberation of sound and image from narrative, figurative, and connotative strings, have clearly added to the process initiated by the dramaturgy of sound in the historical avant-garde.

THE ART OF NOISES IN TWENTIETH-CENTURY MUSIC AND PERFORMANCE ART

The exploration of the "unsynthesizable complexity of sound" as artistic material, which was started by Russolo, changed the contemporary approach to the relationship between music and the performing arts. Erik Salzman and Thomas Desi, in their 2008 book *The New Music Theater: Seeing the Voice, Hearing the Body*, proposed an alternative to the customary critical treatment of opera and musical comedy. For them, the most recent music theatre "came to designate a kind of instrumental or instrumental/vocal avant-garde performance associated with composers like Karlheinz Stockhausen and Mauricio Kagel ... [It] is music driven (i.e., decisively linked to musical timing and organization) where, at the very least, music, language, vocalization, and physical movement exist, interact, or stand side by side, in some kind of equality."[36] No longer a *music drama* that by means of music enhances a dramaturgy of plot and character, a new *music theatre* encompasses all elements of stage and performance. Their reasoning is similar to Hans-Thies Lehmann's call for a postdramatic theatre that operates with a stage/scene dynamic (in the case of music theatre primarily defined by sound) as a substitute for dramatic (or operatic) development. The postdramatic and new music theatre intentionally blur the distinction between dramaticity (a way of setting up a conflict) and theatricality (a manner of using the stage), following the trend that Patrice Pavis has recognized as a legacy of the avant-garde.

The new music theatre created in the tradition of Russolo, Varèse, and Cage takes all existing sound as musical. It counts on sound as an element of stage performance and cherishes the achievements of the historical avant-garde's sound poetry and de-semiotization of words. To illustrate this trend, Salzman and Desi discuss the arbitrary word play in Wilson and Glass's *Einstein on the Beach* and the oral rendition of language as pure sound in Kurt Schwitters's *Ursonate*. The authors also find many features of the new music theatre in the works of Christoph Marthaler, Heiner Goebbels, Jan Fabre, and other proponents of a postdramatic mise en scène, musicalization, and the aural – not necessarily only musical – structure of theatre. Clearly, Salzman and Desi's ideas go far beyond the subject matter of musicals and operas, and converge with the conceptualization of aurality in postdramatic theatre.

Russolo's revolutionary creation of noise-music continued in a series of avant-garde endeavours in the field of mechanical sound and machine music. Charles Bérard's *Symphonie des forces mécaniques* (1908), however, was composed before Russolo first addressed the musicalization of noise. It was a piece that combined sounds of engines, whistles, sirens, and electrical rings together with music from traditional instruments. Bérard later conceived a system of recorded noises and participated in the orchestration of sound for the Parisian performance of *L'Angoisse des machines* by Futurist Ruggero Vasari.

The machine music and noise vocalizations that were part of Italian synthetic theatre took on a different form in the Futurist and leftist avant-garde works of Russia. In the 1920s, Nikolai Foregger explored an original system of physical movement at his Moscow Theatre Workshop, Mastfor. His 1923 *Machine Dances*, "a plastic exercise in constructivism" as he called it, was a human display of the internal workings of an engine: pistons, flywheels, pumps, and belts. The performers rhythmically mimed mechanical moves of machine parts coordinated by the noise music of an off-stage orchestra that played on metal sheets, rods, and scraps, broken bottles, whistles, cans, etc., producing rattles, jangles, shrieks, and other mechanical sounds. A Soviet critic, amazed by the group performance, spared no words of praise for "the divine service of these 'machine-worshipers' ... a noise orchestra of a crowd of motors ... a complicated signalling apparatus ... [and] reckless gymnastics zealously performed with chopped movements mechanized as far as possible, on all kinds of gymnastic apparatus, under, in, on, between, before, and beside various machine structures."[37]

The Futurist love of machine sound and modern dance met in *The Steel Step* (*Le Pas d'acier*), a ballet by Sergei Prokofiev, based on his and Soviet designer Georgi Yakoulov's libretto, which echoed Foregger's exercises. Initially devised in 1925 for the Meyerhold Theatre in Moscow, Diaghilev commissioned the ballet after he heard Prokofiev's dissonant *Second Symphony*, which the composer described as "a symphony of iron and steel." Hence, *The Steel Step* premiered in 1927 at the Parisian Théâtre Sarah-Bernhardt, performed by the Ballets Russes. Erik Levi finds "the Futurist aspects of this work striking ... [since it included] hammers, revolving transmissions, flywheels, flashing electric signals and choreography in which the dancers portrayed the communal joy of industrial labour by copying the movement of machinery against the backdrop of scenery modeled on machines."[38] The festivity of machines evidenced in this first performance of *The Steel Step* has survived through the 2005 "recreation of a lost ballet" directed by musicologist Simon Morrison at Princeton University, which also featured a reconstruction of the original set.[39]

Arseny Avraamov's 1922 *Symfonia gudkov* (Symphony of Sirens), a counterpart to Nikolai Evreinov's 1920 *The Storming of the Winter Palace*, epitomized another instance of the use of concrete noise in Russian avant-garde monumental proletarian performances. The spectacular celebration of the fifth anniversary of the revolution took place in the port of Baku and ultimately across the whole city. The foghorns of the entire Caspian flotilla, two batteries of artillery guns, machine gun salvos of two full infantry regiments, the flights of seaplanes, and the sirens of all the factories in the town provided an appropriate dramatic soundscape for this massive event.

A couple of years later, George Antheil, an American in Paris who was already notorious for his *Airplane Sonata* and *Mechanisms* (1921), composed *Ballet mécanique* as a soundtrack for the Dadaist film of the same name, released on 24 September 1924. The film was directed by painter Fernand Léger and experimental filmmaker Dudley Murphy, with cinematography by Man Ray. The score combined industrial sounds with atonal and jazz music syncopated in a brutal and almost unplayable rhythm. Regrettably, the score could not be used in the original film because of its complicated orchestration, which called for sixteen player pianos (instruments that execute pre-programmed music operated by a mechanism with punched-paper roles), two grand pianos, four bass drums, three xylophones, a tam-tam, seven electric bells, a siren, and three different-sized airplane propellers (high wood, low wood, and metal). Introduced as a masterpiece by Frederick Kiesler at the 1924 International Exposition for New Theater Technique in Vienna, *Ballet mécanique* premiered without sound. Unfortunately, the soundtrack, in a simplified but still too-long version – thirty minutes instead of the seventeen needed for the film – had to be performed separately. Finally, in 2000, with the help of electronic and digital sound equipment, the integrated version of the film has been reconstructed. Antheil, who the French called *un futurist terrible*, treated his instruments literally as intonarumori. For instance, he used the piano exclusively as a percussion instrument that sounds mechanically and captures "the true significance and atmosphere of these giant engines and things that move about us."[40] His own laconic description of *Ballet mécanique* reads: "All percussive. Like machines. All efficiency. No LOVE. Written without sympathy. Written cold as an army operates. Revolutionary as nothing has been revolutionary."[41]

The anti-melodramatic use of noise in avant-garde theatre, celebrated in Futurist and Dadaist circles, remained sporadic in Surrealism, as the production history of *Parade* makes clear. This ballet, with a libretto by

Jean Cocteau, music by Erik Satie, and set and costumes by Pablo Picasso, performed by Diaghilev's Ballets Russes, premiered on 18 May 1917, at the Théâtre du Chatelet. *Parade* is distinguished by the fact that Guillaume Apollinaire coined the term *surréalisme* in its program notes, in an effort to fully describe the piece's multimedia nature, which integrated music, ballet, painting, costuming, and literature. The piece involved a range of innovative, avant-garde attitudes: Cubist breaking of perspective, Picasso's adoration of circus characters, Dadaist irreverence, Futurist rumorismo, popular use of ragtime, and vaudeville. Christopher Schiff describes the sonority of *Parade* as "a compromise of French theatrical music and Futurist noise."[42] As we can learn from the production history, from the very beginning the creators wavered between two separate scores – one of music (Satie) and the other of noise (Cocteau). As the two approaches clashed, compromises plagued the work. In the wake of his and Diaghilev's visit to Rome, where he got acquainted with the Futurist art, Cocteau, possibly for the sake of provocation, included in his script a large number of mechanical noises instead of words. Satie was none-too-happy to compose music that would, he thought, serve as a background for incidental noises. The score thus ended as a mediocre achievement, the biggest innovation being its orchestration, which was enriched by an assortment of noisemakers such as milk bottles, typewriters, Morse tickers, airplane propellers, and a foghorn. Unfortunately, not all of these rehearsals survived to appear on the opening night.

A month after *Parade*, another surrealist attempt at *bruitism*, Apollinaire's *Les Mamelles de Tirésias* (The Breasts of Tiresias), directed by Pierre Albert-Birot, premiered at the Théâtre Maubelle. One could expect quite a noisy play from Apollinaire, whose inclinations toward unconventional use of sound were known from his verbo-voco-visual poetry and 1914 manifesto "L'antitradizione futurista," published in *Lacerba*. Nevertheless, in the play, he uses noise insufficiently – and mainly through a character of "People of Zanzibar," who produces sound accompaniment for most of the stage actions and acts as the chorus. As a noisy commentator, he unabashedly brandishes all sorts of noisemakers: a revolver, a bass drum, a thunder sheet, a musette, and sleigh bells – whatever is handy. He even breaks dishes. Other characters at times produce vocal sound effects such as the onomatopoeia of a train ride, sneezes, and cackles. Although noise in *The Breasts of Tiresias* was not illustrative but – as in Dadaist pieces – ironic and alogical, the main merit of the play is not in the realm of the dramaturgy of sound but in the realm of its grotesquely absurd dramatic situation.

Tristan Tzara's subversive performances at the 1920s Dada soirées in Paris illustrate another way of using noise. They aimed "to frustrate the passive audition of expected sounds by the performance of unexpected and usually aggressive sounds ... In *Vaseline Symphonic*, a work whose title is more scandalous than its content, twenty people sang ascending scales first on the syllable *cra* followed by ascending scales one third higher on the syllable *cri* ... etc. ad infinitum."[43] The audience responded with chanting in unison, screams, and whistles, which only added to the intended cacophonous pandemonium in the theatre. The similarity of this performance to a Futurist serata is indisputable. Marinetti, of course, resented the growing success of Dada, while Dadaists demonstrated their hostility interrupting Russolo's intonarumori concerts in Paris with shouts: "Kill it! Kill it! ... Fiii-Fiii ... Frrr-Frrr." However, in spite of the Dadaists bragging that they, not the Futurists, were now the leaders of the avant-garde, Hans Richter had to admit: "We had swallowed Futurism – bones, feathers and all. It is true that in the process of digestion all sorts of bones and feathers had been regurgitated."[44]

Tzara thus wrote some lines of his plays as noise-musical verses. The dialogue of *The First Celestial Adventure of Mr Antipyrine, Fire Extinguisher* (1916; a second play of the same name was published in 1920) was discontinuous: the lines were no longer meaningful exchanges of logical sentences but rather exchanges of vocal gestures carrying different energies and attitudes shaped in sound. Here, characters bore allegorical names like Mr Blueblue, Mr Cricri, The Pregnant Woman, Mr Absorption, and Mrs Interruption. They delivered lines made of mixed phonetic material: combinations of logical or pathetic sentences, abstract vocalizations, onomatopoeias, lyrical verses and so on. Like Marinetti in the "Variety Theatre" manifesto, Tzara envisions a theatre that "stands as a metaphor for the circus ... The theatre. Since it forever remains attached to a romantic imitation of life, to an illogical fiction, let us give it all the natural vigour that it first had: be it amusement or poetry."[45] Here is a sample of such disruption of traditional dramatic dialogue:

Mr. CRICRI: there is no humanity there are the lamplighters and the dogs dzin aha dzin aha bobobo tyao ...
Mr. BLEUBLEU: (incontestably) toubo matapo the viceroys of the nights ...
THE PREGNANT WOMAN: a big bird alive tyao ty a a ty a o ty a o ...

Mr. CRICRI, Mr. BLEUBLEU, PIPI, Mr. ANTIPYRINE:
zdranga zdranga zdranga zdranga
di di di di di di di di di
zoumbai zoumbai zoumbai zoumbaidzi
dzi dzi dzi dzi dzi dzi dzi dzi dzi dzi dzi[46]

Russolo's experiments with noise provided the inspirational background for Pierre Schaeffer's musique concrète as well. Schaeffer wrote, recorded, and assembled music that operates with sounds as concrete, discrete parcels of material – that is, sonic objects. "The *objet sonore* is to be accepted for its sonic, acoustic properties; for its texture, its grain, for all the qualities it carries in excess of, or prior to, its traditional musical values."[47] A manipulation of these sonic objects in a manner similar to the art of noises gives structure to the compositions of musique concrète. Although the era of electronic and digital recording, amplification, treatment, and broadcast of sound has brought different issues into the discourse of musical composition, the basic principles of the art of noise remain viable. They influenced essential works of twentieth-century musicians such as John Cage, Arthur Honegger, Krzysztof Penderecki, and György Ligeti. A major figure in early electronic music, French-American composer Edgard Varèse, thus described his music as "organized sound." Its organization, as oppose to composition, is based on timbre and rhythm, elements that are more related to noise than to music proper and thus more to the art of noise than to the art of harmony. Torben Sanglid explains, "Varèse tried to emancipate noise from its mimetic function; abstracting it as purely aesthetic … He used sirens because of their glissando-possibilities rather than alluding to an emergency. By shifting the focus from the notes to the sound, by seeing music as layered, organized sound rather than melodic-harmonic development and by experimenting with electronic instruments."[48]

According to Levi, Varèse's work was closest to the spirit of Futurism. Varèse knew of Marinetti and Russolo and admired their ideas about the capability of noise to change listeners' auditory powers. At one of his 1929 concerts in Paris, he was first to introduce the russolophone, a newly invented keyboard-operated noise intoner. His piece for percussion ensemble, *Ionisation* (1931), outraged the audience by breaking conventional rules of musical structure. Its "scoring, which features writing for mechanical sirens arranged in high and low pitches, is especially pertinent in that respect, since the division of sonorities appears to follow the procedure adopted by Russolo in *Risveglio di una città*."[49] The most interesting argument for Varèse's Futurist spirit, Levi attests, lies in musicologist

Jonathan Bernard's suggestion that the composer may have gleaned more from the manifestos written by Futurist painters and sculptors than from those by musicians: "Bernard draws convincing analogies between Futurist painting and the violent anti-episodic, anti-sentimental, spatial aspects of Varèse's work."[50] Here one should recall Russolo's theoretical dictum: "I am not a musician but a Futurist painter using a much loved art to project my determination to renew everything." Concomitantly, one might also ask whether it is merely a coincidence that Russolo's first composition bears the title *Awakening of a City*, which resembles the name of Boccioni's painting *The City Rises* (*La città che sale*, 1910).

Apparently, the most significant Futurist contribution to contemporary music was the noise-incurred disturbance of its harmonic structure. But it cannot be restricted to the changes in orchestral music. Innovators of electronic media, whose new sonic realities literally include previously undetected murmurs of the human body and unattended sounds of the environment, have freely adopted it as well. Foreseeing these developments in 1937, John Cage began his *Credo: The Future of Music* with Russolo-like lines: "Wherever we are, what we hear is mostly noise. When we ignore it, it disturbs us. When we listen to it, we find it fascinating. The sound of a truck at fifty miles per hour. Static between the stations. Rain. We want to capture and control these sounds, to use them not as sound effects but as musical instruments."[51]

LA RADIA: A MANIFESTO OF A PURE ACOUSTIC ART

"La Radia" (1933), a manifesto of Futurist radiophonic theatre by Marinetti and Pino Masnata, was a step toward the synthesis of media and materials in a new technological environment. Marinetti and Masnata professed that radio, as a novel and superior medium, would transcend the naturalism, sentimentalism, and narration of theatre, cinema, and the book. It would abandon conventional staging for a more abstract artistic form that uses "the reception, amplification and transformation of vibrations released by living or dead beings, dramas of states of mind, full of sound effects but without words."[52] In addition, the manifesto exhibited, as might be expected, a typically Futurist disruptive tendency: "*La Radia* abolishes / the space and stage necessary to theatre / time / union of action / dramatic character / the audience as self-appointed judging mass systematically hostile and servile always against the new, always retrograde." Instead, this new art brings about the "compressed dramas comprising an infinite number of simultaneous actions."[53] "La Radia" looked like the synthetic theatre manifesto squared.

At the same time, "La Radia" represented a continuation of Russolo's art of noises in the electronic medium of recording, montage, and the transmission of sound, that is, radio. Marinetti and Masnata envisioned a realm of radio art in which "*parole in libertà*, daughters of the aesthetics of the machine, contain a whole orchestra of sounds and sound harmonies (realistic and abstract) which, single-handedly, can assist the colourful and pliable word in its flash representation of what cannot be seen."[54] Encouraged by technological advancements, Marinetti and Masnata supercharged their Futurism. Not only did they suggest the inclusion of environmental noise as artistic material, but also predicted the recording of a wider spectrum of sounds, even those that cannot be heard by the human ear. These sounds were to be registered by ultra-sensitive equipment able to catch an infinite variety of noises, vibrations of human, animal, vegetal, and inanimate bodies, extensions of voice and breath, and interference between radio stations, celestial bodies, or other radio emitters. Thus the microphone, a new tool for capturing sound, enabling its amplification and radio broadcast, would become a powerful means of immense wireless communication based on the Futurist "wireless imagination," which until then had relied solely on intuition.

Microphone recording and the art of radio married the art of noises with concrete sound poetry and musique concrète. Radio provided laboratories for acoustic research for many notable composers of the twentieth century. At Radio Television Française in Paris, Pierre Schaeffer directed the Concrete Music Research Group (*Groupe de recherche de musique concrète*), which started recording patches of "concrete" noises and experimenting with sounds abstracted from them as the elements of their musical compositions. Thus, as Marinetti and Masnata proposed in "La Radia," the microphone entered into undiscovered fields of sonority. By the recording and the manipulation of an infinite variety of sounds, including those that had previously been inaccessible to the human ear, Schaeffer strove to achieve *musique acousmatique*. Acousmatic listening got its name from Pythagoras, who lectured to his students (*acousmatcoi*) behind the curtain so that they could concentrate on the sounds of his words without seeing him. The term came to denote an aural experience of listening to sounds whose source is unknown. "Acousmatic listening involves a naïve, blank reception of the auditory," comments Seth Kim-Cohen. "We are asked to let sounds in the door without first asking 'Who's there?' Pursuing acousmatic *epochē*, we are then responsible for bracketing out all information that might shade our auditory experience with signification, with historical contingency, with social import. From this reduction, we can identify that which, within the sound, simply *is.*"[55]

Schaeffer's ideas and the technological advancement in sound recording played a significant role in the work of contemporary sound poets as well. Sensitive microphone capturing and electronic amplification of a whisper, a breath, or a cry helped Henri Chopin to discover the *terra incognita* of the human body's dark cavities and Bernard Heidsieck to insert "biopsies" of human utterance into the texture of pre-recorded ubiquitous sounds. Finally, radio became the home of an acoustic art that, contrary to representational radio drama, allowed for a symbiosis of sound (music and noise) and speech, a tonal organization (in Cagean terms) of recorded and electronically prepared material. Klaus Schöning describes it in this manner: "The sensitive, receptive ear of this technology is the microphone, and its storage media are the tape, cassette, record, and microchip. Its speaking mouth is the loudspeaker. One of its utopias is an acoustic space accessible to everyone: the radio."[56] "LA RADIA", a muse of a still little-known "art without time or space, without yesterday or tomorrow," helped Marinetti and Masnata envisage a utopian, but in our age of mass media omnipresent, "immensification of space."[57] They were scouts of an electronic age of global communications that would replace the industrial age of machines they inhabited. "Marinetti's claims for the radiomorphic sensibility of *La Radia*," writes Schöning, "anticipate some of the claims made more recently for the cybernetic sensibility of postmodernism. *La Radia*, he declared, would go beyond time and space, since the possibility of receiving broadcast stations situated in various time zones and the lack of light will destroy the hours of the day and night."[58]

Historically, radio broadcast began to draw virtual maps detached from the now-deserted lands of reality, even before Jean Baudrillard analyzed the concepts of simulacra and simulation as symptoms of the postmodern estrangement from real life. On the other hand, due to its power to cross borders of real time and space, radio created a virtual co-presence of different aural environments from all over the world. In one of his radiophonic syntheses, *Drama of Distances*, Marinetti turned this communicational feature of the radio medium into an aesthetic device. In this piece, he made an audio collage of seven different soundscapes, each one limited to a length of eleven seconds. One after another, we hear a military march in Rome, a tango danced in Santos, religious music played in Tokyo, joyful peasant singing in the fields near Varese, a boxing match in New York, street noises in Milan, and a jazz rendition of a Neapolitan *canzone* at the Hotel Copacabana in Rio de Janeiro.[59] A series of exotic but real sound events liberated from the constraints of local time are shaped into an acoustic art piece. The piece itself is a sonic event in the virtual sphere of radio broadcast, a live performance of the "synthesis of pure radio phonic sensations" as depicted in "LA RADIA". These soundscapes of distant locations function as interpenetrating states of mind rhythmically organized in blocks of noises and sounds. The dramatic clash of juxtaposed sound textures captured in different geographical milieus actually happens in a unique field of aurality, in the combination of timbres, intensities, and densities of sound. Every eleven seconds, the listener is forced to adopt a new level of sensibility required by a new sound attraction that obliges him or her to pulsate with the drama of the material. Clearly, then, the radiophonic synthesis *Drama of Distances* relies more on the materiality of sounds than on the nature and location of their sources.

In 1933 Rudolf Arnheim, a Gestalt psychologist and art theorist known for his influential books on film and visual arts, wrote a less-known book called *Der Rundfunk sucht seine Form* (Radio Searches for its Form). Herbert Read translated it into English in 1936 as *Radio: The Art of Sound*. Arnheim's argument in favour of radio art begins with the depiction of a global sound-sphere where radio connects distant places, emotions, and people, which is, in a way, almost identical to Marinetti's *Drama of Distances*. Soon after, however, Arnheim abandons his exploration of the "wireless as a means of transmission and dissemination" (as he refers to radio) and turns instead to the "wireless as a means of expression." In radio, he believes, an "art that makes use of the aural only"[60] has become for the first time fully accessible. The real subject of his book is an appeal for an aesthetic of pure sound. "In wireless the sounds and voices of reality claimed relationship with the poetic word and the musical note; sounds born of earth and those born of spirit found each other ... so that reality presented itself much more directly, objectively and concretely than on printed paper: what hitherto had only been thought or described now appeared materialized, as a corporeal reality."[61]

Together with acknowledging sound as a corporeal reality, Arnheim conceives of an "acoustic bridge" that connects different kinds of sounds in a unique artistic device: "By the disappearance of the visual, an *acoustic bridge* arises between all sounds: voices, whether connected with a stage or not, are now the same flesh as recitations, discussions, song and music. What hitherto could exist separately now fits organically together: the human being in the corporeal world talks with disembodied spirits; music meets speech on equal terms."[62] His concept of the "acoustic bridge" parallels the ideas of "flash representation of that which cannot be seen" and "an endless variety of concrete versus abstract, of real versus imagined, through *a community of sounds*" conceived in "LA RADIA."[63]

By establishing "a community of sounds" in radio Marinetti determines the field of a new acoustic art similarly to Arnheim. Both of them insist on expressive characteristics of sound that affect us directly. Arnheim's notion of the acoustic art of radio is consistent with the fundamental recognition of the materiality of sound in Futurism. He even claims explicitly that radio sounds are "comprehensible without any experience by means of intensity, pitch, interval, rhythm and tempi, [and all other concrete] properties of sound which have very little to do with the objective meaning of the word or the sound."[64] Arnheim praises the blindness of radio as its utmost creative power. The aural exclusiveness of radio is its advantage: paradoxically, its blindness extends the listener's visual imagination beyond the physical reality ordinarily known to him. "The sounds coming from the box next to my bed," comments Salomé Voeglin, "would have nothing to do with the visual world around me." They appear as noise, "sound that is truly not, and never was, related to any visual source and might lead the listener to invent a 'visuality' beyond his visual imagination … Such a blind 'noise' radio surpasses and stretches out of … its representational task into a generative presentation: intensively always now, clasped in a continuous present, nothing else and nowhere else."[65] This is what Wilson had in mind when he called for a juxtaposition of "a radio image over the [silent] film's voice," each maintaining its full autonomy. Only the full, self-sufficient sound of radio, which Arnheim and Voeglin describe as "blind 'noise,'" together with the self-sufficient visuals of silent film were able to extend the imaginative realm of Wilson performances. As we will find in the analysis of a few cases in point in the final chapter, this dramaturgy of sound method, in association with Glass's music and Hans Peter Kuhn's electroacoustic (one may say radiophonic) design, ushered the art of sound into the inventory of postdramatic theatre methods.

RADIO SINTESI: PREFIGURING CAGE'S CONCEPT OF SILENCE IN MUSIC AND PERFORMANCE

In 1939, six years after his 1933 manifesto "La Radia" that repudiated all previously existing forms of performance, Marinetti published five short radiophonic syntheses.[66] Although he never mentioned Arnheim's name or ideas and most likely never crossed paths with him, Marinetti employed Arnheim's principles of pure acoustic art in his radio syntheses. In one of them, *A Landscape Heard* (*Un paesaggio udito*), he combines several concrete sounds of nature composed/organized in a musical fashion. The synopsis at the top reads: "The whistle of a blackbird, envious of the crackling of a fire, ends by extinguishing the gossip of water."[67] At first it looks as if it promises a psychological motivation and narrative resolution of a dramatic plot (the blackbird is envious and the gossip of the water gets stopped). But the noises – the babbling of a brook, the crackling of a fire, and the cry of a blackbird – that arise one after another are juxtaposed in shape of an arbitrary rhythmical structure independent of psychological idiosyncrasies. Their durations are strictly measured in the script; the blocks of babbling – ten, eight, five, nineteen, twenty-five, and thirty-five seconds long – are interrupted by cracklings of one second, while the blackbird's call at the end lasts six seconds. Apparently, Marinetti's synthetic radio piece is atechnical – the major distinctive feature of the synthetic in contrast to the naturalist theatre as professed by the Futurists was to be atechnical – and there is no traditional dramaturgy in it. Instead, it displays sounds and noises of different timbres along a fixed timeline, following the rules of radiophonic creation "in the field of pure and no longer representational sound," which, as Arnheim claims, "demands no interpretation of the sound, but only the apprehension of the sound itself and of its expression!"[68]

Another of Marinetti's short radio pieces, *I Silenzi parlano fra di loro* (Silences Speak among Themselves), consists of several sound blocks; periods filled with sound are counterpointed to periods emptied of sound with exactly measured durations of eight to forty seconds. In the sounding periods, we hear either music – single notes or brief sequences of notes played on piano, trumpet, and flute, or noise – the roar of an engine, a baby wailing, and so on. In the non-sounding passages, we hear silence. Marinetti deliberately extends the duration of the silent blocks to make silence an active element of the aural drama. In fact, silences are those who speak. Clearly, he draws the aural architecture of the piece from a dramatic clash between silence and sound. He actually applies his own idea from the manifesto "LA RADIA", the idea of an acoustic art capable of the "delimitation and construction of silence." As a result, as Michael Kirby notices, in Marinetti's radio pieces "silence stops functioning as a neutral ground ... Silence is heard against the background of sound; silence becomes equal to sound as an aesthetic tool. Obviously, thoughts of this kind have much to do with the ideas of John Cage."[69]

Similarly, in *Battaglia di ritmi* (Battle of Rhythms), we first hear an electric bell ringing for a short while, and then we "listen" to three minutes of silence. Then we hear the turning of a key in a lock and again "listen" to a minute of silence. This is the end. Curiously enough, there is nothing to be heard after the last block of silence placed at the end of the piece to mark its conclusion, only silence. There is no full stop at the end of a phrase or a story. Obviously, Marinetti was dealing here with a different syntax, if not an absence of syntax. He believed that silences did not need sonic borderlines to be noticed. In his poetics of matter, silence was neither a sign of absence nor a break from the sensation of hearing, but an indistinguishable part of the flux available for listening. Marinetti thus appears as a follower of Bergson's philosophy of duration and a precursor of Cage in his concept of duration as the essence of a music that encompasses sound, noise, and silence.

La Costruzione di un silenzio (The Construction of Silence) is a conceptual piece of radio art that deals directly with silence. Paradoxically, in the piece there is no silence at all but only four juxtaposed blocks of sound, each coming from a different direction and distance. The four blocks of sound are supposed to create the floor, two walls, and the ceiling of an imaginary room of silence – housing for a hollow sculpture of sound, that is, a sculpture of silence reminiscent of Marcel Duchamp's idea of making a sculpture of the *Venus de Milo* exclusively by surrounding the listener with sounds.[70]

Marinetti's *radio sintesi* might seem like mere witticisms, but they were real promulgators of a new audio/radio art that we find now in the works of Bill Fontana, Klaus Schöning, and other soundscape, acoustic environment, and *Ars Acoustica* practitioners. Playing with sound as construction material and using long silences audaciously, Marinetti once again underlined the notion that aurality encompasses sound and silence, time and space. As "LA RADIA" professed new artistic possibilities beyond film and theatre, radio sintesi extended the realm of aural creation beyond the traditional forms of music, speech, and drama. His radiophonic dramaturgy proved that sculpting sonic matter is possible.

Marinetti's equal treatment of sound and silence in radio prefigures some of John Cage's principles of sound composition. Throughout Cage's musical compositions, poems, sound installations, and performances runs his conviction that there is no such thing as silence, only our failure to pay attention to sound. Cage redefined silence after his experience in an anechoic chamber at Harvard University. Athough the complete absence of sound was simulated in the chamber, what he *did* hear was a constant high-pitched ring and a low-pitched pulse: the singing tones of his nervous system and the throbbing noises of his blood. Therefore, silence is not a sonic vacuum but a medium of non-intentional, non-musicated, and non-pitched sound. In other words, there is no empty silence. "Music is continuous," he declared; "only listening is intermittent." Understood in this sense, music encompasses tonal forms together with noise and silence, all of them participating in the realm of aurality that is always around us, but it is up to us whether we listen to it or not.

The young pianist David Tudor first performed John Cage's paradigmatic silent piece *4'33"* on 29 August 1952, in Woodstock, New York. It was a stunning debut. Tudor walked onstage, sat down at the piano, opened the score, raised the lid of the keyboard, and remained motionless. He repeated the action three times since the piece is composed of three silent movements of different lengths. With the "music" piece liberated from any premeditated composition or any externally imposed meaning, the lack of performed sound served as a metaphor for the wholesale elimination of the usual sound-silence opposition. All that listeners had to do was to let themselves go with the unintended and previously unattended sounds of silence to be found in their environment. Cage's intention was, as he said, to let sounds be themselves and to expose listeners to their own and the piece's aurality.

In spite of Cage's radical ambitions, it remains an open question whether sounds can ever simply be themselves. His *4'33"*, Seth Kim-Cohen maintains, is more a conceptualist installation than a piece of music, as it tries to answer the fundamental question of what sound/silence is beyond its perceptive aspect. It challenges our listening rather than hearing. It is not about our audition but our conscious decision to give attention to the potential of sound/silence to be itself, that is, to accept and live through Cage's conception of attended and unattended sound/reality. A version of the tale of how it came to be "takes its cue not from bio-ontological or phenomenological stimuli but from visual art. In 1982, Cage said of his silent performance/music piece: "actually what pushed me into it was not guts but the example of Robert Rauschenberg. His white paintings … When I saw those, I said, 'Oh yes, I must; otherwise I'm lagging, otherwise music is lagging.'"[71] Another "precedent for a more conceptual reading of *4'33"*… resides in Rauschenberg's [1953 canvas] *Erased de Kooning Drawing* … which is simultaneously an exercise in discourse, narrative, and performance."[72] Repeating the painter's unsuccessful routine in trying to turn his colleague's work into a blank canvas by erasing his brush strokes, Cage tried to erase all traditional components of music from his piece. However, like bruises on the canvas, resilient unattended noises kept populating the silent performance. Kim-Cohen criticizes Cage for "failing to realize the fundamental thought of a non-cochlear sonic practice: sound is bigger than hearing." However, one must admit that Cage entertained this very concept in his collaboration with Marcel Duchamp, whose belief in a non-retinal visual art preceded Kim-Cohen's proposition for a sound art as a conceptual and contextual construct beyond actual hearing.

In his sound poetry and short performance pieces of the 1960s, Cage attempted to escape the logocentric patterning of language in a fashion reminiscent of the Italian and Russian Futurists, who had abolished syntax to set words free. After a period of experimentation with irregular words, punning, and allusion, he opted for what the sounds of elementary words could offer. "I hoped to let words exist," he said, "as I have tried to let sounds exist."[73] Abandoning his quest for bizarre words, he tried using ordinary language, but freeing it from the constraints of syntax – a process Cage regularly referred to as the "demilitarization of the language." To discover "the music of verbal space" and to deal with words as sounds, Cage looked for the cadence inscribed in the words' natural inflection: "Speaking without syntax we notice that cadence takes over. Therefore, we tried whispering. Encouraged we began to chant ... To raise language's temperature we not only remove syntax: we give each letter undivided attention, setting it in unique face and size; to read becomes the verb to sing."[74]

Cage thus developed oral performance pieces that use only a single instrument – the human voice – and a single medium – language and its verbo-vocal structure. He wrote a series of sound poems for performance called "mesostics" so named because of their centrally aligned acrostic running through the body of the poem. Since their unpredictably positioned middle letters now aligned the verses, the poems assumed an asymmetrical hieroglyphic form similar to the ideograms of Japanese haiku poetry. This method offered a visual presentation of a poem that would let the sounds of words exist in a new verbo-voco-visual environment. Like Marinetti's synoptic tables of parole in libertà and the Russian Cubo-Futurist stencilled books of zaum poetry, Cage's mesostics reflected sounds iconically by the graphic layout of letters. In that sense one can appreciate Cage's poems as a minimalist version of a Futurist typographical sound poem, as in this fragment:

Me?
I sleep eAsily
undeR
any aCoustic condition.
as hE said:
Lullaby.[75]

A follower of Zen philosophy, Cage found inspiration for his mesostics in the poetry of Matsuo Basho, the renowned haiku master of seventeenth-century Japan who shaped his poems in the form of ideograms:

old pond
a frog jumps
the sound of water

Cage wanted to free language from the grip of Western, syntactical, linear thought, and to bring it more in line with poetry like Basho's, which, as he says, "floats in space ... [and] only the imagination of the reader limits the poem's possible meanings." This "floating in space" of haiku poems is comparable to the sensation that a spectator of Noh theatre feels when a performer with subtle vocal modulations and slow body movements chants, "sculpts," "writes," or "paints" the poem/play in the air while conquering the silence around him and the emptiness of the naked stage. The meaning of Noh performance lies no less in the sculpture that the actor creates in time and space than in the words he utters. The aural, visual, and kinetic elements of Noh performance interact in a manner reminiscent of Basho's famous haiku, in which the sound of the poem is embedded in the shape of an ideogram as a blueprint of a sound sculpture.

In *Sculpture Musical*, a sound poem that Cage performed in Tokyo in 1986, the mesostic string consisted of Marcel Duchamp's words: "sons durant et partant de différent points et formant une sculpture sonore qui dure" (sounds enduring and coming from different points, thus shaping a lasting sound sculpture).[76] It was a performance created in the spirit of Duchamp's idea of making a sculpture of the *Venus de Milo* exclusively by surrounding the listener with sounds. Physically, the sculpture would not exist anywhere else but in sound or in the perception of sound by the centrally placed spectator. This positioning of the spectator in the midst of an art installation, inspired by the immersive quality of sound, was well known in Futurist painting. In addition, Duchamp's conceptualization of the sound-sculpture merged the aurality and visuality of its subject; it used sound instead of light to reveal the physical volume of the beautiful Venus's body. Interactive sound/space experiments take place in Duchamp's kinetic sculptures operating in between the plastic arts and the art of noise. His legendary ready-made *Bicycle Wheel* (1913), for example, was supposed to rotate, producing sound that creates its "virtual volume," as Moholy-Nagy put it. The idea that sound is capable of producing the "virtual volume" of a sculpture is unmistakably relevant for theatre as well. It opens a path for the theatrical use of a conceptual non-cochlear sound art and for – as we will see in the next chapter – Balla, Depero, and Prampolini's experiments with set, costumes, noise, and light, which merge the visual, the aural, and the kinetic into a virtual moto-rumoristic complex on the stage.

6

Sound as Structure: Toward an Aural Architecture of Theatre

FROM ONOMATOPOEIA, ANALOGY, AND ICONICITY TO THE PLASTIC MOTO-RUMORIST COMPLEX

Futurist poets substantially disturbed linguistic and literary conventions by turning the spoken, written, and printed word into a verbo-voco-visual ideogram. Both poetic idioms, parole in libertà and zaum, refashioned words into aural and visual icons, sensorial kernels whose intrinsic performance potential made them available for theatre use. Accordingly, Giovanni Lista found it appropriate to include Marinetti's synoptic table *Battle on 9 Levels of Monte Altissimo* (*Battaglia a 9 piani del Monte Altissimo*) in his anthology of theatre. Here the visual setting determined the corporeal, sensory dimension of its declamation and helped the poem/table turn into a synthetic performance by "declamators in motion – Marinetti, Balla and Depero."[1] Turning the link between sonority and visuals of Futurists' poems in an opposite direction, John J. White thought of the synoptic tables and non-linear typography as iconic consequences of their declamation. This view applies to the scripts of Cangiullo's *Piedigrotta* and Depero's *Colori*, also printed as tavole parolibere. Nevertheless, it is hard to say which came first – Futurist vocal performance or its visual representation. Is onomatopoetic declamation a cause or a consequence of the typographical layout of a poem? In any case, the verbo-voco-visual shape of Futurist poetry signalled the heightened audio-visual hybridization of a new performance style that Marinetti described as "dynamic and synoptic declamation." What we can say with certainty is that Futurist poetry, in both its oral and graphical aspects, was paradigmatic for the development of Futurist theatre, particularly in its synthetic phase.

At first intuitive and corporeal, the historical avant-garde's experiments with sound in the theatre started with the diversion of the vocal gesture from syntactic language, but their explorations spread to a more abstract approach to sound per se, as well as to its expressive and semiotic potential. Futurist initial exploration of "forgotten" sound symbolism in poetry was in line with Walter Benjamin's assertion that "the phonetic elements of a sentence represent the basic resources in which, in a flash-like instant, something mimetic can reveal itself out of a sound."[2] Looking for such sudden revelations in their synthetic theatre, Futurists condensed all drama into a "flash-like instant" that would ignite the audience with the energy of direct experience. The inner workings of their idiom of essential brevity relied on the synaesthetic correspondence of visual sensations, vocal and inanimate sound, environmental noise, music, colour, and smell. They followed the same impulses that led words, sounds, and letters of text-sound poetry to achieve their material equivalence with the things they stood for as their aural and visual icons. Adopting the iconic and analogical structuring of the aural, visual, spatial, and kinetic elements of the stage as a creative method for their abstract theatrical sintesi, Futurists cleared the way for concrete experiments with the "plastic moto-rumorist complex" on the kinetic sculpture-like stage, exemplified by the later works of Balla, Depero, and Prampolini.

Fleeing syntactic and narrative structures, Futurist synthetic theatre started to use an anti-dramatic idiom, similar to what Jacques Derrida calls "another form of writing" in Antonin Artaud's theatre. "For the theatre to be neither subjected to this [logocentric] structure of language, nor abandoned to the spontaneity of furtive inspiration, it will have to be governed according to the requirements of another language and another form of writing ... This time, writing not only will no longer be the transcription of speech, not only will be the writing of the body itself, but it will be produced, within the movements of the theatre, according to rules of hieroglyphics, a system of signs no longer controlled by the institution of voice."[3] Futurist demands for a new theatrical idiom were similar to Artaud's vision of "expression in space [in which] objects themselves begin to speak." This was a theatre idiom "of experimental demonstration of the profound unity of the concrete and the abstract," in which "the overlapping images and movements will culminate, through the collusion of objects, silences, shouts, and rhythms, or in a genuine physical language with signs, not words, at its root."[4] Characteristically, searching for an idiom with signs at its root, Futurists never abandoned their exploration of its phonetic sources. Their scenic language remained indebted to the dramaturgy of sound, even when it became abstract; it remained moto-rumorist, that is, kinetic and noisy.

Marinetti's visit to Moscow and St Petersburg in 1914 provides evidence of this aesthetic trend. A telling dialogue between Livshits and the celebrated Italian guest, reported by the former in his memoir *The One and a Half-Eyed Archer*, provides a case in point. Although Livshits and Marinetti engaged in controversy, it was evident that they both held to the elementary notions established in Futurist art.

Livshits criticized Marinetti: "What is the point of piling up amorphous words, a conglomeration which you call 'words at liberty'? … When I heard you reciting I asked myself a question: is it worth destroying the traditional sentence, even the way you do, in order to reinstate it, to restore its logical predicate by suggestive moments of gesture, mimicry, intonation and onomatopoeia?" Marinetti responded: "Recitation is only a transitional stage, a temporary substitution for syntax … The day we manage to put what I call 'wireless imagination' into effect, we will reject the outer layer of analogies … The 'analogies of the second order,' will be completely irrational … All psychology must be expelled from literature and replaced by the lyrical possession of substance."[5]

It emerges that Marinetti's concept of declamation was not aimed at the cowardly reconstruction of syntax, signification, or psychology as Livshits asserted. Marinetti primarily cared for the materiality of signs leading toward "analogies of the second order" that will expose the material in a more concrete and abstract way. His insistence on onomatopoeia, iconicity, and analogy that leads toward an abstract artistic idiom had an undeniable impact on the development of Italian Futurist theatre, in which vocal and gestural declamation were soon replaced by the treatment of sound as an abstract element of the stage complex. These changes were a logical continuation of inherently theatrical concepts formulated in Marinetti's poetry manifestos that promoted the power of analogy to tie together distant, seemingly diverse, hostile things, the potential of different onomatopoeias to shape an abstract structure, and the capacity of "dynamic and synoptic declamation" to express the "geometric splendor and mechanical sensibility."

Marinetti's major programmatic manifestos, published concurrently with *Zang Tumb Tumb* in 1913, transcended the borders of sound poetry and incited innovations in the idiomatic structure of all Futurist art. His concept of poetry making as "an orchestral style, at once polychromatic, polyphonic, and polymorphous [that] can embrace the life of matter only by means of the most extensive analogies,"[6] for example, initiated further

Futurist experimentation within the wider and more complex structures of the plastic arts and theatre. At the same time, painters Umberto Boccioni and Giacomo Balla outlined concepts of the Futurist visual arts, including plastic dynamism, the compenetration of objects and environments, and the use of "force lines" that put the spectator in the midst of a fragmented reality. In 1913 as well, Enrico Prampolini and Carlo Carrà put up a theory of the interference between objects and atmosphere based on chromophony or the synaesthesia of sound, noise, and smell carried by colour vibrations. Finally, that same year saw the publication of Luigi Russolo's "L'arte dei rumori."

In his comprehensive monograph on Italian Futurist theatre, Lista acknowledges this interplay of artistic disciplines and proposes a periodization of the movement's aesthetics into four phases. By suggesting four phases instead of the habitual two, Lista contests the widely accepted belief that the year 1920 marked the single cut-off between a first and second Futurism. According to Lista, a first period of Futurism, pre-1915, encompasses works defined by dynamism of the above-mentioned poetry, painting, and theatre manifestos. In a second period, 1915–20, works were defined by the exploration of the "plastic moto-rumorist complex." This period, Lista suggests, started with Depero and Balla's "Futurist Reconstruction of the Universe" and Prampolini's "Futurist Scenography and Choreography," published in 1915 and 1916, and went on to include their research into abstract plastic art and theatre up to 1920.[7] A third period, during the 1920s, was defined by a mechanical art that set the eradication of the human actor as its goal. A fourth period, initiated by the "aeropittura" (aerial painting and adjacent forms of literature and performance), was integral to the spatial and spectacular extension of theatre. Lista's diachronic summary of Futurist theatre aesthetics points to an increasing awareness of the materiality of signs – including the oral/aural ones – in poetry, art, and performance. It indicates the growing tendency toward an abstract theatre based not on literary drama but on concrete, scenic material. The influence of Marinetti's poetics of matter is evident throughout, from the interconnected experiments with sound and colour in poetry and painting to the conception of an abstract, tactile theatre of pure sensation. More importantly it entered into a fruitful compenetration and simultaneity (to borrow these two favourite Futurist/Dadaist terms) of the ideas, concepts, and performance practice that have permeated avant-garde theatre theory and production from the beginning of the twentieth century to our postmodern era. Günter Berghaus, for one, considers avant-garde attempts at a non-literary total theatre, which are integral to the methods of contemporary live performance and art in the domain of electronic technologies, as a major thrust of Futurist theatre theory.[8]

DADAIST SOUND AND SCHWITTERS'S *MERZ-STAGE*: PRELUDES TO TOTAL THEATRE

The ideas conceived in Italian Futurism spread to the anarchist and nihilist aesthetics of Dada in Zurich, Paris, New York, Berlin, and Hanover. Richard Huelsenbeck, one of the performers of the famed simultaneous rendition of the poem "L'amiral cherche une maison à louer" at the Cabaret Voltaire, admits to borrowing the methods of bruitism and noise music from Marinetti. "*Le bruit* – noise with imitative effects, was introduced into art (in this connection we can hardly speak of individual arts, music or literature) by Marinetti, who used a chorus of typewriters, kettledrums, rattles and pot-covers to suggest the 'awakening of the capital'; at first it was intended as nothing more than a rather violent reminder of the colorfulness of life."[9] It is not clear why Huelsenbeck failed to mention Russolo, the real author of *Awakening of the City*. Did he think that Marinetti's contributions epitomized the whole Futurist revolution? In any case, he shared Russolo's belief in the expressive power of noise in contrast to the limitations of tonal music. Maintaining a noisy and arrogant stage presence, Huelsenbeck performed "accompanied by a big drum, shouts, whistles and laughs ... [in] an attempt to capture in a clear melody the totality of this unutterable age, with all its cracks and fissures, with all its wicked and lunatic genialities, with all its noise and hollow din."[10] There is a marked similarity between parole in libertà and Huelsenbeck's *Fantastic Prayers*: "Plane pig's bladder kettledrum cinnabar cru cru cru / Theosophia pneumatica / ... Or or birribum birribum the ox whizzcs round in a circle or contracts for / Casting light hand grenade parts 7.6 cm chaser."[11] Enthralled by the noise of the mechanical age himself, in *En Avant Dada: A History of Dadaism* Huelsenbeck was able to properly diagnose symptoms of the Futurist predilection for noise: "While numbers, and consequently melody, are symbols presupposing a faculty for abstraction, noise is a direct call to action. Music of whatever nature is harmonious, artistic, an activity of reason – but *bruitism* is life itself ... *Bruitism* is a kind of return to nature. It is the music produced by circuits of atoms; death ceases to be an escape of the soul from earthly misery and becomes a vomiting, screaming and choking."[12] His reasoning clearly reflects the growing interest, among Expressionists and Dadaists, in a "literalness" inspired by the Futurist intoxication with matter and Russolo's inclusion of everyday sounds/noises in music.

Raoul Hausmann, a central figure of the Berlin Dada group, created *Seelen Automobile*, a series of sound poems he recited in June 1918 at the Café Austria. "The sound poem is an art consisting of respiratory and auditive combinations firmly tied to a unit of duration," he explained, "In order to express these elements typographically, I had used letters of varying sizes and thickness which thus took on the character of musical notation."[13] Hausmann began writing "optophonetic" poetry (*optophonetische Gedichte*) before learning of Ball's poems without words in 1920. He was evidently familiar with the techniques of Marinetti, Tristan Tzara, and Huelsenbeck, that helped him delve deeper into the abstraction of sound-text art. As if acting under a Futurist spell of "geometric and mechanical splendor and numerical sensibility," he was able to envision its ultimate consequence in the abstract letterism of a printed page or a poster (poster poetry, *Plakatgedichte*, was one of his later inventions) as we can see in this illustration:

kp' eriOUM **lp'er**iOum
Nm' **p** *eriii* pERnounnurn
*bprE***ti B***erree e* RR**Ebe**e e
ONNOo gplanpouk
konmpout pERIKOUL
R*R* EE***e***e E E e ***e*** rree*eee* **A**
oapAerrre E E **E**
mgl *ed* padANou
MTNou **tn***ou*m ***t*** [14]

By defining his poems, made solely of letters in different sizes and shapes, as optophonetic, Hausmann emphasized the synergy of their optic and phonetic features. For him this was "the first step towards poetry that is perfectly non-objective and abstract. This is where I differ from Ball ... His poems created new words, sound and above all musically arranged onomatopoeia; mine are based on letters, therefore excluding all possibility for creating language with a meaning or with coordinated movement."[15] Hausmann insisted on a sharp delineation between his "alphabet poems," directly and exclusively based upon letters – that is to say, "letterist" – and Ball's poems based upon words. The optophonetic architecture of Hausmann's letters represented a score for an abstract vocalization of sound, timbre, stress, and pitch: "A poem for me is the rhythm of its sounds. So why have words? Poetry is produced by rhythmic sequences of consonants and diphthongs set against a counterpoint of associated vowels, and it should be simultaneously phonetic and visual. Poetry is a fusion of dissonance and onomatopoeia ... Spiritual vision, spatial form and material sound form are not poetry in themselves but they all make up the poem."[16] His abstract vocalizations, like *bbbb* and *fmsbw*, *kperioum*, and *pggifmu*, proved to be seminal for the French *lettrism* of the 1950s, while his manifesto of the "lawfulness of sound" influenced the purely acoustic approach of contemporary radio and audio art. In terms of the dramaturgy of sound, Hausmann's simultaneous use of abstract visual, spatial, and phonetic elements opened up a possibility for a synthetic art no longer exclusively motivated only by synaesthetic correspondences.

Hausmann's introduction of a pure acoustic art dependent on the graphic disposition of letters was crucial for the work of his colleague, Dadaist painter and collage artist, Kurt Schwitters. For twelve years, from 1920 until its final publication in 1932, Schwitters had been writing/collaging/composing and performing his sound poem "Sonate in Urlauten" (Sonata in Primordial Sound), or "Ursonate."[17] He ended up with a very precise typographical score for a thirty-five-minute vocal performance, organized into four movements with prelude and cadenza. Subsequently performed and recorded by the author for Radio Stuttgart, "Ursonate" finally appeared as a vinyl LP record, which has proved to be inspirational for many contemporary musicians and performance artists. Musician Brian Eno, for instance, included its sampled version in his 1977 album *Before and after Science*, which explored avant-garde and environmental sound, while Christoph Marthaler used its method to counterpoint and discredit the celebratory recitation and documentary presentation of the positive outcome of the Second World War in his 1995 staging of *Stunde Null*, discussed earlier.

Schwitters started from the letterist structure of Hausmann's alphabet poetry and, by breaking it down into a vocal texture, played on the exclusively musical characteristics of the chosen consonant clusters, vowels, and syllables. He conceived the poem as an abstract vocal sonata written according to musical parameters. Schwitters actually borrowed the initial letters of Hausmann's poem, *f b m s b w*, and used them as his first theme in "Ursonate." Hausmann, however, was not impressed: "I severely reproached him at the time for having made out of my invention ... *a classical sonata*, which seemed blasphemy to me and contrary to the phonetic meaning of the letters I had chosen."[18] But "Sonate in Urlauten" was far from a classical music form. It was a collage of sounds available for a surprising, aleatoric, truly Dadaist rendition. When performed at the time, the sonata challenged the perceptions of the audience; listeners did not know whether it was a poetry recital, a variety performance, or a musical piece. Schwitters contributed to the piece's fame by his peculiar stage presence when in the 1920s he, together with Tzara, Theo Van Doesburg, Laszlo Moholy-Nagy, Ed Lissitzky, and Hans Richter, participated in poetry readings all across Europe. Richter remembers one of Schwitters's appearances in a Prussian nobility house in Potsdam:

> Schwitters stood on the podium, drew himself up to his full six feet plus, and began to perform the *Ursonate*, complete with hisses, roars and crowing, before an audience who had no experience whatever of anything modern. At first, they were completely baffled ... Their faces, above their upright collars, turned red then slightly bluish. And then they lost control ... and the whole audience, freed from pressure that had been building up inside them, exploded in an orgy of laughter. ... [But soon] the hurricane blew itself out as rapidly as it had arisen. Schwitters spoke the rest of his *Ursonate* without further interruption. The result was fantastic. The same generals, the same rich ladies, who had previously laughed until they cried, now came to Schwitters, again with tears in their eyes, almost stuttering with admiration and gratitude. Something had been opened up within them, something they never expected to feel: a great joy.[19]

Moholy-Nagy also praised the work as an abstract construction of verbal sound that was able to convey the aesthetic and emotional charge of a work of art: "The words used do not exist, rather they might exist in any language; they have no logical, only an emotional context; they affect the ear with their phonetic vibrations like music. Surprise and pleasure are derived from the structure and the inventive combination of the parts."[20]

In his 1924 manifesto "Consistent Poetry," Schwitters remains adamant that it is absolutely irrelevant whether one recites a written poem or uses any other textual/phonetic structure for his verbo-vocal material: "one can recite the alphabet, a string of purely functional sounds, in such a way that the result is a work of art."[21] For him, in contrast to the standard use of letters and sounds, which when they constitute words are unambiguous, their use in "sound poetry is consistent only in one case, namely when it is created in public performance." The consistency of a poem is assured by its verbal inconsistency. In "Ursonate," therefore, he collaged sound patches irrespective of the possible lyrical or denotative value they could have as syllables of meaningful words. Such use of concrete sound materializes in the reductio ad absurdum of possible meanings of the words *priimiitittiii*, incomplete *primitiv* (primitive), and changeable *tisch/tesch/tusch* (table). Their repetitious phonetic play here resembles Khlebnikov's method in *Incantation by Laughter*:

Priimiitittiii tisch
tesch
priimiitittiii tesch
tusch
priimiitittiii tischa
tescho
priimiitittiii tescho
tuschi
priimiitittiii
priimiitittiii
priimiitittiii
too[22]

Later in "Ursonate," Schwitters goes even further in abstract structuring of phonemes released from their verbal context. On page after page strings of phonemes, syllables, consonant clusters, and multiplied vowels are carefully arranged configuring a score for an abstract vocalization. "It is better to hear the sonata than to read it ... I myself like to and often perform my sonata," explains Schwitters: it is a "rondo with four themes" composed of different verbal/musical motifs spreading "from the pure lyric of the sung [syllabic tune] 'Jüü-Kaa' to the strict military rhythm of the third theme which sounds totally masculine compared to the trembling, sheepishly tender fourth theme."[23] Never abandoning the poem's musical scheme, his strings of "words" veer between chants and incantations of an *ur*-language, and sophisticated aural forms.

Although far more abstract than Marinetti's onomatopoeia of war, Schwitters's loud poetry readings were consistent with the tradition of bruitism that characterized the avant-garde. It continued to influence recent performances by François Dufrêne, Bob Cobbing, Steve McCaffery, and other poets oriented to concrete sound and the disintegration of language. Laszlo Moholy-Nagy's wife Sybil (one of Robert Wilson's favourite teachers) recounted an anecdote that speaks to this tradition, celebrated on both Futurist and Dadaist sides of the ideological barricade. The event took place in Berlin in 1934 at a formal banquet for a delegation of Italian artists, at which all the Nazi dignitaries short of Hitler were present: Goebbels, Göring, Hess, Röhm, and so on. Moholy-Nagy, who received a personal invitation from Marinetti, hesitated to go, but Schwitters, who wanted to honour the Italian poet, insisted, and so they went. They were sitting "sandwiched between the head of the National Socialist Organization for Folk Culture and the leader of the movement *Strength Through Joy*. Moholy was full of resentment, silent … Schwitters drank speedily." Suddenly he started to expound, no holds barred:

> "I love you, your Cultural Folk and Joy … You think I am not worthy of sharing your art chamber for strength and folk? I am an idiot too, and I can prove it." …
>
> The official from the Organization for Folk Culture nodded droolingly, his round cheeks puffed up with wine and amazement. "Oh joyful baby face," Schwitters muttered, tears running down his cheeks, "you will not prohibit me from *MERZing* my *MERZ* art?"
>
> The word *prohibit* had finally penetrated the foggy brain of the *Strength Through Joy* man. "Prohibited is prohibited: *Verboten ist verboten* … And when *Führer* says *Ja*, he says *Ja*, when *Führer* says *Nein*, he says *Nein*. *Heil Hitler!*"
>
> Schwitters looked wildly at Moholy, at me, at Marinetti, but before he could incite anyone to action, Marinetti had risen from his chair. He swayed considerably and his face was purple. "My friends, he said in French, after so many excellent speeches tonight, I feel the urge to thank the great, courageous, high-spirited people of Berlin. I shall recite my poem *The Raid on Adrianople*."
>
> "*Adrianople est cerné de toutes parts SSSSrrr zitzzitzzitzzitzi PAAAAAAgh rrrrrrrrrr*," roared Marinetti "*ouah ouah ouah départ des trains suicides, ouah ouah ouah*"
>
> The audience gasped: a few hushed giggles were audible.
>
> "*Tchip tchip tchip – féééééééééélez*"
>
> He grabbed a wineglass and smashed it to the floor.
>
> "*Tchip tchip tchip … des messages teléphoniques … Piiiiing sssssssssrrrrrr*

> *zitzitzit*" Schwitters had jumped up at the first sound of the poem. Like a horse at a familiar sound the Dadaist in him responded to the signal. His face flushed, his mouth open, he followed each of Marinetti's moves with his own body. In the momentary silence that followed the climax his eyes met Moholy's.
>
> "*Oh Anna Blume*," he whispered and suddenly breaking into a roar that drowned the din of protesting voices and scraping chair legs he thundered:
>
> "*Oh, Anna Blume, Du bist von hinten wie von vorn, A-n-n-a*."[24]

Unfortunately, in the forthcoming carnage of the Second World War, Schwitters and Marinetti would remain worlds apart. The first one's art was designated degenerate by the Nazis of his country so that he had to flee to Norway and England, while the other one, crowned with academic laurels by the Fascists of his country, continued serving them from Libya to the Eastern Front.

Schwitters, who was best known for his collage paintings, christened his own Hanover Dada movement and the magazine he published between 1923 and 1932, *Merz*, after a cut-out from an advertisement for *Kommerz und Privatbank*. The word *Merz* stood for "freedom of all fetters for the sake of artistic creation" in Merz-poetry, Merz-painting, Merz-stage, and so on. The culmination of all these hybrid art forms was an installation, exhibition, sculpture, and performance space called the Merz-building (*Merzbau*). Also known as *The Cathedral of Erotic Misery*, it was an environmental artwork in progress, a growing architectonic construction made of ready-made bric-a-brac that devoured Schwitters's entire two-storey house in Hanover. Layer upon layer, its grotto-like rooms were filled with the endogenous tissue growing from the artist's tumultuous life, documented by saved art objects, debris of popular culture, notes, documents, and trivial scraps, including a sock belonging to Moholy-Nagy and a strand of Richter's hair. All of it was encased by interconnected architectural structures made of plaster and wood that were erected along multiple, irregular axes, a new chamber appearing for each new installation, ad infinitum. Richter remembers one of his many visits to *The Cathedral* when he became aware that "all the little holes and cavities that we [avant-garde artists] had formerly occupied by proxy were no longer to be seen. "They are deep down inside," Schwitters explained, "concealed by the monstrous growth of the column, covered by other sculptural excrescence, new people, new shapes, colors, and details."[25] Never finished "out of principle" and more than ten years in the making before Schwitters fled Nazi Germany in 1936, the *Merzbau* exemplified art that resisted consolidation – always in flux and never purified into an ideal aesthetic form. An Allied bombing raid destroyed it in 1943.

Schwitters's ideas of painting/collage, sculpture, architecture, and theatre were conceived in his abstract/concrete poetry. He saw an uninterrupted link between the rhythmical design of sound-text poetry and the structural design of the plastic arts that, again unfinished "out of principle," flow into each other. "I pasted words and sentences together into poems in such a way that their rhythmic composition created a kind of drawing. The other way around, I pasted together pictures and drawings containing sentences that demand to be read. I drove nails into pictures in such a way that besides the pictorial effect a plastic relief arose. I did this in order to erase boundaries between the arts."[26]

In theatre, this concept called for an intense intermixing and fusion of sound, colour, light, materials, and objects. Consequently, Merz-play was an abstract work of art where, "as in poetry, word is played against word, factor is played against factor, material against material," and which, in contrast to the drama or the opera, "cannot be written, read or listened to; it can only be produced in the theatre."[27] In several of his theoretical texts, published in *Sturm-Bühne* in 1919, Schwitters outlined the Merz-stage as a composite artwork: "The Merz stage knows only the fusion into the total work. Material for stage set are all solid, liquid, and gaseous bodies such as white wall, man [sic], barbed-wire fence, blue distance, light cone. Use surfaces that can become solid or dissolve … Let things turn on themselves and move, let lines broaden into surfaces … The materials for the score consist of all sounds and noises that can be created by violin, drum, trumpet, sewing machine, ticking clock, water stream, etc. … The materials are not to be used logically in their objective relationships, but only within the logic of the work of art."[28]

Additionaly, at the end of his Dadaist poem-book *An Anna Blume*, Schwitters included a manifesto, "To All the Theatres of the World I Demand the MERZ-stage." Here, he goes on to encourage theatre artists to "marry off the materials to each other. For instance marry the oilcloth sheet to the building society, bring the lamp-cleaner into a relationship with the marriage between Anna Blume and the concert pitch."[29] Was this not a Marinetti-inspired thought of escaping the psychological and sentimental "I" and indulging in the life of matter itself? After describing different freely mixed objects, surfaces, and colours, he ironically concludes that in his theatre even humans may be used. "Human beings may be tied to the wings … [They] may appear even in their daily situations, may talk on two legs, even in sensible sentences." As if having in mind opportunities that the dramaturgy of sound offers, he merges disparate sounds in a fiery spinning ball-like crescendo of the aural and the visual in an apotheosis of Merz-stage: "And now begins the glow of musical saturation. Organs behind the stage sing and say 'Phutt, phutt.' The sewing machine rattles on in the front ... A man says 'Bah ...' A water-pipe drips monotonously … Drums and flutes flash death, and a streetcar driver's pipe shines brightly. A jet of ice-cold water runs down the back of the man in one wing into a pot. He sings C sharp, D, D sharp, E flat, the whole worker's song … a melody of violins shimmers pure and as delicate as a girl. A veil spreads latitudes. The glow in the center boils a deep dark red … I demand unity of the forming of space. I demand unity of the molding of time."[30]

Schwitters's vision of *Merz-bühne* as a composite work of art coalesces with the Futurist inclusion of different media and materials in their synthetic theatre, which stems from their preference for materiality, tactility, and abstraction. This idea of an abstract theatre based on the materiality of sound, colour, mass, and movement was advanced by an international group of avant-garde artists who were not limited by national borders. The Bauhaus theory and practice of "total theatre" thus can be traced not only to German Expressionists and Dadaists like Oskar Kokoschka, Lothar Schreyer, or Schwitters. It can also be revealed in works by Italian Futurists like Marinetti, Cangiullo, Balla, Depero, and Prampolini, as well as in works by Russians Malevich, Tatlin, and Kandinsky, all of whom broke ground for the hybridization and synthesis of art forms that constitutes an essential element of contemporary theatricality.

CONFLUENCE OF VERBAL AND STAGE SOUND IN EXPRESSIONISM AND THE BAUHAUS

The German Expressionist theatre that developed in the first decades of the twentieth century, most notably in the period of the Weimar Republic, exhibits three different performance styles: scream or ecstatic Shrei-performance, spiritual or abstract Geist-performance, and self-centred or Ich-performance. Kokoschka's *Murderer, the Women's Hope* (1909), whose hybrid form was discussed earlier, can be considered the source of all three styles. Undeniably the eroticism and physicality of Schrei-performance, in which "sounds became corporal and movements aural," made it suitable material for the dramaturgy of sound. On the other hand, the dramaturgy of sound became integral to Geist-performance in determining an abstract aural dimension, that is, the spirit in performance. In his production of August Stramm's play *Sancta Susanna* in October 1918, Lothar Schreyer shaped a model of Geist-performance in which "setting, sound and action combine on equal terms." This type of performance finds its roots in Kandinsky's theory of "inner sound" that externally differentiates but essentially unites bodily and colour-tone sounds and their movements into a stage composition. Influenced by Kandinsky, Schreyer, a key practitioner of the Sturm-Bühne, developed a particular mise en scène based almost exclusively on the rhythmic and acoustic properties of dramatic language and stage elements. He conceived of drama/performance as "a rhythmic succession of sounds" that echoes the Geist (spirit) of the phenomenal world. Mel Gordon claims that in the Sturm-Bühne's performances we find "bright-color backdrops of black, yellow, green, and red ... oversized cylindrical costumes made from geometrically-painted cardboard and wire ... gigantic ten-foot-high masks ... bizarre instrumentation, like a West African xylophone, glass harmonica, or a violin-solo – all dramatic elements of other avant-garde theatres."[31] This led Gordon to conclude that it was Lothar Schreyer who, albeit unintentionally, "bridged Expressionism's abstractionist beginnings from Kandinsky's Blaue Reiter movement (1911) to Oskar Schlemmer's Bauhaus Theatre Workshop (1923)."[32]

In terms of its oral/aural structure Schreyer's theatre pursued the emphasis that avant-garde poets placed on the sound of words. In keeping with Futurist and Dadist poets, Schreyer eschewed conventional concerns with prosody, tempo, and metre, and instead sought the "fundamental sound" of language. Once liberated from their syntactic fetters, he believed, words would reveal the spirit (Geist) that lies hidden in their inner sound. Historical evidence of the affinity of Expressionist ideas with Marinetti's concept of parole in libertà can be found in Herwarth Walden's *Der Sturm*, an influential Berlin magazine that continued publishing Futurist poetry and manifestos throughout the 1910s. Soon afterwards, a number of German Expressionists started writing poems in strings of rough, elementary words instead of verses, which, once freed from syntax and versification, were able to carry a rich texture of surprising verbal analogies and sonorous combinations. Stramm, for example, as John Willett has noted, destroyed all his previous writings after reading Marinetti's "Technical Manifesto of Futurist Literature" in 1912. His ensuing poetry and dramatic opus, including *Sancta Susanna*, were marked by condensed dialogues in an asyntactical, telegraphic language with emphasis on sound akin to parole in libertà. Schreyer, who joined the *Der Sturm* circle in 1916 and became the editor of the magazine, was also exposed to Futurist influence. Experimenting with bruitist declamation and art-of-noise imported from Italian serate, in two years he organized numerous "sensational, if sometimes incomprehensible" *Sturm* evenings. By the end of 1918 Schreyer had moved to Hamburg, where he formed the *Kampfbühne* ensemble and started to work on short plays resembling Futurist sintesi.

The rhythmic and aural principles of Geist performance, as David Kuhns suggests, come from Schreyer's conviction that "every word has a particular 'sound value' based on its structure of consonants and vowels ... [and] together they determine the unique 'word-tone' of every word. Each word, each sentence, has its unique rhythmic properties; the rhythmic succession of words in drama is a rhythmic succession of sounds."[33] Primarily concerned with the *sound* of performance, Schreyer developed a profoundly meditative program of actor training based on vocal gymnastics, which was a practice of incantation focused on the sound and pace of single words and brief phrases from condensed Expressionist scripts. He taught his students to express various "vibrations of the soul" with their mouths and throats in an act of "sound-speech" different from conventional talk, dramatic dialogue, or operatic singing. "Individual 'sound-speakers' learned to create a 'rhythmically harmonized' ensemble, known as a 'speech-choir.'"[34] This expressive style was employed, more recently, in the postmodern theatre practice of the late Einar Schleef.

In conventional drama, alleged Schreyer, the actor is an agent while the words are the agency. In contrast, Geist actors are an agency allowing word-sounds to become agents. Hence, actors no longer deliver mere dramatic character speech; they consciously help word-sounds to constitute the performance. The actors are now equal to voice, body, sound, and movement: they can be treated as formal materials of poetry and theatre. Acting as "sound figures" they become bearers of "form, color, movement, and sound." Schreyer asked Geist actors not to portray men, but rather to become "animated and resounding color-form." He encouraged the performers to create movement and actions from what they felt in the sounds of the words and the colours of the stage rather than in a dramatic text. They had to follow the internal logic of an abstract/concrete stage composition in which sensory attractions induce one other, stresses Schreyer. In an arc of the performance: "The movement colors the form. The movement forms the color. The sound induces the color-form. The induced color-form produces sound."[35]

Schreyer's Geist-style staging of *Sancta Susanna* was an autonomous stage composition in which these modalities of "inner sound" flowed into each other. Its hybrid form caused consternation among critics, who had some respect for Stamm's script but did not appreciate the actors' "sound-speaking," the mystic changes of music and light, and, most of all, the fact that the character of the rebellious nun, Susanna, was played in the nude. Hebert Ihering's review enumerates the distinct, albeit for him undesirable, aural qualities of the performance: "Before a gaudy black, yellow, green and red wall stands a woman … She speaks, sings, sounds a litany … A second woman answers in a shrill, whistling, giddily high voice. The antiphony continues in harsh dissonances until the woman who is lying on the ground begins to sing a coloratura aria … The acoustic signals of Clementia and Susanna are exchanged again. Now there are trombone flourishes; then later, whistles. One time muffled thuds; another time, clinking glasses. The bodies move like marionettes. Anything dropped to the ground is supposed to be inwardly composed sound, and the nude scene is supposed to be austerely rhythmic. Behind the scenery, Negro drums complete and intensify the orchestration."[36]

Apparently, critics were not ready for Schreyer's foray into sound-colour abstraction and the actors' non-psychological play. Schreyer soon left the Sturm-Bühne for Hamburg to experiment further with sound and rhythm until Walter Gropius called him to be the first teacher of the Bauhaus Theatre Workshop in Weimar in 1921. In his final contribution to the *Sturm-Bühne* magazine, Schreyer offered an apt summation of abstract theatre:

> Art is the artistically logical formulation of optical and acoustic relations.
> Art comes from the senses and appeals to the senses.
> It has nothing to do with understanding.
> The theatre is the formulation of focal color forms.[37]

Schreyer's mystical inclination toward the inner sounds and rhythms of words, people, and the world did not last long in a school that was predominantly oriented to functional design. It was his student, Oskar Schlemmer, who took up his teacher's post and, in his *Triadic Ballet* of 1922, developed a similarly abstract but primarily visual performance technique that was emblematic of the Bauhaus. As Kuhns reports, "Schreyer cautioned that a geometric approach to the principles of theatrical movement tended toward 'undisguised constructivism.'" However, in spite of their stark visuality, Schlemmer's geometrical but fluid choreographies quite musically present pure space in motion. In her recent study *The Theatre of the Bauhaus: The Modern and Postmodern Stage of Oskar Schlemmer*, Melissa Trimingham devotes a full chapter to sound. She finds that sound "engaged and frustrated Schlemmer's genius, as he sought to connect the medium of sound with the 'Gestalten' of the dance which he felt was the origin of all arts. In eventually restricting the sound on the Bauhaus stage to, largely speaking, basic percussion, he sought to understand something very simple that he also sensed was very complex: the relationship of the (moving) body to the making of sound."[38] He sought "impersonal unemotive sound/music which can then be detached from source, moved around and distorted." This sound/music becomes a counterpart to the material forms on stage in the form of, as Futurists would say, a plastic motorumorist complex. Therefore, Hindermith's music for *The Triadic Ballet* was not played by a live musician but executed on a player-piano so that, as Schlemmer notes in his diary, "the exactitude and precision of music, determined by the mechanization, was in extraordinary harmonious rapport with the formal precision of the figures ... parallel to the mathematical costumes, which follow the mechanics of the body."[39] Trimingham concludes that Schlemmer's respect for the physicality of stage made him concentrate "more on periodicity and materiality of sound than its harmony," which is in line with the methods of the avant-garde dramaturgy of sound re-discovered in new music theatre (Salzman) and posdramatic performance (Lehmann).

The truth is that the Bauhaus Workshop paid inadequate attention to the sound of language. Schlemmer admitted: "For the time being, we must be content with the silent play of gesture and motion – that is, pantomime – firmly believing that one day the word will develop automatically from it."[40] Yet, from Gropius's introduction to *The Theatre of the Bauhaus*, originally published 1924, one can see that the dramaturgy of sound, in its vocal, corporeal aspect, was alive and well in the celebrated artistic school. Gropius describes the first performances prepared by the theatre class as a synacoustic/synoptic mix of attractions, which remind us of the above review of *Sancta Susanna*:

> The dancers [were] in metallic masks and costumed in padded, sculptural suits ... The silence was broken by a whirring sound ending in a small thump; a crescendo of buzzing noises culminated in a crash followed by portentous and dismayed silence. Another phase of the dance had all the formal and contained violence of a chorus of cats,

> down to the meowing and bass growls, which were marvelously accentuated by the resonant mask-heads. Pace and gesture, figure and prop, color and sound, all had the quality of elementary form … The stage elements were assembled, re-grouped, amplified, and gradually grew into something like a 'play,' we never found out whether comedy or tragedy ... Set of formal elements ... gestures and sounds would become speech and plot.[41]

AURAL DRAMATURGY OF THE FUTURIST SYNTHETIC THEATRE

In 1915, after all their experiences with propagandistic art-as-action (*arte-azione*) events, bruitist declamation at theatrical evenings (serate), hybrid performances at gallery afternoons (*pomeriggi spetacollari*), and attempts at variety theatre, Futurists took a decisive step toward a "real" theatre. They decided to engage professional actors to stage a series of their short experimental plays – sintesi. In 1915 and 1916, several leading actors (*capocomici*) – Ettore Berti, Ettore Petrolini, Luciano Molinari, among others – and their companies, commissioned by Marinetti and friends, toured Italy with full-evening programs of Futurist synthetic theatre. These tours, meant to popularize Futurist theatre, turned out to be an unfortunate step backwards. Encouraging a number of minor artists to write short synthetic plays, Futurists found themselves promoting sintesi of a lower quality. Besides, the old-fashioned acting at the institutional theatres of that time could not adequately represent the radical reform they sought. Inevitably, most of the performances on these tours fell flat. Nevertheless, "The Futurist Synthetic Theatre," a manifesto by Marinetti, Emilio Settimelli, and Bruno Corra published in February 1915 together with two volumes of short plays, several scripted by the strongest talents of Italian Futurism, remains a source of inspiration for the contemporary theatre. Most importantly for my inquiry into the dramaturgy of sound, many of the theatrical sintesi, especially those subtitled as abstract, included sound as their essential component. Drawing from the synaesthetic explorations in painting, poetry, and music the authors of the manifesto announced, "The Futurist theatrical synthesis … will be *autonomous*, will resemble nothing but itself … Above all, just as the painter and composer discover, scattered through the outside world, a narrower but more intense life, made up of colours, forms, sounds and noises, the same is true *for the man gifted with theatrical sensibility, for whom a specialized reality exists that violently assaults his nerves:* it consists of what is called THE THEATRICAL WORLD."[42]

The manifesto's dictum promises an abstraction of the inherent theatricality of the real world "made up of colours, forms, sounds and noises." Theatre, then, was bound to be about the matter that makes up the world rather than about dramatic characters and their psychology, suffering, or joy. It was supposed to compress "fragmentary dynamic symphonies of gestures, words, sounds and lights," capture a mood, a sensation, and a state of consciousness, and create "stage ambiences where different actions, atmospheres, and times can interpenetrate and unroll simultaneously."[43] The new theatre had to be *synthetic*, which meant extremely condensed and short. Some sintesi are only momentary flashes – Cangiullo's *Detonation*, for example, consists of a bullet shot on an empty stage. The synthetic theatre should be *dynamic*, *simultaneous*, *autonomous*, *alogical*, and *unreal* – all features alluding to concepts developed in Futurist painting and poetry. Most of all, it had to be *atechnical*, that is, dismissive of the dramaturgy of passéist, naturalistic playwriting and staging (a good part of the manifesto is devoted to this issue).

The attribute "alogical" used in the manifesto, although consistent with contemporaneous developments in painting and poetry, was a new word in Marinetti's theoretical vocabulary. The manifesto's co-authors, painters Corra and Settimelli, the prime movers of alogical art and abstraction in synthetic theatre, promoted the term. On the other hand, Lista points out, Marinetti's intensified contacts with Russian Cubo-Futurist poets and painters after his 1914 visit to Moscow and St Petersburg influenced his adoption of the term "alogical" for the description of the new dramaturgy.[44] Indeed, as discussed earlier in this chapter, Marinetti's readiness to steer toward abstraction was apparent in his controversy with Livshits during the visit. Consequently, in the manifesto of Futurist synthetic theatre he describes main features of the new theatrical style as "autonomous," "unreal," and "resembling nothing but itself" using the vocabulary of Cubo-Futurist "objectless art."

Giacomo Balla, known for brave experiments with abstract pictorial and aural forms, wrote *Printing Press* (*Macchina tipografica*, 1914) as a score for "*onomatopea rumorista*" with choreographed movement and stipulated duration. He put twelve performers on the stage, in front of a large backdrop/billboard reading *TIPOGRAFIA*, to enact movements of machine pistons and wheels, simultaneously repeating for eleven minutes each a different phoneme in fortissimo:

1st PERSON: setté setté settésetté setté setté
2nd PERSON: nenné nenné nennénenné nenné nenné

3rd PERSON: vùùùùmmùùvùùùùsmùùvùù
4th PERSON: tè,tè,tè, tè,tè,tè, tè,tè,tè, tè,tè,tè, tè
5th PERSON: miaaa **aaaa** navanó ___ miaaa **aaaa** navanó
6th PERSON: sta ____sta ____sta ____sta ____sta
7th PERSON: lalalalalalalalalalalalalalalalalala
8th PERSON: ftftftftftftftftftftft
9th PERSON: riôriôrièrièriôriôrièrièriôriôrièrièriôriô
10th PERSON: chchchchchspsspschchchchchspsps
11th PERSON: vèvèvèvèvèvèvèvèvèvèvèvèvèvèvèvè
12th PERSON: nunnnònònunnnònònunnnònònunnnònò[45]

The manuscript of the sintesi has three folios containing a script for vocalization, a design for the backdrop with huge typographic upper-case letters, a schematic study of the circular movement of the performers' arms with notes for the tempo, and a sketch of the costumes in white, black, and orange. From Balla's drawing, one can see that performers looked like semaphores circularly moving their arms by the rules of Futurist dance and synoptic declamation that required the "fluency of a train wheel and of an airplane propeller." While mimicking the rotation of printing machine parts they produced abstract vocalizations of the mechanical noise. The visual, kinetic, and aural elements of the piece are simple, repetitive, and abstract to the point that, if not for the backdrop, one would be hard-pressed to decide exactly what they represented. Even though it gave an impression similar to Foregger's *Machine Dances*, which appeared almost ten years later, the sound of *Macchina tipografica* was definitely of another kind. It was not produced by metal noisemakers but by vocal onomatopoeia resembling nothing but itself, and it sounded like an accelerated version of Balla's previous attempts at free word poetry, *Verbalizzazioni astratte* (Abstract Verbalizations) and *Mimiche sinottiche* (Sinoptic Mimes). Curiously, depending on which source one refers to, *Macchina tipografica* is considered an onomatopoeic poem, a theatrical sintesi, or a Futurist ballet. Lista, for example, included it in his anthology of Futurist theatre as a ballet script, probably because Balla and friends showcased the piece for Diaghilev in his Parisian drawing room, attempting to convince him to include it in a double bill with *Feu d'artifice*. Unfortunately, that attempt failed. Among Futurists, the piece was regarded as moto-rumorist, in this case performed by people who would soon be replaced by kinetic objects, puppets, or machines.

A later work by Balla, *Disconcerted States of Mind* (*Sconcertazione di stati d'animo*, 1916), represents another stage complex of sounds, colours, forms, and movements. The language of the piece is reduced to simple, phonetic gestures: four individually costumed people stand on a white stage simultaneously talking, gesticulating, and producing abstract vocalizations. What makes the work unusual is the quasi-musical character of its script. Its verbal/sound material is organized into four micro-scenes/stanzas or tempos in an arrangement similar to a music score. The stanzas are separated by lines/bars into four quasi-musical movements of a set length. In the first "movement," each performer loudly recites various rounds of numbers: 666 billions, 666 millions, 666 thousands, and the same again for 333, 444, and 999. In the second, the performers pronounce different letters – *aaa*, *ttt*, *sss*, and *uuu*. The third movement consists of four parallel silent gestures: the first performer raises his hat, the second looks at his watch, the third blows his nose, and the fourth reads a newspaper. The concluding, fourth stanza, in contrast to the restrained and serious tone of the previous ones, serves as a kind of emotional crescendo in which all the characters perform very expressively, delivering their lines loudly and simultaneously. First goes "sadness – aiaiaiaiaiaiaiai'" second "quickness – quickly, quickly," third "pleasure – sí sí sí sí sí'" and fourth "denial – no no no no no no."[46] By the rhythmic play of sounds and gestures, Balla emphasizes the simultaneity and compenetration of states of mind. Human emotion is only permitted at the end, but even then, it is disconnected from the characters, whose lines overlap and lose their relation to individual psychology. The audience's reading of sadness, quickness, pleasure, and denial is thrown off balance as the work verges into the humorous or tragic cacophony of the synthetic piece.

Vowel Refrains (*Storneli vocali*, 1916), a sintesi by Francesco Cangiullo, subtitled "verses of life – music of death," has a similar structure. Five characters line up onstage and respond to the master of ceremonies with the refrains of a dying man, a doctor, the relatives, the brother, and the crowd. The characters answer each with different, lengthy pronunciations of a vowel sound: *aaaah*, *eh*, *iiih*, *oh oh oh oh*, and *uh*. Obviously, any naturalistic "as-if" acting is out of the question here. Even if a performer chooses to emotionally portray the tragic absurdity of his/her individual situation, such an act will be restricted by the fact that the performers are standing in a chorus line. The sarcastic but clearly abstract conclusion comes when the emcee mechanically utters the line "A. E. I. O. U."

In Balla's *To Understand Weeping* (*Per comprendere il pianto*, 1916), two men, one dressed in a white summer suit and the other in a woman's black mourning dress, stand before a square backdrop painted half in red and half in green. They deliver their lines with the utmost solemnity.

Fourteen lines of dialogue repeat a series of nonsensical vocalizations and numbers:

> MAN IN BLACK: To understand weeping …
> MAN IN WHITE: Mispicchiritotiti
> MAN IN BLACK: 48
> MAN IN WHITE: Brancapatarsa
> MAN IN BLACK: 1215 ma mi …
> MAN IN WHITE: Ullurbusssssut
> MAN IN BLACK: 1, seems you are laughing
> MAN IN WHITE: Sgnacarsanipir
> MAN IN BLACK: 111.111.022 I forbid you to laugh
> MAN IN WHITE: Parplicurplotorplaplint
> MAN IN BLACK: 888, for God's sssssake don't laugh! Understand?
> MAN IN WHITE: Iiiiii rrrrr I rr iririri
> MAN IN BLACK: 12344 Enough! Stop it! Stop laughing!
> MAN IN WHITE: I have to laugh.[47]

This could go on indefinitely were it not for the Man in Black's demand that the Man in White stop laughing. But there is no realistically motivated laughter or mourning on the stage, just two parroting performers in contrasting black and white costumes, in front of the backdrop of contrasting colours, talking in the style of parole in libertà. The materials of sound and colour, used to express diametrically opposite states of mind, have overtaken the dramaturgy of characters who might be weeping or laughing for different psychological reasons. In addition to a slightly farcical sense suggested by the cross-dressing of one of the men in a female mourning robe, at the end, the spectator is left wondering whether the piece requires any understanding of weeping at all. Still, through the clash of the visual and aural material, one can perceive an embryonic dramatic form.

The use of nonsense language and the production of noise are the central dramaturgical elements of *Stati d'animo* and *Violenza* (States of Mind and Violence, 1916) by Mario Carli. In *Stati d'animo* ordinary patrons at a typical promenade café speak an extraordinary, nonsensical language. In truth, all the characters express their attitudes appropriately but they do so using an "inappropriate" vocabulary of abstract vocalizations. This apparently serves them well; it lets them express their states of mind by means of pure vocal gestures. Thus, a speculator bites his fingernails and calculates possible gains by uttering clusters of harsh consonants: "astrr ghrrr frr magnakalacafu" while a student at the next table conveys nostalgia and bitterness: "auflin bergin ochiputecio." The coquette, in turn, glances at both of them, flirting: "chono chiono psi psi" while the clerk reads a newspaper: "ito rito marito oro coro coloro." The journalist, the deputy, and the lovers follow the same pattern. Only the poet and the philosopher express a few pseudo-comprehensible words like "shudder mystery sunrise" and "casuistry universal perspicuity," but their phrases sound more like mystifying blunder than meaningful speech. The short scene of an everyday, carefree afternoon abruptly ends when a wrestler rushes in, fighting everyone, overturning tables, spilling drinks, and screaming, "brututum zum pum!"[48] A counterpoint of two blocks of sonority signals a physical clash: the indifferent murmur of the café visitors occupied with their own states of mind is forcefully disrupted by the violent, aggressive noise of the intruder.

Violenza, subtitled "a symphony," represents again an ordinary street soundscape. Everyday people populate the street, but this time, instead of the drone of a café, a much more intense sound permeates the stage. It begins with the offstage sound of a distant drum roll and cymbals that continually intensifies throughout the entire scene. With time, this aural backdrop becomes loud enough to incite a growing frenzy among the people in the street. Vendors loudly advertise their merchandise while a newspaper hawker throws out the headlines: "Killing! Bombardment! Disaster!" A waiter chases a man out of a café. They shout: "You have to pay! I will not pay! You have to pay! I won't pay!" We hear children scream, windows smashed, cracks of a whip, and a tire exploding offstage. While two actors loudly rehearse a quarrel scene, a real couple starts a violent fight that ends with the woman lying stabbed on the pavement. Another man unsuccessfully chases a woman with the words, "Magda! If you don't return I'll kill myself!" and blows his brains out with a pistol. The persistent, ominous sound of drums and cymbals accompanying all stage actions reaches its deafening crescendo in the duels between the couples. Then a sudden silence sends "a shiver of disgust" through everyone on the stage. As all hastily make their exit in different directions, fruitstands and tables with drinks get overturned and food is scattered on the floor. The loud, violent soundscape is abruptly replaced by a deathlike silence; only a distant tremble of the windowpanes can be heard on the now-deserted stage. The glow of a bloody-red sunset appears; night falls. Fairly soon a new dawn arrives and we see an old couple slowly exiting a house with the help of a young boy. The old couple comes to the front exchanging trivial phrases about a peaceful life. The old man is happy; "*La violenza non esiste*," he says. The boy "innocently" points out two corpses lying onstage. This is the end.

There is no standard dramatic development here. Quite the opposite, the actions of the characters are chaotic, fragmented, and unmotivated. Apparently, the piece's aural configuration becomes its main dramaturgical device. The conflict and resolution, if those are still needed in an "atechnical" sintesi, reside in the different aural qualities of the *Violenza*'s three scenes (one should remember that Balla calls three parts of his abstract synthesis *Disconcerted States of Mind* three *tempi*). Although Carli, unlike Balla, did not use bar lines to separate scenes of *Violenza*, he delineated them quite sharply by aural intensity, timbre, and rhythm. They are juxtaposed in the manner of a musical or, rather, noise composition. The first scene, whose irritating, violent sonority reaches its high point in a cacophonous turmoil, ends abruptly with a man and a woman lying dead in the street. The second scene, in contrast to the first, longer scene, is short and silent; nobody moves on the stage and we hear only the gentle but menacing tremble of windows in a soft sunset breeze. The final, third, scene sounds like an ironic idyll – it contains a subdued speech of the old couple and a young boy, a dialogue of the "disenfranchised."

To show the absurdity of the dramatic content, Carli uses sonic textures contrapuntally; he juxtaposes layers of different timbre, rhythm, and intensity, making a collage of soundscapes in a manner close to musique concrète and Russolo's noise compositions. Without a doubt, Carli builds the drama of his *Stati d'animo* and *Violenza* through the compenetration of aural, visual, and kinetic elements. In so doing, he announces a theatre of "the eventful present, the particular semiotics of bodies, the gestures and movements of the performers, the compositional and formal structure of language as soundscape, the qualities of the visual beyond representation, the musical and rhythmic process with its own time" – a theatre of "states and of scenically dynamic formations."[49] Lehmann calls this theatre postdramatic.

Marinetti, a relentless innovator of Futurist poetics, wrote some of the most interesting synthetic pieces. His abstract sintesi, *The Battle of the Backdrops* (*Lotta di fondali*, 1916) is a play with the stage as itself, in which the protagonists are ubiquitous symbols of the theatre. Curtains, for example, are forced into an interactive play with living characters. The first scene unfurls in front of a red backdrop as we hear the shouts of a rebellious, stampeding crowd. Three characters – the Bully, the Sensitive, and the Persuasive – enter one after another, and with different attitudes deliver their incomprehensible speeches to the backdrop. A minute of silence follows.

Then the backdrops change, or, one could say more accurately, one exits and the other enters. Thus, in the second scene, after a red exits, a soft blue appears and we hear:

Four mandolins play a sweet note, offstage.
A minute of silence.
Whispering and repressed laughter, offstage.
A scale played on a flute, offstage.
The voice of an amorous woman, offstage.
A very rending sob, offstage.
Three beats on an invisible bass drum.
The stage lights dim.
In the dark, the loud snoring of a man. [50]

While the first scene contained "characters" who deliver dramatic, though unintelligible, lines, the second contains only sound: music, noise, and silence on an empty stage. It is at this point that Marinetti uses sound alone as the dramaturgical element of his play. Highlighting the dominance of aurality in the play, he places noises offstage and stipulates the exact duration of the pause: a minute of silence. This is a kind of rhythmic juxtaposition of silent and sounded blocks, which reappears in Marinetti's synthetic radio pieces. It is clear that the real characters are the red and the soft blue backdrop; the others are just noisemakers. Indifferent to – and silent in the face of – the futility of human rioting or love affairs, backdrops stoically bear witness to the dignity of matter. They act similarly to the chairs and pieces of furniture in Marinetti's *drammi di ogetti* (dramas of objects) *Il Teatrino dell'Amore* and *Vengono*. Giving character roles to inanimate objects, Marinetti attests to his love for matter, and his wish to abolish the anthropocentrism of bourgeois art.

The Little Theatre of Love (*Il Teatrino dell'Amore*, 1916) is a drama of objects developed in the background of a dreamy, atmospheric love-betrayal plot with real characters: a husband, a wife, a lover, and a little girl. Here the kitchen buffet and the sideboard take over the emotional tension of the show by expressing the "suffering" of the material. Marinetti attends to the tactile features and texture of their materials; through the objects-characters' onomatopoeia we literally hear the noise of shrinking and expanding of their wooden bodies as they are exposed to the touch, weight, pressure, and moisture of their surroundings. Their lines are a mélange of small talk, quasi-objective reports of the physical conditions, and onomatopoetic mimesis rhythmically interspersed with moments of silence:

IL BUFFET: Cric. It will rain in three quarters of an hour (*Silence*). Griiil. They're opening the gate (*Silence*). Cric Cric. The pressure of the silver service is greater than my cohesion!

LA CREDENZA: Crac-crac. On the third floor, the maid is going to bed (*Silence*). On the scale, it's a weight of 154 pounds. (*Silence*). Crac.

———

IL BUFFET: Cric. It's raining ...

LA CREDENZA: Crac. I'm expanding. (*Silence*) ... Craac craac.[51]

The objects/characters in *They Are Coming* (*Vengono*, 1916) are chairs submitted to torture by a majordomo and maids who are nervously preparing a reception for guests who never arrive. It is a choreographed piece of subtle violence in which the sadistic majordomo forces the maids to constantly rearrange the seating plan. The ultimate victims are, in fact, the chairs. Near the end of the play, the panicky majordomo starts to speak nonsensically – "briccatirakamemame" – herding the frightened maids into a corner of the room. At the end, the chairs silently "leave" the stage helped by a beam of light that elongates their shadows as if they were moving toward the exit. Thus, in Marinetti's *dramma di ogetti*, lights, colours, and the disposition of objects join the dramaturgy of sound expressed by onomatopoeia, incomprehensible vocalizations, and strictly programmed silences to create the subtleties of *stati d'animo*. The synthetic essence of these pieces lies in the fact that they replace the dramatic or narrative development with an audio-visual composition of a stage environment that is able to emanate energies. Its architectural composition/construction of sound, light, and objects in motion looks forward to the later Futurist experiments with a moto-rumorist stage complex.

PRAMPOLINI, CARRÀ, AND DEPERO: SYNAESTHETIC THEORIES AND SYNTHETIC STAGES

The path toward the synthetic and moto-rumorist form of Futurist theatre has been opened by the elaboration of synaesthetic correspondences in two 1913 painting manifestos, "The Painting of Sounds, Noises and Smells" by Carlo Carrà and "Chromophony – the Colours of Sounds" by Enrico Prampolini. Carrà maintained that sounds, noises, and smells incorporated in the painterly expression of lines, volumes, and colours can create dynamic, polyphonic architectural entities similar to musical works. Indebted to Kandinsky's theory of synaesthetic and vibrational correspondences of sound and colour, Carrà conceived ideas similar to those of Rayonists Mikhail Larionov and Nataliya Gonchareva, who maintained that vibrations of sound and colour, and their reflections (rays) in the atmosphere, were integral to painting. For them, it was not the representation of a figure or an object but the abstract play of atmospheric vibrations that made a picture. Carrà also tried to objectify colour and sound as carriers of abstract shapes; he claimed, "*From the formal point of view*: there are sounds, noises and smells which are concave, convex, triangular, ellipsoidal, oblong, conical, spherical, spiral, etc. *From the colour point of view*: there are sounds, noises and smells which are yellow, green, dark blue, light blue, violet."[52] On these grounds, Carrà promoted an art of total painting that involved the cooperation of all the senses. His acknowledgment of sound as colour – and vice versa, colour as sound – and his depiction of a work of art as a polyphonic architectural construction were practically realized in Depero's abstract synthesis *Colori*, a pioneering attempt at a kinetic sound sculpture in performance.

Prampolini, an abstractionist painter who became the most successful and internationally recognized stage designer of Futurism, went further in expressing atmospheric and emotional states of mind through the synergy of sound and colour, which he called "chromophony." Chromophony amalgamates the plastic entity of the set with the scenic action, the movement of actors (if they appear on stage at all), light, and sound. Its force and lyrical beauty stem from the intrinsic material quality of these elements. As for sound, he said, "Why have I chosen sound in order to define the basis of chromophony? Because it is the fittest expression for classifying these new manifestations of mankind … A noise, a sound, a word, while arousing in the atmosphere a pure dynamic vibration, arouses within the volatile imagination of the artist the intuitive chromatic stimulus."[53] Prampolini thus tries to give a scientific justification of the artistically productive impact of sound and noise on visual arts. At another point, he describes chromophony by an example of an engine sound that displaces the atmosphere, then rhythmically diffuses in it, and finally rebounds from obstacles and breaks up into a myriad of chromatic scales awakening a multitude of lights and colours. For Prampolini "painting is an aggregation of chromatic vibrations" in the atmosphere able to express the complexity of physical and psychic forces in nature; it is a pure optical visuality that "needs no help from culture." Through "chromophony" the artist, like the spectator, gets hold of the material essence of a work of art and its idiom beyond cultural codification and framing.

In Fortunato Depero's piece *Colours* (*Colori*, 1915), subtitled as an abstract theatrical synthesis, the stage consists of a pale blue cubic room with no doors or windows. Inside this abstract room, or box, four abstract individualities, or objects, make abstract movements manipulated by invisible strings and talk in an abstract, incomprehensible language of babble and noise. The cast members have no human traits: they are described in physical terms. GRAY is "dark, plastic, dynamic ovoid"; RED is "plastic, triangular, dynamic polyhedron"; WHITE is "plastic, long-lined, sharp point"; and BLACK is "multiglobe." This made Lista call the piece "a visualization of psychic forces, a kind of ballet of abstract forms and sounds."[54] It is unclear whether it is a picture/sculpture staged according to the laws of chromophony, or sound transformed into a kinetic stage entity. The four individualities are supposed to produce vocalizations of their *stati d'animo* that in turn correspond by nature and timbre to the relevant chromatic and formal essence of their own shape and colour. BLACK thus speaks with a "very profound, guttural voice," WHITE "has a sharp, thin, brittle voice," GRAY utters "animal-like sounds," while RED's voice is "roaring and crushing." Their lines are written in the manner of parole in libertà; indeed, the whole two-page script looks like a *tavola parolibera sinotica*, containing vertical and horizontal lines of different-sized letters, typefaces, and levels of boldness. Fragments of their speech go:

BLACK: TO COM momomoo dom pom grommo **BLOM** uoco **DLONN** ...
WHITE: ZINN – FLINN fin ui tli tli dlinn ...
GRAY: Bluma dum du clu umu fubulù ...
RED: SOKRA TI BOM **TAM** cò te' to' lico[55]

Near the end of the play, they start to relentlessly repeat their lines in unison, until a whistle interrupts them. As Daniela Fonti asserts, "There is no story; the whole dramatic action is reduced to the presence of four protagonists whose only meaning is to be phonetic-chromatic equivalents; in short, pure self-reference."[56]

Colori represented the dramatization and visualization of Depero's "*onomalingua*," an idiom that he derived from Marinetti's onomatopoeia and Russolo's rumorismo (noisiness). *Onomalingua*, as the author defines it, is an abstract verbalization of colours, forms, materials, speed, light, temperature, space, and states of mind – a kind of "universal abstract poetry." *Colori* replicated its structure in the field of plasticity, aurality, chromaticity, and illumination as a synergetic theatre performance based on the collusion of objects, words, sounds, lights, and movements. The piece was similar to Kandinsky's staging of Mussorgsky's *Images from an Exhibition* in 1928, one of his experiments from the Bauhaus period, in which the flow of the music generated kinetic images of an abstract theatrical tableau radiating its own "inner sound."[57] In Depero's *Colori*, however, there is no musical composition in the background; its sonority is supplied by the objects/characters, who themselves produce the audio-visual structure of the performance. Depero's piece relies solely on the pulsation of the intrinsic energies of the differently shaped/coloured/sounded objects; their dramatic clash is generated in the sphere of their aural, chromatic, kinetic, and plastic features. *Colori*, therefore, can be considered an early, crude, but for that reason radical attempt at the dissociation of anthropocentrism and psychology from matter and form. Most importantly, it led towards further explorations of scenography and choreography and conceptualization of the plastic moto-rumorist complex, the most relevant expressive mode of Futurist abstract theatre. Unfortunately, like the majority of the Futurists' outstanding conceptual works, *Colori* has not been staged by its creators.[58]

THE PLASTIC MOTO-RUMORIST COMPLEX: AN AUDIO-VISUAL STAGE AS AN ACTOR

To claim that it was the recognition of the materiality of sound in Futurist poetry and the ensuing dramaturgy of sound that laid the theoretical and practical groundwork for their abstract painting and stage design might at first seem far-fetched. But Futurist visual artists were the first to share an interest in the texture, density, and treatment of verbal/painterly masses with Futurist poets. Likewise, Futurist visual artists came up with the oxymoronic term "chromophony" to denote the synaesthetic, vibrational interference between colour and sound. Their approach to audio-visual hybridity of art was a crucial step toward the conceptualization of the plastic moto-rumorist complex (*complesso plastico motorumoristo*), a notion broad enough to encompass all the material elements of theatre and to synthesize all that was seen and heard on the Futurist stage. The term was coined by Balla and Depero, in their 1915 manifesto "Futurist Reconstruction of the Universe," to describe the creation of a kind of marionette or robot in a class of "polyexpressive artificial living beings"; but its meaning was extended that same year by Prampolini's "Futurist Scenography and Choreography" to include the creation of an abstract entity equivalent to the scenic action of a theatrical work of art. For Balla, Depero, and Prampolini, the plastic moto-rumorist complex represented much more than stage objects, sets, lights, and sound; it was the plastic equivalent of the simultaneity, compenetration, and dynamism of the theatrical performance. The plastic moto-rumorist complex of stage was born from the dynamic interplay of the fluid phenomena of light, noise, and motion in the time and space of performance. Sound was considered its obvious and inextricable part. Indeed sound was the medium in which motion and noise, key attributes of the performance, amalgamated, creating the materiality and atmosphere of the stage.

The manifesto "Futurist Reconstruction of the Universe" was a result of the growing maturity of Futurist art. Its significance lies in an effort to embrace all possible forms of sensory perception and unite them, formulating "a new aesthetic object – 'the plastic complex' – which marks a leap from a statement of synaesthesia to a concrete reconstruction."[59] Balla and Depero acknowledged having been influenced by Marinetti's words-in-freedom and Russolo's art of noises, which provided a dynamic, simultaneous, plastic, and noisy expression of universal vibration. With the ambition to achieve a synthesis that would revolutionize Futurist sensibility, they defined the "plastic complex" as "poetry + painting + sculpture + music … a noisiest-pictorial-psychic complex plasticism, [which uses] onomatopoeia, graphic equivalents of noises, phonoplastic equivalents, psycho-plastic equivalents."[60] Balla and Depero promised: "We will give skeleton and flesh to the invisible, the impalpable, the imponderable, and the imperceptible. We will find abstract elements of all forms and all elements of the universe … a life-work based on a variety of materials and most of all on its autonomous character of a plastic complex that is similar to itself."[61]

In addition, they suggested all of this be done with joy. Hence, the manifesto initiated the construction of Futurist toys, artificial landscapes, and mechanical animals. The authors proffered an abstract but energetic and optimistic art in which the temporal elements, sound and motion, merged with the spatial ones, forms and plastic objects. They made a list of kinetic categories that determine plastic complexes as "decompositions," "rotations," and "miracle magic." The contraptions, puppets, and robots they imagined and constructed would not only be illuminated but would be illuminating, colourful, and bright by themselves. Two such models made by Balla, the "Plastic Ensemble Coloured with Din + Speed" and the "Plastic Ensemble Coloured with Din + Dance + Gaiety," were reproduced in the manifesto. Although the actual objects might not be that illuminating, the concept of a moto-rumorist plasticity of the Futurist stage has remained inspirational for a type of contemporary theatre that sculpts and constructs an autonomous performance/production in space and time.

Giacomo Balla's stage set for Stravinsky's ballet *Fireworks* (*Feu d'artifice*), was conceived as such a construction. The "ballet" premiered on 24 April 1917 at the Teatro Costanzi in Rome under the direction of Serge Diaghilev, conducted by Ernest Ansermet. There were no human performers on the stage. Instead, a big flower-like sculpture with a heart of sound, an atmosphere of light, and the muscles of abstract forms pulsated on the stage. Balla had lights replace the dancers. He built a complex of abstract sculptures made of prismatic, pointed, half-spherical, and half-cylindrical wooden boxes covered with painted fabric. The lower structures diffracted and reflected beams of coloured lights, while the smaller ones on the top, transparent and translucent, were illuminated from the back and from inside. Balla virtually choreographed Stravinsky's score by changes of lights that blinked on and off. In the show, which lasted a mere five minutes, there were forty-nine light cues so that Balla had to devise a lighting keyboard in the theatre booth. It helped music and colour to synthesize in a dynamic interplay of bursts of sounds and lights. Rays of coloured light that backlit the asymmetrical architectural construction produced surprisingly shaped multidirectional shadows extended toward and around the audience in the rhythm of Stravinsky's music. Actually, the stage itself, a space without actors, became a moto-rumorist "polyexpressive" entity. It became a space-as-actor (*l'attore-spazio*), envisioned by Prampolini in his manifesto "Futurist Scenic Atmosphere" as "a personification of space in the role of the actor, as a dynamic and interacting element between the scenic environment and the public spectator."[62]

Fortunato Depero's *Plastic Ballets* (*Balli plastici*), conceived in Capri in collaboration with Gilbert Clavel (a Swiss poet and Egyptologist from the Cubist circles of Diaghilev and Jean Cocteau), was performed by marionettes at the Teatro dei Piccoli in Rome in 1918. The show consisted of five short musical mime-actions: The Buffoons, The Mustachioed Man, The Savages, The Shadow, and The Blue Bear. The multicoloured, stylized, mechanical wooden characters/marionettes/toys performed strange actions in an oneiric stage atmosphere created by sound and light. In contrast to traditional, more or less naturalistically designed puppets, Depero's figures were made of Cubist geometrical forms painted in bright primary colours.[63] The puppets were not only operated by puppeteers, they were also animated by the play of light and shadow. Their scenic actions were presented through architectural counterpoints of lines, perspectives, and volumes. The rhythm of the performance was created by the exchange of obsessive silences and sudden shots, thuds, and crazy laughs, expressing the "plasticity of noise." In terms of sound, a shadow play *The Shadow* (*Ombre*) was most interesting; it was "a symphony of abstract shapes in black and gray juxtaposed with a light-play of vivid colours, which offered a visual interpretation of a composition by Béla Bartók."[64]

Prampolini advocated such "creation of an abstract entity that identifies itself with the stage action of the play" in his manifesto "Futurist Scenography and Choreography" (Scenografia e coreografia Futurista, 1915).[65] Here he calls for the abolition of painted backdrops and all the other idiosyncratic elements of the naturalist theatre, including actors. Instead, he suggests a complete activation of the stage by the introduction of coloured lights, noise, and kinetic, electromechanical architecture. Prampolini envisions a total theatre in which its physical, spiritual, and emotional content would find architectural, kinetic, chromatic, and plastic valorization onstage. This would revive the stage as an abstract, autonomous reality in which the temporal media of sound and movement, each preserving its autonomy, integrate into a spatial architecture of colour, form, and plasticity. Also in 1915, Prampolini's article "A New Art? Absolute Creation of Noise and Motion" described "a chromatic and sounding architecture in motion which unites material qualities of the individual art forms in an abstract, synthetic theatre."[66] Prampolini here insists on the theatrical legacy of Marinetti's ideas about lyrical substantiality of matter: "We must shape with greater vehemence the impulses and sensations of the infinitesimal world and the universe which surrounds us. This is the foundation of the *absolute construction of sound and motion* which not only unites in itself the material values of all the arts, but also the sensations which until now have been determined by each individual art form."[67] In this way, he reinforces a Futurist synthetic theatre pronouncement that requires a plunge into the "dynamic, fragmentary symphonies of gestures, words, noises and lights" of the world. Prampolini reveals an inclination toward aurality in design and dramaturgy of sound in theatre when commenting on his collaboration with Achille Ricciardi on *The Theatre of Colour* at the Roman Teatro Argentina in 1920. He admits: "For both of us, delivery, mime, music, and stage design converge, not as isolated, predominant elements or as purely decorative motifs, but as values with equal force, they swell into an accord and music stream … a rich, unified rhythm of light, colour, movement, and sound."[68]

Contrary to Michael Kirby and Giovanni Lista who name Adolphe Appia, Alexander Tairoff and, most of all, Gordon Craig, as Prampolini's major influences, Günter Berghaus believes that Kandinsky's seminal essay "On Stage Composition" had a crucial role in laying the groundwork for Prampolini's ideas of stage totality. The revelation of this link also makes a case for the viability of a Futurist dramaturgy of sound. Searching for aural sources of synthetic theatre Berghaus goes as far back as the work of Romantic German painter Philipp Otto Runge (1777–1810) and his notion of a *Gesamtkunstwerk*. Runge held that a union of the arts could only be achieved under the hegemony of music because music uses "an abstract language that speaks directly to the heart of the addressee ... It stimulates his senses synaesthetically. A *Gesamtkunstwerk* based on musical principles elicits vibrations in the recipient that are not the result of objective representation but of subjective imagination. The artwork is not a representation of reality (*Abbild*), but a 'heightened product of nature.'"[69]

Rather than representing anecdotal content or a certain reality, art/music vibrates from the object through the artist to the spectator in a fashion similar to Kandinsky's "inner sound." Futurists shared this concept in Marinetti's sound poetry, where onomatopoeia directly communicates aural sensations to the listener, or Prampolini's plastic complex, where "the rhythms of sound, scenery and gesture create a psychological synchronism in the soul of the spectator."[70] The notion of a vibrational transfer of feeling, spirit, or essence of matter via "inner sound" was also a conceptual building block in Kandinsky's abstract staging of Mussorgsky's *Pictures from an Exhibition*. Its Bauhaus, Craigian manipulation of geometrical shapes and lit screens as synaesthetic reflections of music clearly shows that Prampolini and Kandinsky were artistic soulmates.

In his "Teatro della pantomima Futurista" Prampolini demanded that the decor of the stage be replaced by the active interplay of the performer and the scenery: "It is a question of renouncing the mimic decorativism, which operates on the surface, in order to enter into the domain of architecture which is concerned with depth."[71] Human bodies, objects, lights, and sounds should unite on stage to create an *attore-spazio* (space-as-actor) that pulsates in front of the audience's eyes. In 1927, several Futurist pantomimes were successfully staged at the Théâtre de la Madeleine in Paris and later in Rome, Milan, and Turin. One of them, Prampolini's *Santa velocità* (Saint Speed), has neither words nor actors, just scenery and sound. This "abstract pantomime" is a finer version of the collages of urban life's sensorial attractions, and is reminiscent of Russolo's and Ruttman's noise-music piece and experimental film. *Santa velocità*'s stage set or, rather, its luminescent backdrop, represents a metropolis – with its skyscrapers and neon lights – while its sonic background echoes intense traffic in the enormous streets and the electric frenzy of "cinematographic" nocturnal life with all the accompanying noise. "Only artistic intervention [is] a human song that arrests and subdues the noise of speedy life out there," writes Prampolini in his stage directions, "But after the song slowly finishes, the rhythm of speed and modernity takes over in an extraordinary crescendo, magic, immense and deafening."[72] Dramatic action consists of a dynamic interplay of coloured lights projected onto an empty stage, different sound textures of city life interpreted by Russolo's *intonarumori*, and a solitary human song. Instead of relying on habitual dramatic conflict, dénouement, and resolution, Prampolini achieved a fully theatrical effect just by an analogical interchange of blocks of sound and light.

Ivo Pannaggi and Giacomo Balla's *Balli Meccanici* (1922) worked on the same premise but included human performers. It is a noisy ballet in which two dancers in spiky, metallic costumes "execute actions mimicking the cadenzas of engine rhythms."[73] Their mechanical movements accompany the noise of two motorcycle engines that produced roar-music in the wings. A bright white light that flashes to the rhythm of their "ballet" turns at times into polychromatic swirls to accentuate changes in sound and motion.

Futurists, Dadaists, and Expressionists reached a theatrical style Marinetti called "an abstract and alogical condensed drama of pure elements which, without any psychology, present the forces of life in movement to an audience," and "an abstract synthesis [which] is an alogical and surprising combination of blocks of typical sensations."[74] As we could see from the analysis of *Macchina Tipografica*, *Colori*, *Feu d'artifice*, *Santa velocità*, and *Balli Meccanici*, one of their formative elements was a dramaturgy that used sound as material, equivalent to other plastic and kinetic elements of performance and stage architecture. It reaches out towards a concept of the stage as a plastic moto-rumorist complex and towards Lothar Schreyer's idea of the Bauhaus abstract theatre as a formulation of optical and acoustic relations. To confirm the vitality of this trend, which brought about current multimedia theatre performances and audio-visual stage installations, the final chapter of the book reexamines the workings of the dramaturgy of sound/matter in several newer postdramatic theatre productions.

7

Postdramatic and Avant-garde Theatre Sound

A VIEW THROUGH THE REAR-VIEW MIRROR

The historical avant-gardes were the first to put forward the notion that sound can be something that both *reveals* and *is* a performance – a notion that has found a sympathetic ear among contemporary theatre creators. Indeed this early recognition of the materiality of sound has contributed to a larger "project" that has more recently come to be called the "performative turn" (Erika Fischer-Lichte) and/or the formation of "postdramatic theatre" (Hans-Thies Lehmann). Proofs of this development seem as elusive as its subject, which is the phenomenon of sound itself. One of the leading figures of contemporary theatre semiotics and performance analysis, Patrice Pavis, admits to being stymied by Robert Wilson's play *The Golden Windows* since "it simply comprises vocal and rhythmic material to be used as a plastic element without any claim to semantic referentiality – so it would be quite fruitless to launch oneself into scholarly exegesis."[1] Notwithstanding this comment, the study of sound in postdramatic theatre, in connection with avant-garde sound poetry and performance, remains viable. As Pavis himself makes clear, a theatre semiotics based on the avant-garde's focus on a spatial/visual mise en scène is facing a crisis in contemporary theatre discourse, where "a domination of *another* avant-garde, that of time, rhythm and voice [that is, of sound], is seeking to break."[2]

A heightened concern with stage sound emerged as an extension of the historical avant-garde's general tendency to turn *techné* into *praxis*, the work of art into action, and dramatic text into performance. In the process the materiality of artistic means, such as voice/sound, was brought to the fore. More particularly, the historical avant-garde's experiments with sound, following radical discoveries in the idiom of poetry, took root in scenic "inventions," such as the Futurist moto-rumorist complex or the Bauhaus's "theatre of totality," which anticipate the postdramatic era. Acknowledging this trend, Fischer-Lichte introduced the term "performative generation of materiality," which takes place in a continuous cycle of corporeality, spatiality, and tonality of the stage and provides for a new aesthetics based on the "transformative power" of such performance practice. Accordingly, all stage signs – lights, objects, and audio-visual and stage design – hitherto illustrative of a play's dramatic development, which had already been turned by the avant-garde into a physical display of theatricality, generated a genuine music/painting/sculpture-like theatre form that Lehmann has termed postdramatic.

Laszlo Moholy-Nagy, one of the key theorists of the Bauhaus, describes a line of Futurist, Dadaist, and Merz theatre development stemming from the works of the avant-garde sound poets who, "taking after non-objective painting where the interaction of colour is essential, transformed word-sound relationships into exclusively phonetic sound relationships, thereby totally fragmenting the word into conceptually disjointed vowels and consonants."[3] When applied to the stage, the fragmentation of aural material and the interpenetration of time and space achieved in poetry brought about a "theatre of totality, a great dynamic-rhythmic process, which can compress the greatest clashing masses or accumulations of media as qualitative and quantitative tensions into elemental form."[4] The synacoustic, synoptic, and syncretic concept of stage, promoted by Moholy-Nagy, validates sound as an independent, simultaneously concrete and abstract theatrical element.

Advancing these Futurist, Dadaist, and Bauhaus ideas, Richard Kostelanetz describes the innovative performance of the alternative neo-avant-garde groups of the 1960s as mixed-means theatre, clearly a predecessor of postdramatic theatre. He asserts that "Mixed-means performances differ from conventional drama in de-emphasizing verbal language, if not avoiding words completely, in order to stress such presentational means as sound and light, objects and scenery ... A mixed-means piece usually opens with a sound-image complex that is constantly communicated; and rather than resort to the linear techniques of variation and development, the piece generally sustains or fills in its opening outline. Narrative, when it exists, functions more as a convention than as a revelatory structure or primary dimension."[5]

Among the creators of this kind of theatre, Kostelanetz lists the Open Theatre Group, Robert Wilson, Meredith Monk, Merce Cunningham, and

John Cage. These artists turned away from narrative pretensions of plot development toward a synchronized exposition of different materials. The juxtaposition of visual and aural stage elements in the mixed-means pieces relates to the technique of verbo-voco-visual clash used in avant-garde sound poetry, and to the syncretism, synaesthesia, and abstraction of the futurist plastic moto-rumorist complex. It is worth noting that the promoters of the avant-garde legacy in theatre were not playwrights and directors but primarily poets, painters, and musicians such as Gertrude Stein, Michael Kirby, Robert Motherwell, Dick Higgins (inventor of the term "intermedia"), and John Cage. It is no wonder, then, that Kostelanetz, being one of them, describes the 1963 Living Theatre's performance of Kenneth H. Brown's *The Brig*, directed by Judith Malina, in terms of "intermedia" arts and contemporary music theatre:

> *The Brig* is a music of military noise. As the prisoners individually shout their requests for permission to cross a certain white line, I could hear a fugue developing; then on the right two soldiers are stamping their feet in 4/4 time. The closest analogue in the history of art is Edgar Varèse's *Ionization* (1931), which pioneered in making music entirely of percussive sounds ... Throughout the performance something is always moving and something is always sounding. The narrative line is a day in the brig, but there is little narrative action. The form of the performance is spatial, as meaning comes primarily through the repetition of action, rather than the development of plot. Very much as in musical theatre, movements and sounds are effectively integrated into a coherent kinetic whole.[6]

In spite of the fact that *The Brig* emulated the routines set by *The Guidebook for Marines* in a hyper-naturalistic physical performance inspired by Artaud's theatre of cruelty, Kostelanetz found all elements needed to describe it as a musical abstraction. Seemingly incongruous, his critical note is apt; it rightly identifies the continuum of the oral and aural aspect of the theatre performance in the parallel exercise of a libidinal voice and an abstract sound structure. True, the Living Theatre celebrated the Artaudian idiom of "the collusion of objects, silences, shouts and rhythms" by their exaggerated vocal mime of the US marine prison drill – a visceral cry against brutality and repression. But the aural elements of the performance that the critic describes as structured noise – its 4/4 time (duration), repetition of convulsive rhythmic movements, and absence of narration – converge into "a coherent kinetic whole" reminiscent of a musical piece/installation. Malina remembers: "Reading the disembodied commands, the numbered shouts that evoke the machine but remain transcendentally human outcries, I heard clearly in my ears the familiar metal scraping prison sounds and the stamp of the booted foot on concrete ... I urged the actors to listen to this sound; to strain to catch its modulations ... [and] they built it into a steady crescendo."[7] It was as if the Living Theatre took Russolo's art of noises and Varèse's organization of sound, and merged them with Artaud's "cries born of the *subtlety* of the marrow" and Marinetti's fisicofollia. *The Brig*, for Kostelanetz at least, presented an ideal example of aurality that made it an icon of innovative performance in the 1960s. Its semiosis – powered by the excessive vocal gestures, shouting of reports, commands, submissions, revolt, and suffering – produced an abstract sound structure in which two streams of the avant-garde dramaturgy met: the corporeality of physical theatre and the abstraction of music theatre. As proved by this confluence, the dramaturgy of sound had the capacity to materialize both the sensuality/corporeality of the voice in performance (in the sense of Barthes's and Lyotard's explorations) and the concreteness/abstraction of sound onstage (in the sense of the Bauhaus and Wilson).

In his introduction to a collection of essays *Close Listening: Poetry and the Performed Word*, Charles Bernstein states, "the twentieth-century innovative poets work with sound as material, where sound is neither arbitrary nor secondary but constitutive." Their dealing with sound as a materializing dimension of poetry and a subject of vocal performance extends the patterning of poetry into a "more fluid and pluriform aural (post-written) poetic practice." Interestingly, Bernstein's parenthetical adjective, "post-written," is analogous to Lehmann's term "postdramatic." It reflects the fact that just as modern performance poetry destabilizes its linguistic object – the written poem – by its insistence on sound, the modern theatre destabilizes its literary source – the drama – by its anti-Naturalistic staging. This confirms a legacy of the resounding challenge that poets and performers of the historical avant-garde issued to conventional poetry, art, and theatre by promoting the materiality of sound and experimenting with sound patterns in their works.

More importantly, Bernstein's attempt to reconcile the oral and aural aspects of performance poetry provides an innovative and welcome contribution to the contemporary understanding of voice and sound in theatre. He proposes: "By *aurality* I mean to emphasize the sounding of the *writing*, and to make a sharp contrast with *orality* and its emphasis on breath, voice and speech – an emphasis that tends to valorize speech over writing, voice over sound, listening over hearing, and indeed, orality over aurality … Aurality is meant to invoke a performative sense of phonotext or audiotext and might better be spelled *a/orality*."[8] Bernstein's introduction of the composite term *a/orality* acknowledges the performative value of vocal sound patterning without restricting it to speech. In theatre, it allows for a performance/mise en scène independent of the emotional and psychological interpretation of dramatic speech and plot development. The dramaturgy in the field of Bernstein's a/orality pays equal attention to the voice of the performer and stage sound; concerned with an audiotext in place of a conventional drama, it devises a postdramatic performance.

One such attempt at a/orality was the 2000 performance of *War Music*, Christopher Logue's translation/adaptation of Homer's *Iliad*, staged by the theatre company Sound & Fury. It played in the completely darkened auditorium of the Battersea Arts Centre in London for its "Playing in the Dark" season. Critic Martin Welton describes his experience of the event in the essay "Seeing Nothing: Now Hear This …": "I'm sat in the far right corner, at the back … and we are plunged into darkness. A great clap, a rumble of thunder, and Patroclus comes crying to Achilles' tent. There is no light, none at all … Words and sound are more 'concrete' than is ordinarily the case … the word 'Apollo' in the dark takes a musculature all its own; it exists in space … Unsighted, off-balance, surrounded by very real actors and sound effects, how does one construct meaning, make sense of what is going on? … The words of Logue's text were afforded no permanence. In the darkness, they could come into being only in the actors' mouths, in the spectators' ears, and disappear."[9]

In *War Music* Logue sought to reveal the tragic mythos embedded in the sound of the poem's words and verses. He approached Homer as a poet rather than a translator of Greek, with an interest in reviving the performative value of his poetic speech. His aim was to communicate the intrinsic orality and acoustic features of Homer's *epos* to the audience and readers in the form of a textscape/soundscape. In that form, *War Music* was first performed in 2000 and then published in 2002. Emily Greenwood, who titled Logue's translation to performance project "Sounding Out Homer," compares his undertaking to a process of "mapping the oral event onto an augmented textual surface designed to bear more and different kinds of meaning than the conventional printed page," a method used by ethnologists in the transcription of traditional oral works, such as Native American tribal chants. "The layout of his poem is often likened to a script, with the very deliberate alternation of text and blank space controlling the pace at which the reader moves through the text, signalling performance. In fact, Logue's Homer contains a veritable soundscape; to the sound of the dramatic voice we can also add music, insofar as his language strives to reproduce both visually and aurally (on the page and in the ear) the music of war."[10]

Logue's endeavours replicate a kind of poetry-making characteristic of members of the historical avant-garde, Apollinaire, Marinetti, or Hausmann, for instance, who designed the verbo-voco-visual structure of their poems primarily with its acoustic effectiveness in mind. Extending the acoustic effectiveness of Logue's sound-text to stage performance, members of Sound & Fury invented a unique theatrical device of "playing in the dark." In a program note for *War Music*, the artists state their key interest in devising the sound space of theatre that would present their audience with new ways of experiencing theatre by heightening the aural sense. Martin Welton notices that it is in such a sound space, wedged open by focusing on listening to the voice, that "spoken words become 'things' in their own right ... Rather than existing in terms of representation and interpretation, *War Music* can be considered as an embodied event played out sensorially rather than conceptually."[11]

Sound & Fury's next production, *The Watery Part of the World* (2003), played in darkness as well. This time the content of the show offered an ideal justification for the use of an immersive, exclusively aural space. The piece, using fragments of Herman Melville's *Moby Dick*, presents the true grim story of the *Essex* whaling boat that capsized in 1820. According to records, crewmembers fought to survive in the ocean for more than one hundred days. Lyn Gardner reviewed the show in *The Guardian*: "The sea of darkness that envelopes the audience – except for some tiny glimpses of ghost-like faces bleached with guilt – immediately puts us in the same position as the Essex's crew, adrift in the vast expanse of unknowable, never-ending ocean ... I longed to be released from the purgatorial darkness, the sound of creaking timbers, the vast expanse of the becalmed ocean, the tiny snuffling sounds of dying men and, indeed, my own imagination. Playing the piece in the dark concentrates its power."[12] The thick immersive soundscape of the show clearly did not need visuals to enhance its expressiveness: the dramaturgy of sound provided a complete theatrical experience.

Peter Stein's 1980 staging of Aeschylus' *Oresteia* at the Berlin Schaubühne provides another example of the emphasis on orality/aurality achieved by turning off the lights. To expose the tensions between verbal and oral aspects of the tragic trilogy, that is, dramatic speech and stage voice, Stein "devised a darkened and thus primarily aural space" for its first two parts. What the audience heard then was the actors' almost-incomprehensible speech, dissipating into an old men's chorus of murmurs and whimpers. A reviewer in *Die Zeit* describes their rendition of the *ololygmos* (a sacrificial cry – a vocal ritual traditionally used by the tragic chorus) as "a sound shouted out, sung, and tuned with a flittering tongue in falsetto, half cricket chirp and half birdcall … Yet the voices primarily articulated segments of speech. If one of the old men murmured a sentence, others spread across the room and repeated it at varying volumes, pitches, and tempos to emphasize the diverse range of voices … The materiality of the voices became evident. The tense relationship between the particular tonalities of voice and language was sustained throughout."[13] Obviously, the actors aimed at the creation of a sonorous performance rather than the articulation of a syntactic text. Helped by a darkened stage and freed from the boundaries of a strictly dramatic presentation, the speech segments vocalized by the actors acquired an independent reality on the stage as pure sounds; it was the sound of their voices at play.

On the other hand, sounds of words rather than sounds of voices played a crucial role in the structure of Robert Wilson's early plays. In his opera *A Letter for Queen Victoria* (1974), performed without the sophisticated electro-acoustic additions typical of his later work, Wilson opted for a method inherited from avant-garde sound poetry that focused on the phonetic substance of words. He devised the work's script by emulating verbal formulas and utterances of his adolescent friend and collaborator, the autistic poet Christopher Knowles. Knowles spelled and pronounced words in an endless chain of variations that followed his own formal logic. He dissociated words from their conventional meanings and syntax and turned them into mnemonic aids in the form of pure sonic and/or visual patterns. "I became more fascinated with him and what he was doing with language," Wilson recounted in an interview. "He would take ordinary, everyday words and destroy them. They became like molecules that were always changing, breaking apart all the time, many-faceted words, not just a dead language."[14] Thus, in a segment of *A Letter for Queen Victoria* called "The Sundance Kid Is Beautiful,"[15] Knowles and Wilson engage in a word game animated by such unusual speech practice. They "build rhythms by shouting back and forth letters of the alphabet, and by clapping wooden blocks together; they play with certain clusters of letters (HAP, HATH, HAT) and put together words, words letters and sentences like building blocks."[16] The result is a kind of concrete poetry, an aleatoric music score that becomes characteristic of the visual, physical, and mental structure of the whole piece. In another scene, the company members (who had been through rehearsals of endlessly repeating Knowles's vocalizations) pronounced a series of syllables in front of a backdrop printed with the seemingly nonsensical text. At times, this took on direct satiric commentary; so, in front of a backdrop where the words "CHITTER CHATTER" had been written one hundred times, they appeared as café patrons engaged in gibberish conversations that verged on environmental noise. Murmurs, sound effects, scream songs, and contrapuntal shouts, all of them contributing to its musical sound texture, punctuated the performance. A similar use of nonsensical language, creating a sonorous image of an uneventful afternoon in a café patio destroyed by a violently yelling intruder of a different state of mind (presented by a different sound/language texture), appears in the Futurist synthetic theatre piece *Stati d'animo* by Mario Carli discussed earlier.

As Arthur Holmberg claims, the main character of *A Letter for Queen Victoria* is language, which, pushed by Wilson to its limits, collapses into a kind of sonic debris. This phonetic trashing, inspired by Knowles's peculiar pulverization of words, has proved to be a gold mine for oral/aural performance. It carries dramatic tension from the *entr'acte*'s beginning with a pre-verbal, primal shriek that "goes through a phonetic chaos … [of] MNHJUYGTHRD VBNH V B BBNHJ BVG PJER GLOS O CHOCOLATE … to finish with the word – 'chocolate' – clear, recognizable, lovely in the sweet simplicity of its reference to *glâce au chocolat* (chocolate ice cream)."[17] Here, the word play builds on the confrontation of two polarized vocal sound structures: one a mass of "primitive" intuitive vocalizations, the other a cultivated high speech appropriate for a letter to the Queen. This is nature against culture. The dramatic clash evolves from the inherent contradictions of voice, speech, sound, and text. At one point, after actors' initial struggle for proper articulation, "these electro whe whe whe whe whe whe wheeelswheels," comes the question: "What are we doing? / We're doing a letter for Queen Victoria. / We're doing the play. / And you sit on the bench and just wait for me … OK."[18] Is the last line's approval a reassuring clarification or a tacit condescending violence whose utterance bears historical references? Perhaps an answer can be instinctively inferred from the change of tone from an intuitive cacophonic noise to a rational euphonic speech. Wilson explains: "Together we bring to life a verbal text, but one in which the words do not have the function of telling a story or communicating a meaning. The words are like music, devoid of plot: a kind of concrete poetry used as sound and also as image … To define this phrase precisely, I would say that the words make their appearance to be listened to like a noise, a sound, is listened to, as if the atmospheric elements had been gathered together in the room."[19]

The intuitive, music-like words in Caryl Churchill's play *The Skriker* (1994) are dug up from a pre-verbal phonetic chaos. The play begins with the long, almost incomprehensible monologue, chant, and dance of the spider-like fairy Skriker, "a shape shifter and death portent," a screeching river spirit who, according to Northern English folklore, steals and drowns children. Her incantation is reminiscent of avant-garde sound poetry that strove to revive the ancient phonetic roots of language. Skriker's word play, full of puns, nursery rhymes, and ritual rhythms, lets her reclaim the power of speech's forgotten sensuality. Through the free, unabashedly ludic oral composition, Churchill deconstructs ordinary language and creates a primordial idiom appropriate for a creature from the underworld:

> Heard her boast beast a roast beef eater, daughter could spin span spick and spun the lowest form of wheat straw into gold, raw into roar, golden lion and lyonesse under the sea dungeonesse under the castle for bad mad sad adders and takers away. …
>
> Slit slat slut. That bitch a botch an itch in my shoulder blood. Bitch botch itch. Slat itch slit botch. Itch slut bitch slit.[20]

Skriker's depiction of herself, threatening as it is, resounds with the sheer musicality and assonance of sibilants and affricates. Her subliminal language retaliates against logocentrism, consumerism, and the belief in scientific progress – against a world that has forgotten fairies: "bloodmoney is the root of evil eye nose the smell hell the taste waste of money." The pre-symbolic speech of Churchill's female avenger – primitive, infantile, and illogical – resides in the semiotic *chora*, a primordial birthplace of *logos*. The chora is a term that Julia Kristeva, borrowing from Plato's *Timaeus*, uses to denote a space of uncertain, mobile, and provisional articulation. She defines chora as having a profound, bodily root: "indifferent to language, enigmatic and feminine, this space underlying the written is rhythmic, irreducible to an intelligible verbal translation; musical, anterior to judgement."[21] Kristeva criticizes traditional Platonic thought for depriving logos of its originary acoustic pleasure and claims, "the voice precedes and makes possible a language that always bears its traces. Both generating and destabilizing the semantic, the vocalic is therefore – at the same time – the precondition of the semantic function and its uncontrollable excess."[22] Churchill's use of excessive, libidinal vocality to characterize her damaged fairy deprived of the ability to bear children echoes Kristeva's idea of revolution in poetic language that originates from the instinctive sonority of the semiotic, maternal chora.

Different approaches to the concept of chora had marked *The Skriker*'s production history, which has recently leaned toward the oral field of expression. While *The Skriker*'s initial 1994 production by the modern dance company Second Stride emphasized features of physical theatre, the 2006 staging at the Victorian College of the Arts School of Drama in Melbourne, directed and designed by Brian Lipson, demonstrated an increased preoccupation with primordial sound. "Lipson divides the Skriker's speech between the actors of the company, who vocalise it as a sound poem or a spoken oratorio around the audience," wrote critic Alison Croggon. "This is language as thickness, viscera, weight, saliva, sex, violence, the softness of palate and lip: language as spell and enchantment, where meaning constantly threatens to slip its noose and collapse back to animal howl and croon. Here Churchill is pushing theatre hard up against the poem, sense against nonsense, and one can only admire the force of the centrifugal will that keeps the text this side of comprehensible."[23] This newer version of *The Skriker* amalgamates two layers of oral/aural expressiveness, of theatre and of poetry, in a seemingly centrifugal flow, reminiscent of the swirl of force lines that Futurist painters used to put the spectator in the centre of their works. Paradoxically, this flow does not dissipate the sound-image of *The Skriker*. Due to our intuitive, sensual immersion in sound and Churchill's keeping the language in the field of poetry, that is, "this side of comprehensible," the performance and its reception become coherent. The play gathers strength from a poetic return to the sonority of the maternal chora, a practice advanced by the historical and neo-avant-garde's explorations of language.

Peter Brook, a protagonist of the 1960s theatrical avant-garde, in his book *Empty Space* asks, "Is there another language, just as exciting for the author, as a language of words? Is there a language of actions, a language of sounds – a language of word-as-part-of-movement, of word-as-lie, of word-as-parody, of word-as-rubbish, of word-as-contradiction, of word-shock or word-cry?"[24] This question, evidently inspired by Artaud, still looms large in theatre discourse. It motivated theatre artists such as Brook, Eugenio Barba, and Ariane Mnouchkine, whose productions examine not only the individual performer's vocal body but also the expressive style embedded in the authentic oral traditions of different cultures. In 1970, Brook gathered a group of performers from all over the world in Paris and established the Centre

International de Recherches Théâtrales. The company members breathed, spoke, chanted, moved, and acted in different languages and performance traditions. Their first intercultural exercises that targeted the language divide were, naturally, "restricted" to sound. Inventing a vocabulary of syllables to which each actor contributed his own – *bash / ta / hon / do* – they gave birth to the language known as Bashtahondo. The new language, obviously more corporeal than cerebral, eliminated, at least in the rehearsals, the need for understanding the concepts behind different words in different languages. Brook and his international troupe soon embarked upon an ambitious performance project that examined linguistic and theatrical communication: the production of *Orghast,* scripted by the poet Ted Hughes in an *ur*-language of the same name, interactively devised by the playwright and the company.

After roughly a year of preparation, *Orghast* premiered at the 1971 Shiraz-Persepolis theatre festival at two sites of sacred Persian tombs carved into high cliffs. A two-part ritual and physical performance took place in that spectacular environment at dusk, lit by the last rays of sunset, and at dawn, lit by the sunrise. As night started to fall, the light was provided by huge balls of fire lowered from the crag toward the audience. The tragic mythos of *Orghast* consisted of fragments from Aeschylus' *Prometheus Bound*, Avesta hymns, Calderón's *La vida es sueño*, Seneca's *Hercules Furens* and *Thyestes*, and an Armenian play. Whether or not the audiences understood the mythos, they were unquestionably captivated by the sheer sensual enjoyment of the vista, the intriguing sound of the actors' mystical speech, and the stunning physicality of the performance. Tom Stoppard wrote in the *Times Literary Supplement*, "*Orghast* aims to be a leveller of audiences by appealing not to semantic athleticism but to the instinctive recognition of a 'mental state' within a sound. One can hardly imagine a bolder challenge to the limits of narrative."[25] Indeed, in retrospect, the historical avant-garde was full of such challenges. The creation of *stati di anima* (mental states), for instance, was a frequent topic of Futurist non-figurative paintings and non-narrative theatrical syntheses based on pure sound. Clearly, for Brook and Hughes the exploration of sound in *Orghast* was quintessential. One of their program notes reads: "What is the relation between verbal and non-verbal theatre? What happens when gesture and sound turn into word? What is the exact place of the word in theatrical expression? As vibration? Concept? Music? Is any evidence buried in the sound structure of certain ancient languages?"[26] A few random lines from the script illustrate their attempt at such a language:

OARGLAKRIS GLAUR PROGHAST UMLABAOO SHOAR
the eagle overshadows out of sun a new command is flying…
SOYINNABLARG TOTTAHOANYA GROKIDOTUTTU
I was in darkness brought into light I was broken to pieces…
OOOL NEEEE-YAGH OOOL ONEEEAAR NEEY-AGH
Woman has opened woman has opened life…

The dramaturgical use of sound in *Orghast*, during the processes of scriptwriting, rehearsing/devising, and staging, which ran parallel, was consistent with the historical avant-garde practice. Hughes's verbal inventions were encouraged by the linguistic advisers on the project, Geoffrey Reeves and Mahin Tadjadod. Their position was that in ancient Greek tragedy speech "must have been closer to what we know as music than what now passes for acting." Or, that in Avestan readings of Zoroastrian hymns, "no phonetic notation can encompass the range of sounds – guttural, nasal, glottal, explosive, compound consonants, [plus] seventeen vowels … [and] the voice moving suddenly from lips to throat to nose, and shifting abruptly in pitch."[27] Brook and his plurilingual ensemble, which had already adopted these ideas when practising Bashtahondo, devised their rehearsals accordingly. Their exercises comprised a meditative communication between participants through a number of mantra-like syllables closer to music than speech. Schreyer also used this technique, in rhythmic sound-exercises with his actors in the 1920s. Only through a thoroughly meditative process, in which a performer is stripped of individual idiosyncrasies, he believed, could one's fundamental "sound speech" be awakened. In the same vein, *Orghast*'s idiom appears as a fundamental "sound speech," intuitively extracted from what the performers and we, the audience, perceive as an ancient, primal language. "If it doesn't work musically," Hughes concludes, "it doesn't work at all ... The deeper into language one goes, the less visual/conceptual its imagery, and the more audial/visceral/muscular its system of tensions ... In other words, the deeper into language one goes, the more dominated it becomes by purely musical modes, and the more dramatic it becomes – the more unified with total states of being and with the expressiveness of physical action."[28]

Exploring the confluence of the physical and the conceptual, which had already been at work within the oral/aural sphere of language, Hughes followed the path of the avant-garde arts. Richard Peaslee, the sound designer and composer of the piece, who thought that theatre always lags behind the other arts, offers a practical summary: "After ten years of rock now suddenly everyone is trying to write a rock musical. This production

[*Orghast*] is a big leap forward for the theatre, from representational to abstract, abandoning the meaning of words to their sound. It happened in art fifty years ago, when the form of an object was abandoned for colour and shapes."[29] The interaction between abstract painting and sound poetry, exemplified by Giacomo Balla's involvement with Futurist poets and playwrights of parole in liberta and sintesi teatrale in Italy or Kazimir Malevich's involvement with poets of zaum in Russia (discussed earlier in the book), indeed remains characteristic of the avant-garde approach to theatre.

This holds true for Tadeusz Kantor and his adherence to the art of the *informel* in painting and theatre. Kantor, one of the key figures of new avant-garde theatre and visual art (installations, happenings, and conceptual art), directed his pieces using performers' bodies, voices, sounds, space, and rhythm to make a kinetic, sculptural, or aural stage composition. In his famous performance piece *Dead Class* (1975), a theatrical wonder that toured Europe for almost two decades, the stage was emptied or filled up with music, clatter, or silence as conductor/sculptor Kantor called up his dead classmates. Here the theatrical space appeared as "something elastic, not given and inflexible, but something which beats like a heart," asserts Brunella Eruli.[30] Its beat was both corporeal and musical – the sound patterns and rhythm of the performance were produced by the sensorial impulses. Similarly to Marthaler's musicalization of the stage or Wilson's prolongation of performance time, Kantor created a fluid time/space entity that relied on an aesthetic of duration. This aesthetic echoed Henri Bergson's concept of la durée, which, as a representation of the continuum of time and space, was adopted by the historical avant-garde – in Futurist painting and sound poetry – and spread to new avant-garde movements such as Fluxus and Informel, to name just two. Since la durée determines the meeting point of music (or art of sound) and plastic arts, Kantor's hybrid installations and performances indeed may be called time sculptures or sound sculptures.

Kantor has stated that his stage presence as a conductor/sculptor of an energetic performance and/or kinetic installation encapsulates and exemplifies Informel ideas. Michel Tapié coined the term "Art Informel" in *A Different Art* (*Un art autre*, 1952), a book that describes the work of several notable painters, including Jean Dubuffet, Wols, Jean Fautrier, and Alberto Burri, whose common denomination was rebelliousness, spontaneity, irrationality, and freedom of form. More concerned with immediate physical encounter with the material than with the final shape of the work of art, they focused on painterly mass and texture and the act of painting itself. The Informel artists' predilection for palpable material and gestural expression clearly appealed to Kantor. His moulding of an *ur*-matter of language and performance was an oral/aural counterpart to their raw and impulsive painting. His live interaction with the performers on the stage reflected an American variant of Informel "action painting" or "gestural abstraction," epitomized by the works of Willem de Kooning and Jackson Pollock, who spontaneously dribbled, splashed, or smeared paint onto the canvas. In his manifesto *The Informel Theatre* (1961), Kantor embraced the idea of "REALITY in its elementary state: MATTER that is freed from abiding the laws of construction, forever changeable and liquid, escaping every rational measure." This concept let him develop a theatre that turns all elements of performance – actors, objects, space, text, and sounds – into flexible, malleable, raw matter. Kantor described (and occasionally staged) his actors as "degraded, without dignity, hanging motionless like cloths, a heavy mass of sacks in a wardrobe ... [waiting to] earn a chance to become the form." In their speech, "instead of classical linguistic forms, THE COARSE '*BRUTE*' MATTER OF LANGUAGE ... INARTICULATE SOUNDS, and PHONEMES, emerge ... Human articulation resembles the remotest, the wildest forms (howling of the pack of dogs) and cruellest sounds (cracking of bones)."[31]

During the performance of *Dead Class* Kantor stands, sits, walks, and dances around and within the stage space. He conducts a group of old people dressed in plain mourning clothes with corpse-like infant dummies attached to their bodies on a pilgrimage to their childhood classroom: four rows of school benches thrown into a corner of the stage. They roam onstage uttering broken, incomplete, sometimes nonsensical lines in an attempt to recall happier days. As the conductor/teacher directs their grammar drills they "grind words like mills" into the "*raw material of speech:* inarticulate sounds, murmur, stutter, drawl, whisper, croak, whining, sobbing, spitting, phonemes, obscene and syntax-free language."[32] When at the beginning the actors and mannequins sit motionlessly on their benches with crushing apathy visible on their faces, the audience cannot distinguish one from the other. But when the music of a *valse française* temporarily infuses them with life, their still sculptures change into a carnival parade of figures marching around the benches. Animated by the music, their faces brighten, their bodies straighten up in sync with the strokes of Kantor's baton, and they succeed, if only momentarily, in their enormous fight. They climb onto the school benches to reach for the sky: a sculpture of hope builds before our eyes, incited by the swell of the music. Then, in sync with the music's diminuendo, disillusion returns and the edifice disintegrates into a state of formless, suffering matter. Once again, although aware of its ephemeral nature, Kantor tries to give form to inert matter. Aided by the music, he continues sculpting a human pyramid that constantly crumbles. In Kantor's *Dead Class* we do not witness a dramatic representation, just a convulsive pulsation of inchoate matter (actors/sounds/objects/space) struggling to acquire some sort of meaningful shape. Kantor's *Dead Class* represents an instance of the musicalization of theatre as well; he conducts his actors like an Informel painter splashing pigments, manipulating raw matter with the help of the musical flux.

Christoph Marthaler's oeuvre is one of the epitomes of the "musicalization of theatre," a phenomenon recently identified and discussed by David Roesner. The musicalization appears as a staging method devised primarily by the organization of rhythm, sound, and tonality, and by the use of aural features of speech and performance in his works as well as those of Einar Schleef, Robert Wilson, and other contemporary theatre directors. Marthaler, for example, follows the lines of a carefully designed spatial, rhythmic, and auditory score that encompasses all performance elements in the shape of a unique music/stage composition. His stagings thus ideally fit Erik Salzman's description of a new music theatre "that is music driven (i.e., decisively linked to musical timing and organization) where, at the very least, music, language, vocalization, and physical movement exist, interact, or stand side by side, in some kind of equality."[33]

Marthaler's theatre has two distinct characteristics: the dystopian stage space and the preeminent slowness with which the performance unfolds. Anna Viebrock, who has designed the settings for most of his shows, creates cavernous spaces – waiting rooms, institutional halls, gymnasiums, train stations, cafés – in which an individual feels isolated and alienated. As critic Christine Richard of *Theater Heute* wrote, "Marthaler's stage world is a waiting-room at four in the morning, or better, a piano bar at half past one. Dreams and sadness take over and the single light source reveals only self-irony, halfway between sleep and awakening, between tipsy and sober." To this emptiness of space Marthaler affixes an emptiness of time induced by the slow pace of the performance. Dramaturg Stefanie Carp, another of Marthaler's faithful collaborators, has remarked that there has rarely been a director of text-based theatre who has worked so particularly and precisely on rhythm. This practice has drawn Marthaler toward musical expression, and it has allowed him to make a theatre of a continuous present of historical time, empty time, and memory-time. The relentless slowness of his troupe's clownery-cum-melancholic-singing challenges the myth of efficiency and progress and constitutes, as Carp states, "a theatre of victims, never one of perpetrators." The formal, compositional features of Marthaler's music theatre coalesce with his political engagement in the same way that absurd, alogical anti-art stemmed from Dadaists' anti-bourgeois, anti-war stance. It was for good reason that in the early years of his career, when he produced several experimental evenings devoted to Érik Satie, John Cage, and Kurt Schwitters, Marthaler was referred to as a "neo-Dadaist."

The now-legendary piece *Screw the European! Screw him! Screw him! Screw him! Go screw him!* (*Murx den Europäer! Murx ihn! Murx ihn! Murx ihn! Murx ihn ab!*) became the hallmark of Marthaler's performance/staging style. It premiered in January 1993 at Berlin Volksbühne am Rosa-Luxemburg-Platz and remained in the theatre's repertoire until 2007. Ironically subtitled "a patriotic evening," it marked the reunification of the state with a sadly humorous farewell (some call it a requiem) to the German Democratic Republic. The play begins with an extremely long, static, and mute scene where the affectless performers sit on chairs at individual tables, together but alone, in a vast neon-lit waiting-room with a broken clock and the slogan "SO THAT TIME NEVER STANDS STILL," composed of individual letters hanging on the back wall. As the audience, waiting too long for the show to start, becomes irritated by the seemingly never-ending immobility and silence, letters begin to drop to the floor. A sense of abandonment permeates the space on both sides of the ramp. The lonely people on stage start their mindless everyday routines – obsessive, grotesque, and sometimes even violent. Alienation, depression, and melancholy are thick in the air. A few times throughout the performance actors leave their seats at the sound of a buzzer, line up in front of an upstage door, and wash their hands in the toilet room. These repetitive sound calls represent the "musical bars" of the performance's rhythmic structure. The actions that follow are trivial, repetitive, and executed in slow tempo. Mostly taken from the clown repertoire,[34] they depict clumsy, funny, and sad attempts by human beings to connect with each other. These awkward and desperate physical motifs get resolved when the performers break into song. "Singing in Marthaler's theatre occasions acts of collective memory. Mostly sung very quietly, songs grow out of silence bringing individuals from solitude into chorus. They are sung as if half-remembered, very fragile, harmonious and beautiful," writes Benedict Andrews.[35] One by one, the whole company gradually joins in the nostalgic humming of one of the actors, fighting the desolation and hopelessness of the waiting room. Their choral singing of the tunes dug out from the path into oblivion (ranging from the patriotic and romantic Volkslied,

Schubert, and Wagner to trivial German pop songs) makes people on the stage, along with those in the auditorium, rise from their habitual pettiness. Of course, all of them will soon crumble into despair like the human pyramid of hope that Tadeusz Kantor stubbornly keeps sculpting to the swelling music in his *Dead Class*.

Marthaler's recognizable music theatre style has been a mainstay of European and world stages for more than two decades. His recent production *Rising Butzbach: A Sustainable Colony* (*RiesenButzbach: Eine Dauerkolonie*), staged at the 2009 Wiener Festwochen, was co-produced with Napoli Teatro Festival Italia, the Athens Festival, the Avignon Festival, the International Theatre Festival Wroclaw, Theater Chur, and Festival Tokyo.[36] The author calls the piece "a musical-dramatic contemplation of the last days of consumption," and once again we find a cavernous space designed by Anna Viebrock, a temporal collage-dramaturgy by Stefanie Carp, and a musical mise en scène by Marthaler. A huge white bunker-like box, poured in concrete, with the label "Institute of Fermentation Industry" on its top, opens into several rectangular pockets. It epitomizes a painful space laid bare by the current global financial insecurity, foreclosures, and job losses, in which a bedroom, a garage, a bank, a recording studio, a furniture warehouse, and a shopping mall are all literally present at all times. At the beginning of the show, we hear an indistinct sound of tectonic disturbance coming from outside. On the stage, a dozen people, residents of the "rising" city of Butzbach, disempowered and disenchanted like the East German citizens in *Murx den Europäer!*, engage in petty, everyday activities in an environment of surveillance and suspicion. Surrounded by security cameras, alarm systems, and anti-theft devices, they act as mutual spies, closest enemies, and beloved partners who conspire/fight/love to protect their company and family assets. Only in their childish acts and beautiful singing does a common humanity break through. They sob, throwing themselves at the furniture that is to be confiscated. They hide in the garage to let off steam with the disco hit "Stayin' Alive," in spite of a "singing inspector" who directs them to sing Mahler or Beethoven. In the same garage, toward the end of the performance, they all sing the "Prisoners' Chorus" from Beethoven's *Fidelio*: "O welche Lust, in freier Luft" (O what joy to breathe in the free air). During their singing, the garage door modifies the loudness of their polyphonic singing; the sound swells up as it opens and dies down as it closes. Hence, the artistic and political message of *RiesenButzbach* gets delivered not only by the interweaving of short performance acts and singing, but also through the deliberate manipulation and structuring of sound.

In the process of musicalization of theatre and postdramatic staging, "the drama as a literary linguistic reality all but vanishes and makes room for 'something completely different': for the paralinguistic dimension, for voices and intonation, rhythm, speed and slowness of speech, sexual and gendered auditive information, gesture and the expressivity of body language in general,"[37] writes Lehmann. Elfriede Jelinek's drama *A Sport Piece* (*Ein Sportstueck*, 1998), directed by Einar Schleef, is a rich example of the rhythmic, musical organization of the mise en scène that activates the "paralinguistic" dimension of the piece embedded in the script. On opening night, the massive production, with a chorus line of 133 actors/dancers and the conductor planted in the balcony of Vienna's Burgtheater, lasted five hours. As Linda DeMerrit states, after their marathon exercise, the performers were rewarded with a fifty-five-minute standing ovation. Although the critic's assessment of the applause's duration might seem exaggerated, *Ein Sportstueck*, as a provocative argument in the hot public debate over the political swell of Jörg Haider and his nationalist Austrian Freedom Party, no doubt could arouse such an emotional reception.

Upon winning the 2004 Nobel Prize in Literature, Jelinek was praised "for her musical flow of voices and counter-voices in novels and plays that with extraordinary linguistic zeal reveal the absurdity of society's clichés and their subjugating power."[38] Indeed, the script for *Ein Sportstueck* is musically arranged by the rhythmic juxtaposition of different speech/language planes – *Sprachflächen*. Patching together quotes from disparate sources – which run the gamut from tabloid pages and soap operas to the high literature of Kleist and Hofmannsthal – Jelinek assembles a collage of verbal textures. Most sources that are linked, thematically, to sports activity include prompts for training routines, cheers, laudatory speeches, words of competitive encouragement, expressions of triumph and defeat. Into this disquieting clash of verbal layers, she inserts racist, anti-Semitic, and sexist statements to remind the audience of their recent past (and to warn them of their potential future). Rather than celebrating sport as a heroic individual effort, Jelinek portrays it as a violent expression of hostility toward the other, driven by a team/nationalistic mentality.

When writing for theatre, Jelinek breaks the linguistic cadence of her script into different language melodies and rhythms: "I always work with language in a compositional way. It's like a piece of music with different voices that are drawn close in a *stretto* and then also occur in reverse. It is basically a contrapuntal weave of language that I try to produce."[39] Manipulating phonetic and syntactic forms of words and sentences, Jelinek creates an aural weave based on contrasting textures, energies, and rhythms of individual and choral speech. The director of the piece – Einar Schleef, known for his choric staging – went even further in his juxtaposition of aural blocks when he added numerous verbal and musical quotations to the script for the chorus's gestural and vocal performance. Schleef admits that he approached the script of *Ein Sportstueck* as a "phonotext," that is, a blueprint for musicalisation. He explains: "A text consists of rhythmic phases. It can't be just information. On stage I obstruct this consumption of the text as information through the rhythmicisation and the distribution of the text onto several performers. Thus it defies an all too easy availability."[40] Hence, his chorus members, instead of merely delivering script lines, execute gymnastic shouting and stomping drills to expose the aggression that lies at the core of team sports. In one scene, they mime the motions of a physical assault repeatedly kicking and punching an imagined victim for more than a half an hour while happily chanting brutal words, as if they were the lyrics to a rap song. In addition, from time to time during the performance, at a barked command the actors threateningly storm toward the audience. Departing from natural speech, the vocal and physical performance of the chorus becomes an energetic transfer in which, as Roesner notices, "asemantic stresses predominate … As the text is chopped up … the musicalization enters into a conflict with the text."[41] Thus, Schleef resuscitated the paralinguistic dimension of Jelinek's script/score for *Ein Sportstueck* by intentionally enforcing the conflict between the text's signification and its rhythmical sound patterning.

Schleef's choric method of staging originated in his reinvention of the ancient chorus in his 1986 production of *Mothers*, a tragedy devised from Euripides' *The Suppliants* and Aeschylus' *Seven against Thebes* at Frankfurt's Schauspiel. Here the chorus took the dynamics of vocal performance to its extreme, from a subdued whisper to an extended cry. Particularly in the rendition of the phonetic segments of speech containing sounds of ritual lamentation (extant in the ancient Greek verses), the chorus completely abandoned any signifying textual coherence and turned to non-verbal screams encrypted in "crying" syllables. Here, "the tension [between verbal and oral aspects of dramatic speech] disappears as the voice itself becomes language," claims Fischer-Lichte; "The voice no longer transmits language; it *is* language, in which a bodily being-in-the-world expresses him/herself and addresses the audience purely. The materiality of the voice reveals the performance's materiality in its entirety."[42] Besides, leaving the cocoon of dramatic speech, voice meets with music/noise/sound and becomes an independent producer of aural stage space. Consequently, Fisher-Lichte's statement can be broadened to take into account not just voice but all stage sound that constitutes "performance's materiality in its entirety." Thus, in addition to participating in Marthaler's or Schleef's musicalization, voice comes to articulate sound-images of theatre pioneered by Wilson and now apparent in performances by the Socìetas Raffaello Sanzio, the Theatregroep Hollandia, and other such groups.

The Theatregroep Hollandia, founded by dancer, actor, and director Johan Simons and percussionist, composer, and sound artist Paul Koek in the early 1980s, left behind proscenium theatre to perform in dysfunctional places: abandoned factories, churches, scrapyards, and other sites typical of the post-industrial landscape. By infusing sounds, noises, and rhythms into theatrical imagery, the group Hollandia enhances the spectator's bodily awareness of the environment, not only in showing the inhumanity of such places but in making the audiences feel their own displacement. The group's mission statement describes their work as "resisting reality" and providing "a leading part for music": "Sounds of reality (*musique concrète*) are also incorporated into the play, sometimes electronically manipulated ... Non-dramatic and non-literary texts – ordinary texts, speeches, articles, interviews – can be transferred from reality and serve as a basis for or part of a stage performance ... It is not always a text that provides the basis for a play: it may also be music and musical structures. The creation of music-theatre is the main sideline in Hollandia's work."[43]

Their *Industrial PROJECT KLM Cargo* (1998), for example, is a collective exercise based on conveyer-belt work in an airport warehouse; its physical and aural disposition is similar to Schleef's choral theatre. Also reminiscent of Balla's Futurist *Machina Tipografica* and Nikolai Foregger's Constructivist *Machine Dance* with noise orchestra, it furthers some avant-garde performance techniques. But in *KLM Cargo* they go beyond the mime of machinery. In one scene, chorus performs movements choreographed to a sophisticated score of electronic, percussive sounds in front of a video screen showing a mute close-up of a suffering individual. This contrast of two engaged sound-images reinforces hostility of the environment, that is, the industrial area in which the performers and spectators are enclosed. This is typical of the aurally enhanced environmental theatre Hollandia wants to achieve. As a result, the Veenstudio, a music-theatre laboratory under Paul Koek's direction, was established within the company. Its mandate is to workshop and to develop a new language: "Essential to this new language is that all dramatic elements are chosen and interpreted musically. The text is chosen for its rhythm or melody; the tempo of the performance evolves with a musical tension and the music has a substantive role. The text is hence not only chosen for its content but also for a rhythmic or melodic feature, and the visual elements are arranged compositionally in space in relation to one another."[44]

The company's performances of the 1990s and early 2000s were determined by a non-hierarchical organization of auditory, visual, and kinetic stage elements. Henk Oosterling describes Hollandia's performance method as similar to the montage of attractions in the first Russian films, in which "images are cut without anecdotal bridges, sounds are sampled on rhythms, images, words and gestures." In their productions, "voices become instruments that produce new theatrical and dramatic effects ... [so that] sound deconstructs the unity of the images, as the rhythm stresses the intensity of the theatrical gesture."[45] Thus, digitally treated and amplified musical rhythms and sounds in *Su-pa* (1996) are counterpointed to the raw noise of "earthly materials such as wood, iron, grass, vegetables, stones and paper." In *Quick Lime* (1999), a piece about Marinus van der Lubbe – a revolutionary sentenced to death for setting fire to the Reichstag – the protagonist's raging cry, his obsessive repetition of the made-up word/gesture *Gottadusumfing*, and the percussive sounds heard as he repeatedly beats himself, all become acoustic performances in themselves.

Founding members of Socìetas Raffaello Sanzio Chiara Guidi and Claudia and Romeo Castellucci also subscribe to an aural dramaturgy that brings an immediacy and intensity to the performance event. Guidi admits: "The acoustic magma shaking up inside me awaits its dramaturgical catalyzing ... I'd like the cry of an animal or the screech of a machine to cause the sort of commotion that makes me want to intervene, to placate an anguish that doesn't even exist."[46] This fundamentally aural motivation drives all eleven episodes of their huge international project *Tragedia Endogonida* (produced in different European cities from 2002 to 2004). They all open with the sound of human/animal/cosmic breathing: a drone, digitally prepared by sound designer Scott Gibbons, which "spreads through the space like a smoke, creeping into all cavities and passageways of the stage and auditorium, opening them up to their own vibrations."[47] Then the hum evolves into a human voice, becoming screams and groans, whose increasing intensity reaches the limits of the audible. The episodes close with a choral rendition of the text in front of a video projection of letters and spoken words. While the images speed past, blurring into indistinct strobes similar to Rorschach blots, the actors' speech deteriorates into a kind of vocal clamour. In Berlin's episode, remembers Ridout, one could hear the sound of "percussive sucking, breathing, spitting amplified inside of the voice ... all the scraps and shards of breath discarded in the act of forming meaningful phonemes. A language in the negative, the sound of language in tatters and ruins, still desperately, urgently carrying something that must be communicated."[48] This subversive act, emphasizing the limited communicational reach of logocentric speech, is similar to Wilson's trashing of language, and confirms the legacy of the Futurists' liberating words/sounds through the destruction of syntax. The urge to communicate beyond verbal language drives the Socìetas Raffaello Sanzio members to use sophisticated media extensions of the voice and body such as audio-visual capturing, electronic amplification, and digital treatment of sound. Thus, in Shakespeare's *Giulio Cesare* (1997) Romeo Castellucci gave the role of Mark Antony to an actor who had recently undergone a laryngotomy that left him with a screeching voice. Castellucci capitalized on this fact by projecting a live, endoscopic image of the contractions in the actor's damaged throat while he delivered Antony's monologue. The cool, quasi-scientific, audio-visual scrutiny of the performer's vocal body added an uncomfortable physicality to the moving but shrewd funeral oration. In the same vein, the actor playing Brutus inhaled helium to make the pitch of his voice higher. This conscious juxtaposition of corporeal voice and dramatic speech exposed the tension between the orality and the rhetorics of theatre. It might have looked like nothing more than a trick, especially in the case of staging a classic, but Castellucci's practice, deeply rooted in the avant-garde trend toward the materiality of performance, enhanced the drama by means of physical theatricality.

Socìetas Raffaello Sanzio's performance of a concert adaptation of Louis-Ferdinand Céline's 1932 novel *Journey to the End of the Night* at the 1999 Avignon Festival went to another level of para-textual reading. The novel's torrent of language was presented by a vocalization similar to the Futurist declamation of parole in libertà and Artaud's glossolalia in his radiophonic work, *Pour en finir avec le jugement de Dieu*. As Timothy Scheie reports, "during the first of the piece's six 'movements,' four vocalists, standing around a table, whispered, clucked, groaned, and shrieked fragments of Céline's text in tightly orchestrated rhythms, weaving the words into abstract tonalities and percussive noise."[49] In addition, the readers had to compete with a continuous flood of sound effects and film clips projected on three circular screens. The visual stream, in the style of Expressionist and surrealist cinema, led the spectators on a journey through a First World War battlefield, a bordello, an American automotive factory, and a Parisian suburban slum. The unrestricted torrent of sounds and images from Céline's novel assaulted the audience's senses with bursting fragments of life, as the Futurists would say. But this intense collage of aural and visual attractions was achieved by a technical sophistication unknown to the Futurists. It was a concerto of *musique concrète* for the new media, reflecting a world reduced/elevated to cacophony.

The oral/aural performance style of contemporary theatre has been substantially enriched by its technological sophistication. The aural environment of the theatre event is now created by the use of wireless microphones, constellations of loudspeakers, electronic/digital equipment for sound treatment, and a whole set of paraphernalia known to contemporary sound designers and theatre-makers. Today, "less than an organ or an instrument [...] the voice in theatre appears more as a producer of a sound space with multiple sources, relying both on the *bodies* on stage and *recordings* and *samples*."[50] In companies like Theatregroep Hollandia and Socìetas Raffaello Sanzio, sound designers and music producers/performers are crucial contributors to the artistic team. Aside from composer Philip Glass, who organizes musical sound in counterpoint to the author's architectural ideas, one of the most celebrated of Wilson's collaborators has been the sound designer Hans-Peter Kuhn. Kuhn's specialty is building environmental noise into a complete layer of acoustics. Through a sophisticated maze of loudspeakers, he disperses sound around the performance/audience space, fortifying an immersive soundscape in the production. Kuhn's work follows earlier attempts at spatialization of sound in musique concrète, and what "Varèse had even earlier imagined as 'a series of sound projections in space by means of the emission of sound in any part or in many parts of the hall.' In his *Poème Électronique*, realized at the Brussels World's Fair in 1958, a tape piece of bells, sirens, treated voices, and piano traveled in various routes through four hundred loudspeakers spread throughout the Philips Pavilion designed by Le Corbusier."[51]

In the Schaubühne production of *Death Destruction & Detroit II* (1987), for instance, Kuhn created a sonic cocoon for the performance: "We had a line of 10 little speakers grouped around the sides and back of the auditorium. There were nine separate spots in the house, four for voices and five for taped sound effects. We also had speakers in the ceiling, the proscenium and backstage. So you were completely covered with sound."[52] Kuhn's architectural dispersal of sound sources ideally fulfilled John Cage's goal of a "total sound space." Working with a massive archive of recorded sounds, which were sampled, treated, and mixed with voices and noises produced by the actors, Kuhn structured an aural counterpart to

Wilson's theatre of images. Throughout the performance of *Death Destruction & Detroit II*, Wilson forced the audience to change their viewing angle by raising walls (China's Great Wall or the walls of Berlin's Spandau Prison) into position, interchangeably on all four sides of the theatre. Acting in response to the logic of the piece's three-dimensional design rather than illustrating stage events, Kuhn produced a soundscape that made the audience feel the space of the sound itself three-dimensionally as well. By a masterly disposition of the loudspeakers, he dispersed voices and sounds to become autonomous plastic and dynamic elements of performance. Andrzej Wirth commented in *Theatre Heute*: "The speaker is accompanied by, but never identical to, his voice. His statements are produced by him, but do not belong to him; they belong to space ... Separated from the actor, language and speech are elements of a spatial, not written text." The audience of the 1983 Rotterdam production of the *CIVIL wars* must have felt a similar impression. Here "the tiny figure of William the Silent sat in the hand of the world's largest woman reading the Edict of Nantes while his voice [helped by a chain of invisible loudspeakers] traveled in a nearly perfect circle around the perimeter of the auditorium."[53]

The visual and aural configurations of Robert Wilson's theatre can be considered a consequence of the spatialization of sound. Although Wilson's theatre has often been called "a theatre of images" because of his creative process, which starts with the sketching of semi-abstract (one might say hieroglyphic) storyboards, the truth is that in his staging, Wilson always returns to the organization of sound and the deconstruction of language. His involvement with the dramaturgy of sound is undeniable. It includes several aspects: Wilson's probe into the communicational power of language by fragmentation of words and their sound/graphic patterns (*A Letter to Queen Victoria*); his exploration of silence (*Deafman Glance*); the rhythmical organization of musical and visual structures (*Einstein on the Beach*); and the production of dense soundscapes correlated to the architectural volumes of his stage sets (*Death Destruction & Detroit II* and *the CIVIL wars*).

In his production of Heiner Müller's *Hamletmachine* (New York, Hamburg, and Berlin, 1986), Wilson organized a parallel rhythmical structure of blocks of sound and silence, carefully choreographed movements, and ninety-degree rotations of the set for each consecutive scene. Small, incremental changes – repetition, variation, and reversal of motives, all typical of minimalist music – were applied to the change of visual perspective for each tableau. The silent prologue to *Hamletmachine* begins with the percussive sounds of two claves hit together that cut time into pieces. Later in the performance, these sharp beats initiate all major changes in a technique borrowed from Japanese Noh theatre, employed to mark the merciless evolving of time. In a poorly lit, deep rectangular stage space, we see an old woman in white rags sitting in a wheelchair. Across from her there is a long table diagonally dividing a large stage floor in two. Three identically dressed women enter and sit at the table. They scratch or knock the table with rhythmical, monotonous persistence. Their non-negotiable, authoritarian position makes the spectator think of a courtroom or a prison ward. The washed-out old woman, perhaps a prisoner or a defendant, tied to her chair, looks like a character from Samuel Beckett's *Endgame*. She slowly moves her limbs with spasmodic jerks, screams silently, and freezes with her mouth wide open. A simple piano tune, romantic and almost childish, drips into the space. A yellow-clad boy comes in playing hopscotch and stops in mid-flight, balancing on one leg. We hear wolves howling in the distance, a train passes. All this "silent" ballet, lasting around thirty minutes, repeats in the next, sounded scene in which the scraps of Müller's text are finally uttered: "I was Hamlet. I stood at the shore and talked with the surf, BLABLA, the ruins of Europe in back of me."

Hamletmachine is what Lehmann calls, using the words of Wilson's role model Gertrude Stein, a postdramatic "audio landscape" where "the passing of time turns into a 'continuous present' … [and] theatre becomes similar to a kinetic sculpture, turning into a *time sculpture*."[54] Wilson's dramaturgy of sound and silence, rotation of the stage, and figural games with objects and performers require a "landscape-response" from the audience, suggests Elinor Fuchs. That is the only reception fully appropriate for a dispersed perceptual field reinforced by the repetition and slow-motion transformations of its aural and visual perspective. Here, one should remember a brief observation from Thornton Wilder's journal: "A myth is not a story read from left to right, from beginning to end, but a thing held full-in-view the whole time. Perhaps this is what Gertrude Stein meant by saying that the play henceforth is a landscape."[55] A piece of theatre like Wilson's, mounted onstage to expose its phonetic, aural, visual, and plastic materiality to our eyes and our ears, is an offering for our senses, mind, and emotions, a spatial and musical disposition, an "audio landscape" that does not rush to tell a story. It is a spatial text, a play/performance/production physically "held full-in-view the whole time." It is, as Kostelanetz has aptly noted, a sound-image complex that is constantly communicated or, in terms of postdramatic theatre, an exposition of a purely "scenic dynamic."

The phenomenon of the spatialization of sound on the contemporary stage must not be solely regarded as an achievement of new technologies. It has a long history within the avant-garde theatre's struggle to detach speech, voice, and vocal gesture from the written text and to liberate physical sound from voice trapped in the corporeal, emotional, and psychological intricacies of the individual. The postdramatic theatre of Sound & Fury, Schleef, Castellucci, and Wilson inherted methods of the historical avant-garde's sound poetry and performance in which vocal gesture has been used to dislocate verbal meaning and make words/sounds resonate both within the body and in the space. They are indebted to Artaud's acknowledgment of the expressive and dynamic spatial potential of voice. Artaud believed that words detached from horizontally laid out concept-bearing lines of dialogue "will be construed in an incantational, truly magic sense – for their shape and their sensuous emanations."[56] In contrast to the way logical speech flattens theatrical space – as Derrida interprets Artaud's point – sound reinstates the volume of theatrical space. "Once aware of this language in space, language of sounds, cries, lights, and onomatopoeia, the theatre must organize it into veritable hieroglyphs."[57] Postdramatic theatre artists accepted the hieroglyphic writing and performance that coordinate phonetic elements of language with visual, pictorial, and plastic elements of staging. Hence, quite programmatically describing the "textscape" and a "theatre of voices," Lehmann states that "the new variants of text should carry the connotation of the 'spacing' understood in the sense of Derrida's *espacement*: the phonetic materiality, the temporal course, the dispersion in space."[58]

The significant echo of the sound explorations from the historical avant-garde found in contemporary performance proves a continuum in the centrality of the orality/aurality in our theatrical discourse. Its shift towards the concept of self-sufficient sound started in the early part of the twentieth century – the era of Futurist, Dadaist, and Expressionist experiments – when promoters of an anti-Naturalistic mise en scène rejected the language of character, plot, and dramatic development and opted for a "speech" of stage materials, one of which was sound. Their understanding of "speech" meant a communication by sensory attractions, rather than intellectual concepts, aimed at the audience's participation in a performance event. This required attending to a performance's complex audiovisual theatricality and its non-verbal idiom while forgoing the narrative and figurative frameworks of a standard drama. Consequently, a core medium of such an idiom, sound, which the avant-garde recognized as a substantial rather than an illustrative element of theatre, has become vital to the performance/staging style of the twenty-first century.

A spectrum of the postdramatic performances examined here, in one way or another, follow the avant-garde's tendency to disarticulate Cartesian logocentrism by oral/aural means. They take part in the process that Helga Finter calls "the theatricalization of voice," which "on the one hand, takes the written (the seen) as spoken sounds and transforms sight into hearing and kinesthesia and, on the other hand, takes tone and sound as spatially written, thus transforming hearing to sight."[59] Voice thus becomes a concrete sound that crosses sensory borders by virtue of its own materiality. As one among the material elements of a performance, it shapes an abstract/concrete piece of art – as much a theatre event as an image, sculpture, construction, or composition. Looking back at its sources, we can see in postdramatic theatricality a realization of Kandinsky's concept of "the human word as an abstract means developing in time and space to the disposition of theatre. In the same way plastic arts find their place in architecture, poetry finds its place in music."[60] In an interview given to Sylvère Lotringer, Wilson explains that in his theatre "words weren't used to tell a story. They were used more architecturally: for the length of the word, of the sentence, for the sound. They were constructed like music."[61] Thus the circle, from explorations of the phonetic materiality of words to the temporal and spatial displacement of sounds, closes with a claim that the theatricality of today's performance greatly relies on its own orality/aurality. Additionally, the notion of *espacement* that is always already contained in language helps us understand postdramatic theatricality, not only in terms of the musicalization of performance, but more profoundly in terms of a concretization/materialization of the theatrical sign, which allows for a revival of its aural, visual, and physical aspects.

Epilogue

When a cry, a moan, a chuckle, a cough, a mumble, or a stutter emerges from its secure place amid the lines of dramatic dialogue – when the voice springs from the dramatic character, abandoning its cocoon for stage space – it is reborn as part of an evolving theatrical noise/sound pattern that has a life of its own. As an audience member I no longer face only psychologically motivated actions of madness, joy, or grief, but also theatrical sound itself. To my ears and my mind the sound appears emotionally engaging, empathetic, but at the same time concrete and abstract, naked in its materiality. Needless to say, this relationship with sound becomes even more complicated when mediated, recorded, instrumental, electronic, and digital extensions of sound flood the stage. And when sound's rhythmic, durational, and contrapuntal workings start to determine stage visuals, the relationship between theatre and sound becomes still more complicated. But the point of origin remains: I and a cry in the theatre.

That is how my journey into sonic matters of theatre now and its sources then (in the historical and neo-avant-garde) began. It started rather intuitively – I was immersed in sound and felt its palpability as a radio director/dramaturg and a theatre sound designer – but turned into a more rigorous exercise in my effort to retrace, theoretically and historically, the legacy of the avant-garde treatment of sound in the postdramatic theatre. Finding the urgency of the topic of sound in theatre – which up to now was regarded mostly as an ancillary marker of the dramatic plot – rooted in the recognition of its materiality and the oral/aural experiments of the historical avant-garde, this book argues for a place for the dramaturgy of sound within postdramatic theatre practice.

The parameters of an emerging dramaturgy of sound, primarily concerned with time, rhythm, voice, and other aural aspects of theatre, cannot easily be pinned down by citing a direct line of influences. Yet the dramaturgy of sound *is* both ubiquitous and multifaceted. One has only to glance at the theatre of the past few decades, revisited here, to notice just how crucial the dramaturgy of sound has been. It has been evident in the return to pre-verbal and corporeal impulses embedded in the sound of words in the Living Theatre's *The Brig* (1963), Peter Brook and Ted Hughes's *Orghast* (1971), and Caryl Churchill's *Skriker* (1994); in the music-like staging method of Tadeusz Kantor's *Dead Class* (1975) and Christoph Marthaler's *Murx the European!* (1993); in the exploration of aural and physical values of choric performance of Elfriede Jelinek and Einar Schleef's *Ein Sportstueck* (1998); in the emphasis on aurality in Peter Stein's *Oresteia* (1980) and Sound & Fury's *War Music* (2000) played in darkness; in the expansion of the sonic sphere into a kinetic sculptural space in Robert Wilson's productions; and in the intermediality of works reaching into the twenty-first century like those of the Socìetas Raffaello Sanzio and the Theatregroep Hollandia.

All these productions/performances feature an "'auditive stage' [that] around the theatre image opens up 'intertextual' reference to all sides or complements the scenic material through musical motifs of sound or 'concrete noise.'"[1] A few of the most recent performances discussed here exhibit an architectural/kinetic extension of sound into space achieved "in the sense of the *espacement*: the phonetic materiality, the temporal course, the dispersion in space, the loss of teleology and self identity,"[2] which Derrida holds necessary to break the closure of the dramatic text. They concur with my initial hypothesis that the dramaturgy of sound, from its avant-garde sources to its current practice, unfolds in two never-separated, intertwined strains – the gestural, corporeal power of the performer's voice and the structural qualities of stage sound.

The phenomenon of listening itself, however, turns us back to the archetypal situation of I and a cry in the theatre revamped in many postdramatic performances, where "breath, rhythm, the opaque actuality and intensity of the body's visceral presence take precedence over logos, disturbing and interrupting all semiosis."[3] Listening "reads" theatre performance without semantic pretensions; it discovers the flux of "phonotext" or "genotext" (Julia Kristeva) or "the grain of the voice" (Ronald Barthes) that reveals the materiality of language from within. Therefore, Lehmann suggests a new theatre "in ways similar to a modern *language poétique* – an attempt toward a restitution of *chora* as a 'space' and discourse without telos, hierarchy and causality," a theatre that "tends toward something like a *chora-graphie*."[4] A closer look at Lehmann's neologism reveals manifold connotations of this word, which precludes its fixity. First, chora denotes a pre-verbal space and an aural flux, but then, at least phonetically, it calls to mind *chorus* and *chorea*, ritual singing and dancing in the theatre; and finally, a *graph* denotes something visual embedded in this compound of writing, drawing, and performace.

At the end of my journey, having in mind the twofold, gestural/structural development of the dramaturgy of sound, I can plead together with Robert Wilson: "Listen to the pictures!" It is not a call for mere synaesthesia or a postmodern theatrical trickery; it is an affirmation of "chora-graphie" as a substantial way of approaching theatre. My book's trajectory has taken it from the exploration of the autonomous use of sound and voice in the historical avant-garde, as it breaks with logocentric literature and dramatic theatre, to an analysis of its "echoes" in current performance practice. It is my hope that its final destination, the rediscovery of the pronounced orality/aurality of the postdramatic theatre, may initiate the inclusion of the aesthetics and phenomenology of sound in contemporary theatre study.

Notes

INTRODUCTION

1 Jim Drobnick, "Listening Awry," in *Aural Cultures* (Toronto: YYZ Books, 1994), 20.

2 The term "pulsion/al" figures in several English translations of Jean-François Lyotard's books, representing the French *pulsion/èle*, which is, in turn, used for Sigmund Freud's German term *Trieb*, whose standard English translation is "drive" or "instinct." Writing about sound in theatre, I have opted to use "pulsion" for its euphonic value, which connotes a pulsating rhythm of performance.

3 Patrice Pavis, *Languages of the Stage: Essays in the Semiology of the Theatre* (New York: PAJ, 1982), 190.

4 Eugenio Barba, "The Nature of Dramaturgy: Describing Actions at Work," *New Theatre Quarterly* 1, no. 1 (February 1985): 75.

5 Eugenio Barba, "The Deep Order Called Turbulence: The Three Faces of Dramaturgy," *The Drama Review* 44, no. 4 (Winter 2000): 60.

6 Together with Fuchs's notion of "the theater of difference," concepts such as Barba's "dramaturgy of changing states," Bonnie Marranca's "theatre of images," and Helga Finter's "theatricalization of voice" overlap as the descriptors of "postdramatic theatre."

7 Elinor Fuchs, *The Death of Character* (Bloomington and Indianapolis: Indiana University Press, 1996), 175–6.

8 Hans-Thies Lehmann and Patrick Primavesi, "Dramaturgy on Shifting Grounds," *Performance Research* 14, no. 3 (2009): 3.

9 Peter Szondi, *Theory of the Modern Drama: A Critical Edition*, ed. and trans. Michael Hays (Minneapolis: University of Minnesota Press, 1987), 7.

10 Markus Wessendorf, "The Postdramatic Theatre of Richard Maxwell," *Norsk Shakespeare–og teatertidsskrift* (Oslo) 1 (2006): 29–33. http://www2.hawaii.edu/~wessendo/Maxwell.htm, last accessed 20 January 2012.

11 Hans-Thies Lehmann, "Word and Stage in Postdramatic Theatre," in *Contemporary Drama in English: Drama and/after Postmodernism*, vol. 14 (Trier: Wissenschaftlicher Verlag, 2007): 42.

12 Hans-Thies Lehmann, *Postdramatic Theatre*, trans. Karen Jürs-Munby (New York: Routledge, 2006), 25.

CHAPTER ONE

1 Paul Allain and Jen Harvie, eds, *The Routledge Companion to Theatre and Performance* (London and New York: Routledge, 2006), 167.

2 See Lynne Kendrick and David Roesner, eds, *Theatre Noise: The Sound of Performance* (Cambridge: Cambridge Scholars Publishing, 2011). Introduction at http://www.c-s-p.org/flyers/978-1-4438-3440-7-sample.pdf, last accessed 22 January 2012.

3 See Matthias Rebstock and David Roesner, eds, *Composed Theatre: Aesthetics, Practices, Processes* (Bristol and Chicago: Intellect, 2012). The project's website represents a virtual hub for international research into theatre sound/music. Visit http://spa.exeter.ac.uk/drama/staff/roesner/projects/composedtheatre/welcome.shtml, last accessed 17 January 2012.

4 The word "dramatic" is used here in a sense that connotes the dynamics of sound's supposed life, not the form of theatrical representation.

5 David Burrows, *Sound, Speech, Music* (Amherst: University of Massachusetts Press, 1990), 21.

6 Patrice Pavis, "The State of Current Theatre Research," *Applied Semiotics/Sémiotique appliquée* 1, no. 3 (1997): 213.

7 Robert Wilson, *The Theater of Images* (New York: Harper, 1984), 101.

8 Frederick J. Ruf, *Entangled Voices: Genre and the Religious Construction of Self* (New York: Oxford University Press, 1997), 67.

9 Euripides' *The Phoenician Women*, directed by Paolo Magelli, a production of the Theatre Marin Držić, Dubrovnik, performed at the 1988 MESS festival in Sarajevo.

10 See Thanos Vovolis, "The Voice and the Mask in Ancient Greek Tragedy," in *Soundscapes*, eds Larry Sider et al. (London and New York: Wallflower Press, 2003): 83–102; and Torbjörn Alström, "The Voice in the Mask," *The Drama Review* 48, no. 2 (2004): 133–5.

11 Andrei Serban, "The Life in a Sound," *The Drama Review* 20, no. 4 (1976): 25.

12 Murray Schafer, "I've Never Seen a Sound," in *S:ON – Le son dans l'art contem-*

porain canadien/Sound in Contemporary Canadian Art, ed. Nicole Gingras (Sherbrooke: Éditions Artextes, 2003), 68.

13 Don Ihde, *Listening and Voice: A Phenomenology of Sound* (Athens: Ohio University Press, 1976), 45.

14 Maurice Merleau-Ponty, *The Primacy of Perception*, ed. James M. Edie (Evanston: Northwestern University Press, 1964), xvii, emphasis in original.

15 David Roesner, "The Politics of the Polyphony of Performance: Musicalization in Contemporary German Theatre," *Contemporary Theatre Review* 18, no. 1 (2008): 54.

16 Ibid., 31.

17 Erika Fischer-Lichte, *The Transformative Power of Performance: A New Aesthetics*, trans. Saskya Iris Jain (London and New York: Routledge, 2008), 17.

18 Ibid., 75.

19 See *Acoustic Turn*, ed. Petra Maria Meyer (Tübingen: Wilhelm Fink, 2008).

20 Hans-Thies Lehmann, *Postdramatic Theatre*, trans. Karen Jürs-Munby (New York: Routledge, 2006), 68.

21 Ibid., 92.

22 Robert Bean, "Polyphonic Aurality and John Cage" in *Aural Cultures*, ed. Jim Drobnick (Toronto: YYZ Books, 1994), 127, 134.

23 See www.youtube.com/watch?v=Z5sB_YvvSS4, last accessed 24 May 2010.

24 Steve McCaffery, *Carnival, the second panel 1970–1975* (Toronto: Coach House Press, 1976), no pagination.

25 Steve McCaffery, "Voice in Extremis," in *Prior to Meaning: The Protosemantic and Poetics* (Evanston: Northwestern University Press, 2001), 161.

26 Claudia Castelucci et al., *The Theatre of Socìetas Raffaello Sanzio* (New York and London: Routledge, 2007), 24–5.

27 Lehmann, *Postdramatic Theatre*, 18.

28 Kazimir Malevich, "From Cubism and Futurism to Suprematism: The New Painterly Realism," in *Russian Art of the Avant-Garde: Theory and Criticism, 1902–1934*, ed. John E. Bowlt (New York: Viking Press, 1976), 130.

29 Antonin Artaud, *The Theatre and Its Double*, trans. Mary Caroline Richards (New York: Grove Press, 1958), 80.

30 Günter Berghaus, ed., *F.T. Marinetti: Critical Writings* (New York: Clarendon Press, 2006), 391.

CHAPTER TWO

1 I am using this twofold word according to Michael Kirby's definition, which adheres to the avant-garde predilection for the materiality of the sign/sound/light: "The word 'affect' rather than 'effect' was used [... because]

theatre seeks not merely an effect – a response – but an affective response, an emotional and ultimately nonintellectual one. ('Bright light,' says Webster in defining the word, 'affects the eyes.')." Michael Kirby, *A Formalist Theatre* (Philadelphia: University of Pennsylvania Press, 1987), xiv.

2 Douglas Kahn, *Noise, Water, Meat: A History of Sound in the Arts* (Cambridge: MIT Press, 1999), 2.

3 Umbro Apollonio, ed., *Futurist Manifestos* (London: Thames and Hudson, 1973), 22.

4 Günter Berghaus, *Avant-Garde Performance: Live Events and Electronic Technologies* (New York: Palgrave Macmillan, 2005), 23.

5 Jules Romains, *La vie unanime* (Paris: L'Abbaye, 1908). Quoted in Marianne W. Martin, "Futurism, Unanimism and Apollinaire," *Art Journal* 28, no. 3. (Spring 1969): 261.

6 Apollonio, *Futurist Manifestos*, 22.

7 Steven Connor, "Feel the Noise: Excess, Affect and the Acoustic," in *Emotion in Postmodernism*, eds Gerhard Hoffman and Alfred Hornung (Heidelberg: Universitätsverlag C. Winter, 1997), 152.

8 *Futurist Manifestos*, 182, 195.

9 Ibid., 24.

10 F.T. Marinetti, "The Founding and Manifesto of Futurism," in *Futurist Manifestos*, 23.

11 D. Burliuk, V. Khlebnikov, A. Kruchenykh, and V. Mayakovski, "A Slap in the Face of Public Taste," in *Words in Revolution: Russian Futurist Manifestoes 1912–1928*, trans and eds Anna Lawton and Herbert Eagle (Washington: New Academia Publishing, 2004), 51–2. Originally *Russian Futurism through Its Manifestos, 1912–1928* (Ithaca: Cornell University Press, 1988), 51–2.

12 Hugo Ball, *Flight out of Time: A Dada Diary*, trans. and ed. John Elderfield (Berkeley: University of California Press, 1996), 61.

13 Camille Saint-Saens's letter quoted in Anne d'Harnoncourt, *Futurism and the International Avant-Garde* (Philadelphia: Philadelphia Museum of Art, 1980), 11.

14 It is a laconic definition of expressionist drama penned by Kurt Pinthus in 1918. Quoted in Aviel Roshwald and Richard Stites, *European Culture in the Great War: The Arts, Entertainment and Propaganda, 1914–1918* (Cambridge: Cambridge University Press, 2002), 48.

15 Matei Calinescu, *Five Faces of Modernity: Modernism, Avant-Garde, Decadence, Kitsch, Postmodernism* (Durham: Duke University Press, 1987), 119.

16 Ball, *Flight Out of Time*, 66.

17 Francesca Bacci, "In Your Face: The Futurists' Assault on the Public's Senses,"

in *Art, History and the Senses*, eds Patrizia Di Bello and Gabriel Koureas (Surrey and Burlington: Ashgate, 2010), 83.

18 Robert Motherwell, *The Dada Painters and Poets: An Anthology* (Cambridge: Harvard University Press, 1981), 26.

19 Ibid., 26.

20 John D. Erickson, *Dada: Performance, Poetry, and Art* (Boston: Twayne, 1984), 97.

21 Quoted in Steve McCaffery, *Carnival*, no pagination.

22 Luigi Russolo, *The Art of Noises* (New York: Pendragon Press, 1986), 50.

23 Torben Sangild, *The Aesthetics of Noise* (Copenhagen: DATANOM, 2002) www.ubu.com/papers/noise.html, last accessed 24 May 2010.

24 Jacques Attali, *Noise: The Political Economy of Music* (Minneapolis: University of Minnesota Press, 1985), 2.

25 Ibid., 5.

26 Ibid., 7.

27 Ibid., 3.

28 Balilla Pratella, "Manifesto of Futurist Musicians, 1910," in Apollonio, *Futurist Manifestos*, 30.

29 Jonathan Sterne, *The Audible Past: Cultural Origins of Sound Reproduction* (Durham: Duke University Press, 2003), 3.

30 Hermann von Helmholtz, *On the Sensations of Tone as a Physiological Basis for the Theory of Music*, trans. Alexander J. Ellis (New York: Dover Publications, 1954), 1.

31 Ibid., 2.

32 Don Ihde, *Sense and Significance* (Pittsburgh: Duquesne University Press, 1973), 25, 27.

33 Andrew M. Kimbrough, *Dramatic Theories of Voice in the Twentieth Century* (Amherst: Cambria Press, 2011), 7.

34 Ibid., 19.

35 Walter J. Ong, *Orality and Literacy: The Technologizing of the Word* (London: Routledge, 2002), 8.

36 Ibid., 33.

37 Garett Barden, "Method in Philosophy," in *The New Bergson*, ed. John Mullarkey (New York: Manchester University Press, 1999), 38.

38 Ihde, *Sense and Significance*, 28.

39 Aristotle, *Metaphysics*, trans. John Warrington (London: Dent, 1956), 51.

40 René Descartes, *Discourse on Method, Optics, Geometry, and Meteorology*, trans. Paul J. Olscamp (Indianapolis: Bobbs-Merrill, 1965), 65.

41 Ross Brown, *Sound: A Reader in Theatre Practice* (London: Palgrave Macmillan, 2010), 58.

42 Steven Connor, "Windbags and Skinsongs," http://www.bbk.ac.uk/english/skc/windbags/, last accessed 17 August 2011.
43 Steven Connor, "The Strains of the Voice," http://www.bbk.ac.uk/english/skc/strains, last accessed 17 August 2011.
44 Roland Barthes, "The Grain of the Voice," in *The Responsibility of Forms*, trans. Richard Howard (New York: Hill and Wang, 1985), 269.
45 Barthes, *The Responsibility of Forms*, 270.
46 Pierre Fédida, *Le Corps, le texte et la scène* (Paris: Delarge, 1983), 252.
47 *Rimbaud Complete*, trans., ed., and with an introduction by Wyatt Mason (New York: Modern Library, 2002), 104.
48 *Words in Revolution: Russian Futurist Manifestoes 1912–1928*, 52.
49 Mikhail Larionov, "Pictorial Rayonism," in *Russian Art of the Avant-Garde: Theory and Criticism, 1902–1934*, ed. John E. Bowlt (New York: Viking Press, 1976), 101.
50 Enrico Prampolini, "Chromophony – The Colors of Sounds," in *Futurist Manifestos*, 115.
51 See Jeff Edwards, "Steiner, Thought Forms, and Kandinsky," in *Beyond Kandinsky: Revisiting Spiritual in Art*, a New York School of Visual Arts online symposium at http://www.beyondkandinskyblog.net/2011/04/steiner-thought-forms-and-kandinsky.html.
52 Wassily Kandinsky and Franc Mark, eds, *Blaue Reiter Almanach*, trans. Henning Falkenstein (New York: Viking Press, 1974), 92.
53 Wassily Kandinsky, *Complete Writings on Art*, eds Kenneth C. Lindsay and Peter Vergo, (Boston: G.K. Hall & Co., 1982), 364.
54 Mel Gordon, "Songs from the Museum of the Future: Russian Sound Creation 1910–1930," in *Wireless Imagination: Sound, Radio, and the Avant-Garde*, eds Douglas Kahn and Gregory Whitehead (Cambridge: MIT Press, 1992), 203.
55 See Janet Tassel, "Staging a Kandinsky Dream," *New York Times*, 7 February 1982. The work reached out to the cybersphere as 'an animated digital object' produced by the Gertrude Stein Repertory Theatre, New York, http://www.glopad.org/pi/en/record/digdoc/1004283, last accessed 24 May 2010.
56 Kandinsky, *Complete Writings on Art*, 281.
57 Ibid., 263.
58 Ibid., 264.
59 David F. Kuhns, *German Expressionist Theatre: The Actor and the Stage* (Cambridge: Cambridge University Press, 1997), 150.
60 Kuhns, *German Expressionist Theatre*, 267.
61 *Marinetti: Selected Writings*, trans. R.W. Flint and Arthur A. Cappotelli (New York: Farrar, Straus and Giroux, 1972), 117.

62 Kandinsky, *Complete Writings on Art*, 261.

63 Marjorie Perloff, *The Futurist Moment: Avant-Garde, Avant Guerre, and the Language of Rupture* (Chicago and London: University of Chicago Press, 1986), 38.

64 See a detailed case study of the performance by Dorothy Pam in *The Drama Review* 19, no. 3 (1975): 5–12.

65 *Words in Revolution: Russian Futurist Manifestoes 1912–1928*, 51–2.

66 Ibid., 70.

67 Ibid., 73.

68 Ibid., 66.

69 F.T. Marinetti, "Technical Manifesto of Futurist Literature," in *F.T. Marinetti: Critical Writings*, ed. Günter Berghaus (New York: Farrar, 2006), 112.

70 Velimir Khlebnikov, "The Word as Such," in *Collected Works of Velimir Khlebnikov*, ed. Charlotte Douglas (Cambridge: Harvard University Press, 1987), vol. 1, 257.

71 Antonin Artaud, "First Letter on Language," *Collected Works,* trans. Victor Corti (London: Calder and Boyars, 1968), vol. 4, 83.

72 Steve McCaffery, "From Phonic to Sonic: The Emergence of the Audio-Poem," in *Sound States: Innovative Poetics and Acoustical Technologies*, ed. Adalaide Kirby Morris (Chapel Hill: University of North Carolina Press, 1997), 155.

73 See Veit Erlmann, ed., *Hearing Cultures: Essays on Sound, Listening and Modernity* (Oxford and New York: Berg, 2004).

74 Steven Connor, "The Modern Auditory I," in *Rewriting the Self: Histories from the Renaissance to the Present*, ed. Roy Porter (London: Routledge, 1997), 213.

75 Connor, "The Modern Auditory I," 212.

76 Erika Fischer-Lichte, "The Avant-garde and the Semiotics of the Antitextual Theatre," in *Contours of the Theatrical Avant-Garde*, ed. James M. Harding (Ann Arbor: University of Michigan Press, 2000), 92.

77 Patrice Pavis, *Languages of the Stage: Essays in the Semiology of the Theatre* (New York: PAJ, 1982), 190.

78 Steve McCaffery, "From Phonic to Sonic," 155.

79 Fischer-Lichte, *Contours of the Theatrical Avant-garde*, 79.

80 Christopher Innes, "In the Beginning Was the Word: Text versus Performance," in *The Performance Text*, ed. Domenico Pietropaolo (Ottawa: Legas, 1997), 9.

81 Antonin Artaud, *The Theatre and Its Double*, 91.

82 Christopher Innes, *Avant Garde Theatre, 1892–1992* (London: Routledge, 1966), 15.

83 See R.S. Gordon, "The Italian Futurist Theatre: A Reappraisal," *Modern Language Review* 85, no. 2 (1990): 349–61.

84 Jacques Derrida, *Writing and Difference*, trans. Alan Bass (Chicago: University of Chicago Press, 1978), 240.

85 Ibid., 174.

86 Ibid., 189 and 247.

87 Quoted in Jon Erickson, "The Language of Presence: Sound Poetry and Artaud," *boundary 2* 14, no. 1/2 (Autumn 1985–Winter 1986): 280.

88 Patrice Pavis, "Avant-garde Theatre and Semiology: A Few Practices and the Theory Behind Them," in *Languages of the Stage: Essays in the Semiology of the Theatre* (New York: PAJ, 1982), 186.

CHAPTER THREE

1 For a complete chronology and programs, see Simona Bertini, *Marinetti e le 'eroiche serate' (con antologia di testi)* (Novara: Interlinea edizioni, 2002), 47–9, 158–60.

2 *I poeti futuristi* (Milano: Edizioni Futuriste di *Poesia* 1912), 372.

3 Giovanni Lista, ed., *Théâtre futurist italien, anthologie critique* (Lausanne: La Cité/L'Age d'Homme, 1976), vol. 1, 49. Also at http://ubu.artmob.ca/sound/balla_giacomo/Balla-Giacomo_Discussione.mp3, last accessed 20 January 2012.

4 Simona Bertini, *Marinetti e le 'eroiche serate'* (*con antologia di testi*) (Novara: Interlinea edizioni, 2002), 145.

5 Günter Berghaus, *Avant-Garde Performance: Live Events and Electronic Technologies* (New York: Palgrave Macmillan, 2005), 33.

6 "The Synthetic Futurist Theatre," in Apollonio, *Futurist Manifestos*, 183.

7 Michael Webster, "Words-in-Freedom and the Oral Tradition," *Visible Language* 23, no. 1 (1989): 69.

8 Ong, *Orality and Literacy*, 44.

9 Quoted in Marjorie Perloff, *The Futurist Moment: Avant-Garde, Avant Guerre, and the Language of Rupture* (Chicago and London: University of Chicago Press, 1986), 81.

10 *Marinetti: Selected Writings*, 89.

11 Ibid., 125.

12 Richard J. Pioli, *Stung by Salt and War: Creative Texts of the Italian Avant-Gardist F.T. Marinetti* (New York: Farrar, 1972), 41. Original in *I poeti futuristi* (Milano: Edizioni Furutiste di "*Poesia*," 1912), 29.

13 Apollonio, *Futurist Manifestos*, 112. Original in *I Manifesti del futurismo*, lanciati da Marinetti et al. (Firenze: Lacerba, 1914), 154.

14 Ibid., 112.
15 Sound alignment and ideophone language practices are discussed in Veit Erlmann, ed., *Hearing Cultures: Essays on Sound, Listening and Modernity* (Oxford and New York: Berg, 2004).
16 Steve McCaffery, "Introduction," in Steve Mccaffery and bpNichol, eds., *Sound Poetry: a Catalogue* (Underwich Editions, Toronto, 1978), no pagination.
17 Luigi Russolo, *The Art of Noises* (New York: Pendragon Press, 1986), 56–7.
18 Jon Erickson, "The Language of Presence: Sound Poetry and Artaud," *boundary 2* 14, no. 1/2 (Autumn 1985–Winter 1986): 279.
19 Ibid., 281.
20 Christopher Middleton, "The Rise of Primitivism and Its Relevance to the Poetry of Expressionism and Dada" in *Bolshevism in Art and Other Expository Writings* (Manchester: Carcanet New Press, 1978), 28.
21 Quoted in Susan Hiller, ed., *Myth of Primitivism* (Florence: Routledge, 1991), p 86.
22 Andrew M. Kimbrough, *Dramatic Theories of Voice in the Twentieth Century* (Amherst: Cambria Press, 2011), 68.
23 Ibid., 108.
24 Quoted in Middleton, "The Rise of Primitivism," 31.
25 Richard Kostelanetz, "Text-Sound Art: A Survey," *Performing Arts Journal* 2, no. 2 (1977): 62.
26 Hugo Ball, *Flight out of Time: A Dada Diary*, 61.
27 Quoted in Günter Berghaus, "Dada Theatre or the Genesis of Anti-bourgeois Performance Art," *German Life and Letters* 38, no. 4 (1985): 297.
28 Ball, *Flight out of Time*, 68.
29 Ibid., 25.
30 Ibid., 68.
31 Ibid., 226.
32 Ibid., 236.
33 Ibid., 70.
34 Ibid., 71.
35 Walter Arndt, "Preface," in Christian Morgenstern, *Songs from the Gallows* (New Haven: Yale University Press, 1993), xii.
36 http://ubu.artmob.ca/sound/morgenstern_christian/ Morgenstern-Christian_Das-Grosse-Lalula.mp3, last accessed 20 January 2012.
37 Paul Scheerbart, *Gesammelte Werke*, herausgegeben von Thomas Bürk, Joachim Körber, Uli Kohnle (Linkenheim: Phantasia, 1986–1996), v. 1, 576. Also at http://ubu.artmob.ca/sound/scheerbart_paul/Scheerbart-Paul_Kikakoku-Zauberspruch-I.mp3, last accessed 20 January 2012.

38 Raymond Federman, "The Language of Dada: Intermedia of Words," *Dada/Surrealism* 2 (1972), 19.

39 Ibid., 19.

40 Antonin Artaud, *The Theatre and Its Double*, 93.

41 Jacques Derrida, *Writing and Difference*, trans. Alan Bass (Chicago: University of Chicago Press, 1978), 189.

42 Sonia Delaunay-Terk was the wife of Robert Delaunay, a painter, and a propagator of *simultaneisme*, whose supposedly innovative *Orphism* was a subject of a bitter controversy between Cubists and Futurists at the time.

43 Mel Gordon, ed., *Dada Performance* (New York: PAJ, 1987), 38–9. Gordon uses a facsimile of its original publication in *Cabaret Voltaire, Recueil littéraire et artistique*, ed. Hugo Ball, Zurich, Meierei Spiegelgasse 1, June 1916.

44 Apollonio, *Futurist Manifestos*, 99.

45 This is an anglicized version of *compenetrazione* that appears in Flint and Kirby's translations of Marinetti's texts. I use the term accordingly.

46 Marinetti, *Selected Writings*, 164.

47 Ibid., 332–3.

48 The original edition is reprented in F.T. Marinetti, *Teoria e invenzione futurista*, a cura di Luciano De Maria (Milano: Arnoldo Mondadori Editore), 1968, 641–779. *Zang Tumb Tumb* has many textual versions with different titles. Its two basic texts, "Bombardamento" (Bombardment) and "Adrianopoli assedio orchestra" (Adrianople-siege-orchestra), were published in *Lacerba* in 1913. The title of these very first versions clearly demonstrates that Marinetti was aware of possibilities for the orchestration of a poem, not only as an onomatopoeic sound report from the battlefield, but also as an extension beyond mimetic rendition, toward an independent cacophonic structure that might have inspired Luigi Russolo's art of noises.

49 Steve McCaffery, "From Phonic to Sonic: The Emergence of the Audio-Poem," in *Sound States: Innovative Poetics and Acoustical Technologies*, ed. Adelaide Kirby Morris (Chapel Hill: University of North Carolina Press, 1997), 151.

50 "The Battle of Adrianopolis" was recorded in April 1924 for *La Voce del Padrone* as R6916 [78 rpm] and later reissued on the CDs *Musica Futurista* and *Futurism and Dada Reviewed*.

51 "Geometric and Mechanical Splendour and the Numerical Sensibility" in Apollonio, *Futurist Manifestos*, 155.

52 Ibid., 155–6.

53 Marinetti, *Selected Writings*, 88.

54 Bertini, *Marinetti e le 'eroiche serate*,' 146. Also in *Teoria e invenzione futurista*, 689.

55 Ibid., 147. Original reprinted in F.T. Marinetti, *Teoria e invenzione futurista*, a cura di Luciano De Maria (Milano: Arnoldo Mondadori Editore, 1968), 111.

56 Zbigniew Folejewski, *Futurism and its Place in the Development of Modern Poetry: A Comparative Study and Anthology* (Ottawa: University of Ottawa Press, 1980), 183–5. Also in *Teoria e invenzione futurista*, 694–5; Pioli, 78; Bertini, 144.

57 Clara Orban, *The Culture of Fragments: Words and Images in Futurism and Surrealism* (Atlanta: Rodopi, 1997), 45.

58 László Moholy-Nagy, *Vision in Motion* (Chicago: P. Theobald, 1969), 306.

59 Ibid., 301.

60 Ibid., 304.

61 Folejewski, *Futurism and Its Place in the Development of Modern Poetry*, 35.

62 Marinetti, *Selected Writings*, 85.

63 Pioli, *Stung by Salt and War*, 41.

64 Bertini, *Marinetti e le 'eroiche serate,'* 146.

65 Pioli, *Stung by Salt and War*, 50.

66 Don Ihde, *Listening and Voice: A Phenomenology of Sound* (Athens: Ohio University Press, 1976), 83–4.

67 Walter Benjamin, "On Mimetic Faculty," *Reflections*, ed. Peter Demetz (New York: Schocken Books, 1986), 335.

68 Raymond Chapman, *The Treatment of Sounds in Language and Literature* (Oxford: Blackwell and Deutsch, 1984), 38.

69 Ibid., 38.

70 Patrizia Violi, ed., *Phonosymbolism and Poetic Language* (Turnhout, Belgium: Brepols, 2000), 7, 9.

71 Quoted in White, *Literary Futurism*, 25.

72 Apollonio, *Futurist Manifestos*, 154, 158.

73 Marinetti, *Selected Writings*, 144.

74 "Manifesto of Futurist Playwrights, 1911," in Marinetti, *Selected Writings*, 113.

75 Giovanni Lista, *La scène futuriste* (Paris: Editions du Centre national de la recherche scientifique, 1989), 142.

CHAPTER FOUR

1 Anna Lawton, "Introduction," in *Words in Revolution: Russian Futurist Manifestoes 1912–1928*, trans and eds Anna Lawton and Herbert Eagle (Washington: New Academia Publishing, 2004), 8. Originally *Russian Futurism through Its Manifestoes, 1912–1928* (Ithaca: Cornell University Press, 1988), 8.

2 Ibid., 52.

3 Victor Shklovsky, "The Resurrection of the Word," in *Russian Formalism: A Collection of Articles and Texts in Translation*, eds Stephan Bann and John E. Bowlt (Edinburgh: Scottish Academic Press, 1973), 41.
4 Ibid., 42.
5 Krystyna Pomorska, *Russian Formalist Theory and Its Poetic Ambience* (The Hague, Paris: Mouton, 1968), 120.
6 Velimir Khlebnikov, *Collected Works*, trans. Paul Schmidt, ed. Ronald Vroom (Cambridge: Harvard University Press, 1997), vol. 3 (1997), 34. In this case, and later in *Zangezi*, I took the liberty of discussing Schmidt's translations because they follow the phonetic principles applied in the original poem. However, my use of English translation does not deny the primacy of original Russian text.
7 Ibid., 38. Original in Velimir Khlebnikov, *Tvoreniia*, eds V.P. Grigor'ev and A.E. Parnis (Moscow: Sov. Pisatel', 1986), 54.
8 Paul Schmidt, a prominent translator of Russian literature into English, coined the word "beyonsense" to denote zaum – the Futurist idiom of poetry. I am using it accordingly.
9 Ladislav Matejka and Krystyna Pomorska, eds., *Reading in Russian Poetics: Formalist and Structuralist Views* (Cambridge: MIT Press, 1971), 11.
10 Ibid., 11.
11 Andrey Bely, "The Magic of Words," *Selected Essays of Andrey Bely*, ed., trans. Steven Cassedy (Berkeley: University of California Press, 1985), 98.
12 Ibid., 93.
13 Ibid., 97.
14 *Words in Revolution: Russian Futurist Manifestoes 1912–1928*, trans and eds Anna Lawton and Herbert Eagle (Washington: New Academia Publishing, 2004), 80. Originally *Russian Futurism through Its Manifestos, 1912–1928*, (Ithaca: Cornell University Press, 1988), 80.
15 Ibid., 80.
16 "New Ways of the Word: The Language of Future, Death to Symbolism," 1913, in *Words in Revolution: Russian Futurist Manifestoes 1912–1928*, 71.
17 *Words in Revolution: Russian Futurist Manifestoes 1912–1928*, 61.
18 Ibid., 60.
19 Ibid., 68.
20 *Marinetti*: *Selected Writings*, 89.
21 Ibid., 89.
22 Nils Åke Nilsson, "Kruchonykh's Poem 'Dyr bul shchyl,'" *Scando-Slavica* 24 (1979): 145.
23 Ibid., 75–6.
24 Pomorska, *Russian Formalist Theory*, 120.
25 Khlebnikov, *Collected Works*, vol. 3, 30. Original in Khlebnikov, *Tvoreniia*, 54.

26 Velimir Khlebnikov, *The King of Time: Selected Writings of the Russian Futurian*, ed. Charlotte Douglas, trans. Paul Schmidt (Cambridge: Harvard University Press, 1985), 20.
27 Pomorska, *Russian Formalist Theory*, 97.
28 See Nils Åke Nilsson, "How to Translate Avant-garde Poetry: Some Attempts with Khlebnikov's 'Incantation by Laughter,'" *Velimir Khlebnikov: A Stockholm Symposium* (Stockholm: University of Stockholm, 1985), 133–50; and "Futurism, Primitivism and the Russian Avant-garde," *Russian Literature* 8 (1980): 469–82.
29 Ong, *Orality and Literacy*, 44.
30 Christopher Innes, *Avant Garde Theatre, 1892–1992* (London: Routledge, 1966), 3.
31 Antonin Artaud, *The Theatre and Its Double*, 70.
32 Velimir Khlebnikov, *Snake Train: Poetry and Prose*, ed. Gary Kern (Ann Arbor: Ardis, 1976), 59.
33 Viktor Shklovsky, "On Poetry and Trans-sense Language," trans. Gerald Janecek and Peter Mayer, *October* 34 (Autumn 1985): 9.
34 Nilsson, "Kruchonykh's Poem 'Dyr bul shchyl,'" 144.
35 Shklovsky, "On Poetry and Trans-sense Language," 20.
36 Roland Barthes, *The Responsibility of Forms: Critical Essays on Music, Art, and Representation* (New York: Hill and Wang, 1985), 269, 280.
37 Ibid., 280.
38 Ibid., 283–4.
39 See Silvija Jestrovic, *Theatre of Estrangement: Theory, Practice, Ideology* (Toronto: University of Toronto Press, 2006), 52–7.
40 Pomorska, *Russian Formalist Theory*, 78.
41 *Words in Revolution: Russian Futurist Manifestoes 1912–1928*, 53–4.
42 See the complete list in Mel Gordon, "Songs from the Museum of Future: Russian Sound Creation (1910–1930)," in *Wireless Imagination: Sound, Radio, and the Avant Garde*, eds. Douglas Kahn and Gregory Whitehead (Cambridge: MIT Press, 1992), 206.
43 Gordon, "Songs from the Museum of Future," 209. The article includes a compiled table of Khlebnikov's universal phonetic/colour alphabet. See 216.
44 John E. Bowlt, ed., *Russian Art of the Avant-Garde: Theory and Criticism, 1902–1934* (New York: Viking Press, 1976), 101.
45 *Words in Revolution: Russian Futurist Manifestoes 1912–1928*, 14.
46 Ibid., 37.
47 Robert Benedetti, "Reconstructing 'Victory over the Sun,'" *The Drama Review* 28, no. 3 (Autumn 1984): 17.
48 Alexei Kruchenykh, *Our Arrival* (Moscow: Archive of Russian Avantgarde , 1995), 66.

49 Charlotte Douglas, "Introduction," in Velimir Khlebnikov, *The King of Time: Selected Writings of the Russian Futurian*, trans. Paul Schmidt, ed. Charlotte Douglas (Cambridge: Harvard University Press, 1985), 4.
50 "Victory over the Sun," trans. Ewa Bartos and Victoria Nes Kirby, *The Drama Review* 15, no. 4 (Autumn 1971): 107–25.
51 *Words in Revolution: Russian Futurist Manifestoes 1912–1928*, 76.
52 Kruchenykh, *Our Arrival* 67.
53 Benedetti, "Reconstructing 'Victory over the Sun,'" 17.
54 Kruchenykh, *Our Arrival*, 67. The actual costumes can be seen at http://www.russianavantgard.com/kazimir_malevich.html#theatre, last accessed 20 January 2012
55 Susan P. Compton, *The World Backwards: Russian Futurist Books 1912–16* (London: British Museum Publications, 1978), 57.
56 K. Tomashevsky, "Victory over the Sun," *The Drama Review* 15, no. 4 (Autumn 1971): 102.
57 Ibid., 103.
58 Quoted in Gerald Janacek, *Zaum: The Transrational Poetry of Russian Futurism* (San Diego State University Press, 1996), 190.
59 Benedikt Livshits, *The One and a Half-Eyed Archer*, trans. John E. Bowlt (Newtonville: Oriental Research Partners, 1976), 164.
60 Paul Schmidt, "Introduction," in Khlebnikov, *Collected Works*, vol. 2, xi.
61 Khlebnikov, *Zangezi* in *Collected Works*, vol. 2, 331. Original in Khlebnikov, *Tvoreniia*, 473.
62 Khlebnikov, *Mrs Laneen* in *The King of Time*, 61–7.
63 Khlebnikov, *The World in Reverse* in *The King of Time*, 68–75.
64 Khlebnikov, *Collected Works*, vol. 2, 338, 341.
65 Ibid., xi.
66 Ibid., 277.
67 Ibid., 345.
68 Roland Barthes, *The Responsibility of Forms: Critical Essays on Music, Art, and Representation* (New York: Hill and Wang, 1985), 270.
69 *Dokhlaya Luna. Stikhi, Proza, Stat'i, Risunki, Oforty* [Croaked Moon: Verse, Prose, Essays, Drawings, Etchings] (Moscow: Pervyi Zhurnal Russkikh Futuristov), 1914. Quoted in Zbigniew Folejewski, *Futurism and Its Place in the Development of Modern Poetry: A Comparative Study and Anthology* (Ottawa: University of Ottawa Press, 1980), 76.
70 Barthes, *The Responsibility of Forms*, 269.
71 *Khlysty*, a commonly accepted name of an underground church sect of Russian Spiritual Christians active from the late seventeenth century, is a corrupted version of *Khristy*, meaning The Christ's Ones. Thus, the attribution of their devotion has been turned into the denunciation of their flagellant prac-

tice: the word *khlyst* means a whip. It resulted in the prosecution of their rituals, which would often end in sexual orgies. Their connecting of body and soul, stemming from Russian paganism, made glossolalia, as an irrational and spontaneous sound creation, even more attractive to the Futurists.

72 Quoted in Gerald Janacek, *Zaum: The Transrational Poetry of Russian Futurism* (San Diego: State University Press, 1996), 301.

73 "Destruction of Syntax – Wireless Imagination – Words in Freedom" in Richard J. Pioli. *Stung by Salt and War: Creative Texts of the Italian Avant-Gardist F.T. Marinetti* (New York: Farrar, 1972), 47.

74 Ibid., 75.

75 Antonin Artaud, *Selected Writings*, ed. Susan Sontag, trans. Helen Weaver (New York: Farrar, Straus and Giroux, 1976), 110.

76 *Russian Art of the Avant-Garde: Theory and Criticism*, 130, 133–4.

77 Ibid., 129.

78 Kazimir Malevich, *Essays on Art*, ed. Troels Andersen (Copenhagen: Borgen, 1968), vol. 1, 73.

79 Artaud, *The Theatre and Its Double*, 110.

80 Ibid., 287, 124.

81 Helga Finter, "Experimental Theatre and Semiology of Theatre: The Theatricalization of Voice," *Modern Drama* 26, no. 4 (1983): 501.

82 Ibid., 504.

CHAPTER FIVE

1 Günter Berghaus, *Italian Futurist Theatre, 1900–1944* (New York: Clarendon Press, 1997), 235.

2 Berghaus, *Italian Futurist Theatre*, 236.

3 Quoted in Lista, *La scène futuriste*, 132.

4 Ibid., 132.

5 Francesco Cangiullo, *Piedigrotta, parole in libertà* (Milano: Edizioni futuriste di "Poesia"), 1916.

6 Apollonio, *Futurist Manifestos*, 144.

7 Danela Fonti, "Depero 'mimismagico' (mimica, declamazione, teatro cabaret, marionette) e motorumorismo," *Depero: Dal Futurismo alla Casa d'Arte*, Il catalogo (Milano: Ed. Charta e MART, 1994), 61.

8 Lista, *Le Théâtre Futuriste Italien*, vol. 1, 49. Lista made "la transposition phonétique" from a facsimile while in my quote, his French spelling is replaced by the Italian found at http://www.paoloalbani.it/BiblioNazionale.html. Audio available at http://ubu.artmob.ca/sound/balla_giacomo/Balla-Giacomo_Discussione.mp3, last accessed 27 May 2010.

9 www.ubu.com/sound/balla.html, last accessed 27 May 2010.

10 Luigi Russolo, *The Art of Noises* (New York: Pendragon Press, 1986), 23.
11 Russolo, *The Art of Noises*, 23.
12 Connor, *Emotion in Postmodernism*, 156.
13 Russolo, *The Art of Noises*, 27.
14 *Marinetti: Selected Writings*, 87.
15 Russolo, *The Art of Noises*, 23.
16 Michael Kirby, *Futurist Performance* (New York: PAJ, 1986), 33.
17 Russolo, *The Art of Noises*, 57.
18 Ibid., 28.
19 Ibid., 87.
20 John J. White, *Literary Futurism: Aspects of the First Avant-Garde* (Oxford: Clarendon Press, 1990), 344.
21 Russolo, *The Art of Noises*, 60.
22 Wassily Kandinsky, *Complete Writings on Art*, eds Kenneth C. Lindsay and Peter Vergo (Boston: G.K. Hall & Co., 1982), 261.
23 Russolo, *The Art of Noises*, 32. For a detailed description and analysis see Hugh Davies, "The Sound World, Instruments and Music of Luigi Russolo: The Expanding Medium," *Lmc*, 2, no. 2 (1994) at http://creativegames.org.uk/modules/Art_Technology/theory/authors/hugh_davies.htm, last accessed 29 January 2012.
24 An article in *L'Hérault Beliers*, October 1913, quoted in Russolo, *The Art of Noises*, 18.
25 Marinetti's letter to Pratella quoted in Lista, *La scène futuriste*, 78.
26 See Stephen D. Press, *Prokofiev's Ballets for Diaghilev* (Burlington: Ashgate, 2006), 207–8.
27 Russolo, *The Art of Noises*, 29.
28 Quoted in Hugh Davies, "The Sound World, Instruments and Music of Luigi Russolo: The Expanding Medium," *Lmc* 2, no. 2 (1994) at http://creative games.org.uk/modules/Art_Technology/theory/authors/hugh_davies.htm, last accessed 29 January 2012.
29 See Francesco Cangiullo, *Le serate futuriste: romanzo storico vissuto* (Milano: Ceschina, 1961), 87.
30 Russolo, *The Art of Noises*, 26.
31 Ibid., 5.
32 *Weekend* (Ein Film ohne Bilder/Film without pictures) Regie: Walter Ruttmann. Premiere: 15 Mai 1930 (Berlin/Haus des Rundfunks) – Radio Sendung "Hörspiele auf Tonfilmen" am 13 Juni 1930. Available on Youtube at www.youtube.com/watch?v=O34DaUfmjI4&NR=1, last accessed 31 May 2010.
33 Alan Licht, *Sound Art: Beyond Music, between Categories* (New York: Rizzoli International Publications, 2007), 36.

34 *Koyaanisqatsi* (Life out of Balance) has two sequels *Powaqqatsi* (Life in Transformation) and *Naqoyqatsi* (Life as War). It has been released on DVD by MGM in 2002. Its trailer can be seen at www.youtube.com/watch?v=PirH8PADDgQ, last accessed 20 January 2012. Note the fragment between 1:35 and 1:42: it makes you recognize a recent event and think about the fact that art knows more about life than history does.

35 See Reggio's interview at www.koyaanisqatsi.org, last accessed 4 June 2010.

36 Eric Salzman and Thomas Desi, *The New Music Theater: Seeing the Voice, Hearing the Body* (New York: Oxford University Press, 2008), 5.

37 Mel Gordon, "Songs from the Museum of the Future: Russian Sound Creation (1910–1930)," in *Wireless Imagination: Sound, Radio, and the Avant-Garde*, eds Douglas Kahn and Gregory Whitehead (Cambridge: MIT Press, 1992), 223.

38 Erik Levi, "Futurist Influences upon Early Twentieth-century Music," in *International Futurism in Arts and Literature*, ed. Günter Berghaus (Berlin and New York: Walter de Gruyter, 2000), 338.

39 See http://www.pasdacier.co.uk/project.htm, last accessed 10 May 2012.

40 Quoted in Levi, "Futurist Influences," 339.

41 Carol Oja, "George Antheil's Ballet Mécanique and Transatlantic Modernism," in *A Modern Mosaic: Art and Modernism in the United States*, ed. Townsend Ludington (Chapel Hill: University of North Carolina Press, 2000), 185.

42 Christopher Schiff, "Banging on the Windowpane: Sound in Early Surrealism," in *Wireless Imagination: Sound, Radio and the Avant-Garde*, eds Douglas Kahn and Gregory Whitehead (Cambridge: MIT Press, 1992), 140.

43 Schiff, "Banging on the Windowpane," 151.

44 Richter, *Dada: Art and Anti-Art*, 33.

45 Erickson, *Dada: Performance, Poetry, and Art*, 76.

46 Mel Gordon, *Dada Performance*, 55.

47 Seth Kim-Cohen, *In the Blink of an Ear: Toward a Non-Cochlear Sonic Art* (New York and London: Continuum, 2009), 9.

48 Torben Sangild, *The Aesthetics of Noise* (DATANOM/UBUWEB, 2002), 9, www.ubu.com/papers/noise.html, last accessed 29 May 2010.

49 Levi, "Futurist Influences," 351.

50 Ibid., 352.

51 John Cage, *Silence: Lectures and Writings* (Middletown: Wesleyan University Press, 1961), 2.

52 Levi, "Futurist Influences," 412.

53 F.T. Marinetti and Pino Mansata, "La Radia," in *Wireless Imagination: Sound, Radio, and the Avant-Garde*, eds Douglas Kahn and George Whitehead (Cambridge: MIT Press, 1992), 265.

54 F.T. Marinetti, *Critical Writings*, ed. Günter Berghaus (New York: Farrar, 2006), 413.
55 Kim-Cohen, *In the Blink of an Ear*, 13.
56 Klaus Schöning, "The Contours of Acoustic Art," *Theatre Journal* 43, no. 3, Radio Drama (October 1991): 312.
57 *Wireless Imagination*, 266.
58 Steven Connor, "The Modern Auditory I," in *Rewriting the Self: Histories from the Renaissance to the Present*, ed. Roy Porter (London: Routledge, 1997).
59 *Le Théâtre Futuriste Italien*, vol. 2, 57.
60 Rudolf Arnheim, *Radio: The Art of Sound*, trans. Herbert Read (London: Faber & Faber, 1936), 14.
61 Ibid., 15.
62 Ibid., 195.
63 Marinetti, *Critical Writings*, 413.
64 Arnheim, *Radio*, 29.
65 Salomé Voeglin, *Listening to Noise and Silence: Towards a Philosophy of Sound Art* (New York and London: Continuum, 2010), 201.
66 See *Le Théâtre Futuriste Italien*, vol. 2, 55–7. Two are published in Kirby, *Futurist Performance*, 292–3.
67 Kirby, *Futurist Performance*, 292.
68 Arnheim, *Radio*, 196.
69 Kirby, *Futurist Performance*, 144.
70 Marcel Duchamp, *Notes*, arr. and trans. Paul Matisse (Boston: GK Hall and Co.,1983), n. 183.
71 Kim-Cohen, *In the Blink of an Ear*, 161.
72 Ibid., 163.
73 Marjorie Perloff, "The Music of Verbal Space: John Cage's 'What you Say …'" in *Sound States: Innovative Poetics and Acoustical Technologies*, ed. Adelaide Morris (Chapel Hill, London: University of North Carolina Press, 1997), 129.
74 Ibid., 131.
75 "36 Mesostics Re and not Re Duchamp," in John Cage, *M: Writings, '67–'72* (Middletown: Wesleyan University Press, 1973), 27.
76 Marjorie Perloff, *Poetry On & Off the Page: Essays for Emergent Occasions* (Evanston: Northwestern University Press, 1998), 294.

CHAPTER SIX

1 Giovanni Lista, ed., *Le Théâtre Futuriste Italien, anthologie critique* (Lausanne: L'Age d'Homme, 1976), vol. 1, 178.
2 Walter Benjamin, "On the Mimetic Faculty," *Reflections: Essays, Aphorisms,*

Autobiographical Writing, ed. Peter Demetz (New York: Schocken Books, 1986), 335.

3 Jacques Derrida, *Writing and Difference*, trans. Alan Bass (Chicago: University of Chicago Press, 1978), 191.

4 Artaud, *The Theatre and Its Double*, 108, 119, 124.

5 Benedikt Livshits, *The One and a Half-Eyed Archer*, trans. John E. Bowlt (Newtonville: Oriental Research Partners, 1976), 191.

6 *Marinetti*: *Selected Writings*, 85.

7 Giovanni Lista, *La Scène Futuriste* (Paris: Editions du Centre de la recherche scientifique, 1989), 10.

8 See Günter Berghaus, "A Theatre of Image, Sound and Motion: On Synaesthesia and the Idea of Total Work of Art," *Maske und Kothurn* 32, no. 2 (Universität Wien: Institut für Theaterwissenschaft, 1986): 7–28.

9 Robert Motherwell, ed., *The Dada Painters and Poets: An Anthology* (Cambridge: Harvard University Press, 1981), 25.

10 Hugo Ball, *Flight out of Time: A Dada Diary*, 56.

11 *Blago Bung Blago Bung Bosso Fataka: First Texts of German Dada*, ed. Malcolm Green (London: Atlas Press, 1995), 55.

12 Motherwell, *The Dada Painters and Poets*, 26.

13 Raoul Hausmann, "Poeme phonétique," *Courrier Dada* (Paris: Le Terrain Vague, 1958), 59.

14 Raoul Hausmann, "Poeme phonétique" in *Courrier Dada*, édition établie par Marc Dachy (Paris: Éditions Allia, 2004), 57. My illustration emulates the poem's typeset found at http://www.artpool.hu/Poetry/soundimage/Hausmann.html, last accessed 8 November 2011.

15 Hausmann, *Courrier Dada*, 1958, 60.

16 Ibid., 59. Poems are available for listening at www.ubu.com/sound/hausmann.html, last accessed 8 June 2010.

17 Magazine *Merz*, no.13, 1925, included a *Merz-Grammophon-platte*, a recording of Schwitters reciting his *Scherzo der Ursonate*. A later recording, a result of his cooperation with the Suddeutscher Rundfunk Stuttgart in 1932, is preserved in the German Radio Archive in Frankfurt/Main. Fragments of *Ursonate*, published by WERGO, Mainz are also available at www.ubu.com/sound/schwitters.html, last accessed 10 June 2010. In 1958 Lords Gallery, London, produced a record that, together with a selection from *Ursonate*, includes Schwitters's recitation of *An Anna Blume*.

18 Hausmann, *Courrier Dada*, 1958, 116.

19 Kurt Schwitters, *PPPPPP: Poems, Performances, Pieces, Proses, Plays, Poetics*, Jerome Rothenberg and Pierre Joris, eds. (Philadelphia: Temple University Press, 1993), xxi.

20 Motherwell, *The Dada Painters and Poets*, xxviii.

21 Klaus Schöning, "The Contours of Acoustic Art," *Theatre Journal* 43, no. 3 (Radio Drama, Oct., 1991): 311.
22 Motherwell, *The Dada Painters and Poets*, xxix. See Appendix, Figure 20 (and 20a).
23 Schwitters, *PPPPPP*, 236.
24 Motherwell, *The Dada Painters and Poets*, xxix.
25 Hans Richter, *Dada Art and Anti-Art*, trans. David Britt (London: Thames and Hudson, 1965), 152.
26 Schwitters, *PPPPPP*, 218.
27 John D. Erickson, *Dada: Performance, Poetry, and Art* (Boston: Twayne, 1984), 98.
28 Schwitters, *PPPPPP*, 218.
29 Mel Gordon, *Dada Performance*, 100.
30 Ibid., 100.
31 Mel Gordon, *Expressionist Texts* (New York: Performing Arts Books, 1986), 18.
32 Ibid., 210.
33 Kuhns, *German Expressionist Theatre*, 153.
34 Kuhns, *German Expressionist Theatre*, 156.
35 Ibid., 154.
36 Quoted in Kuhns, *German Expressionist Theatre*, 166.
37 Quoted in Gordon, *Expressionist Texts*, 18.
38 Melissa Trimingham, *The Theatre of the Bauhaus: The Modern and Postmodern Stage of Oskar Schlemmer* (New York and London: Routledge, 2011), 129.
39 Ibid., 136
40 Kuhns, *German Expressionist Theatre*, 57.
41 Walter Gropius, ed., *The Theatre of the Bauhaus*, trans. Arthur S. Wensinger (Baltimore: Johns Hopkins University Press, 1996), 9.
42 Apollonio, *Futurist Manifestos*, 195.
43 Quoted in Günter Berghaus, *Italian Futurist Theatre, 1909–1944* (New York: Clarendon Press, 1997), 178.
44 See Lista, *La Scène Futuriste*, 196.
45 *Le Théâtre Futuriste Italien*, vol. 2, 97.
46 Michael Kirby, *Futurist Performance* (New York: Dutton, 1971), 232.
47 *Le Théâtre Futuriste Italien*, vol. 2, 51. Originally in *Il teatro futurista sintetico*, a supplement to *Gli avvenimenti*, vol. 2, no. 15 (2–9 April 1916), Milano. My translation.
48 *Le Théâtre Futuriste Italien*, vol. 2, 52. Kirby, Futrist Performance, 256–7.
49 Lehmann, *Postdramatic Theatre*, 35, 68.
50 "Marinetti's Short Plays," trans. V.N. Kirby, *The Drama Review* 17, no. 4 (December 1973) 124.
51 Ibid., 118–9. Also in *Il teatro futurista sintetico creato da Marinetti, Settimelli, Bruno Corra* (Piacenza: Ghelfi Costatino, 1921), 24–6.

52 Apollonio, *Futurist Manifestos*, 114.
53 Ibid., 118.
54 Lista, *La Scène Futuriste*, 206.
55 Kirby, *Futurist Performance*, 278.
56 Daniela Fonti, "Depero 'mimismagico' (mimica, declamazione, teatro cabaret, marionette) e motorumorismo," in *Depero: Dal Futurismo alla Casa d'Arte* (Milano: Ed. Charta e MART, 1994), 63.
57 See http://www.wassilykandinsky.net/pictures.php, last accessed 20 January 2012.
58 A video animation of Depero's *Colori* by Gabriele Marino from 2009 is available at http://www.youtube.com/watch?v=ict51WbO3AI, last accessed 20 January 2012.
59 Pontus Hulten, *Futurism and Futurisms* (London: Thames and Hudson, 1992), 548.
60 Apollonio, *Futurist Manifestos*, 199.
61 Ibid., 197.
62 Kirby, *Futurist Performance*, 230.
63 See http://www.google.ca/search?q=balli+plastici+depero&hl=en&prmd=imvns&tbm=isch&tbo=u&source=univ&sa=X&ei=CXoxT_DEIanhogGyiOnIBw&ved=0CDcQsAQ&biw=1165&bih=750, last accessed 20 January 2012.
64 Berghaus, *Italian Futurist Theatre*, 313.
65 Kirby, *Futurist Performance*, 203.
66 Quoted in Günter Berghaus, "A Theatre of Image, Sound and Motion: On Synaesthesia and the Idea of Total Work of Art," *Maske und Kothurn* 32, no. 2 (1986): 24.
67 Ibid., 24.
68 Enrico Prampolini, *L'impero*, 11 July 1923.
69 Berghaus, "A Theatre of Image, Sound and Motion," 14.
70 Filiberto Menna, *Prampolini* (Rome: De Luca Editore, 1967), 111.
71 Ibid., 111.
72 *Le Théâtre Futurist Italien*, vol. 2, 120.
73 Ibid., 118.
74 Marinetti, "The Abstract Psychological Theatre of Pure Elements and Tactile Theatre," 1924, in *Critical Writings*, 391.

CHAPTER SEVEN

1 Patrice Pavis, *Analyzing Performance*, trans. David Williams (Ann Arbor: University of Michigan Press, 2003), 207.
2 Patrice Pavis, *Languages of the Stage: Essays in the Semiology of the Theatre* (New York: PAJ, 1982), 186.

3 Laszlo Moholy-Nagy, "Theatre, Circus, Variety," in Oskar Schlemmer, *The Theatre of the Bauhaus* (Baltimore: Johns Hopkins University Press, 1996), 52.
4 Ibid., 52.
5 Richard Kostelanetz, *On Innovative Performance(s): Three Decades of Recollections of Alternative Theatre* (Jefferson: McFarland & Co., 1994), 8.
6 Ibid., 73.
7 Judith Malina, "Directing *The Brig*," in *The Brig*, Kenneth H. Brown (New York: Hill and Wang, 1965), 106.
8 Charles Bernstein, ed., *Close Listening: Poetry and the Performed Word* (New York and Oxford: Oxford University Press, 1998), 13.
9 Martin Welton, "Seeing Nothing: Now Hear This …" in *The Senses in Performance*, eds Sally Barnes and André Lepecki (New York: Routledge, 2007), 146–55.
10 Emily Greenwood, "Sounding Out Homer: Christopher Logue's Acoustic Homer," http://journal.oraltradition.org/files/articles/24ii/14_24.2.pdf, last accessed 20 May 2010.
11 Welton, "Seeing Nothing," 154.
12 Lyn Gardner, "The Watery Part of the World," *The Guardian*, 28 June 2003.
13 Quoted in Fischer-Lichte, 128.
14 See www.ubu.com/ubu/wilson_opera.html, last accessed 10 September 2010.
15 The audio recording of the scene is available at www.ubu.com/sound/big_ego.html, last accessed 20 July 2010.
16 Bonnie Maranka, *Theatre of Images* (New York: Drama Book Specialists, 1977), 43–4.
17 Arthur Holmberg, *The Theatre of Robert Wilson* (New York: Cambridge University Press, 1996), 45.
18 Quoted in Holmberg, *The Theatre of Robert Wilson*, 45.
19 Maria Nadotti, "Teatro d'artista: Conversazione de Robert Wilson," *Teatro in Europa*, no. 7, 1990. Quoted in Miguel Morey and Carmen Prado, *Robert Wilson* (Barcelona: Ediciones Poligrafa, 2003), 31.
20 Caryl Churchill, *Plays, 3*, introduced by the author (London: Nick Hern Books, 1998), 2.
21 Julia Kristeva, *Revolution in Poetic Language*, trans. Margaret Waller (New York: Columbia University Press, 1984), 34.
22 Adriana Cavarero, *For More Than One Voice: Toward a Philosophy of Vocal Expression*, trans. Paul Kottman (Stanford: Stanford University Press, 2005), 148.
23 See http://theatrenotes.blogspot.com/2006/09/skriker.html, last accessed 20 July 2010.
24 Peter Brook, *Empty Space* (London: MacGibbon & Kee, 1968), 49.
25 A.C.H. Smith, *Orghast at Persepolis* (London: Methuen, 1972), 46.

26 Ibid., 42.
27 Ibid.,172, 179.
28 Quoted in Smith, *Orghast*, 45.
29 Ibid., 120.
30 Brunella Eruli, "The Space of Emotions," at http://www.dramforum.com/?articleid=32, last accessed 16 May 2008.
31 Tadeusz Kantor, *A Journey through Other Spaces: Essays and Manifestos, 1944–1990*, ed. Michal Kobialka (Berkeley: University of California Press, 1993), 54.
32 Ibid., 51, 54.
33 Eric Salzman and Thomas Desi, *The New Music Theater: Seeing the Voice, Hearing the Body* (New York: Oxford University Press, 2008), 5.
34 After the revolutionary May of 1968, Marthaler, a Swiss teenager trained as an oboist and a flutist, left for Paris, where he learned the principles of the École Jacques Lecoq: *le jeu* (playfulness), *complicité* (togetherness), and *disponsibilité* (openness).
35 Benedict Andrews, "Christoph Marthaler: In the Meantime," http://www.realtimearts.net/article/issue76/8246, last accessed 20 January 2012.
36 See www.festwochen.at/index.php?id=eventdetail&detail=412 and www.teatrofestivalitalia.it/Napoli_Teatro_Festival_Italia_Programme_Riesenbutzbach_Eine_Dauerkolonie-1014.1091.7.html?v=1&y=2009, last accessed 12 September 2010.
37 Lehmann, "Word and Stage in Postdramatic Theatre," in *Drama and/after Postmodernism*, 37.
38 See http://nobelprize.org/nobel_prizes/literature/laureates/2004, last accessed 10 June 2010.
39 Karen Jürs-Munby, "The Resistant Text in Postdramatic Theatre: Performing Elfriede Jelinek's *Sprachflächen*," *Performance Research: A Journal of the Performing Arts* 14, issue 1 (2009): 49.
40 Quoted in David Roesner, *Theater als Musik* (Tübingen: Narr, 2003), 197; translated in Jürs-Munby, "The Resistant Text," 51.
41 Roesner, *Theater als Musik*, 197; translated in Jürs-Munby, "The Resistant Text," 51.
42 Fischer-Lichte, *The Transformative Power of Performance*, 129.
43 See the company's website, www.zthollandia.nl, last accessed 20 July 2010.
44 Ibid.
45 Henk Oosterling, "Hypocritical Theatre: Hollandia's Intermedial Multiverse," *Performance Research 'Navigations,'* eds Ric Allsopp & David Williams 6, no. 3 (Winter 2001) at http://www2.eur.nl/fw/cfk/PDF/HO/art.hollandia.pdf.

46 Claudia Castelucci, Romeo Castelucci, Chiara Guidi, Joe Kelleher, and Nicholas Ridout, *The Theatre of Socìetas Raffaello Sanzio* (New York and London: Routledge, 2007), 25.
47 Ibid., 84.
48 Ibid., 85.
49 Timothy Scheie, "Voyage au Bout de la Nuit," *Theatre Journal* 52, no.1 (March 2000): 128–9.
50 Helga Finter, "Mime de voix, mime de corps: L'intervocalité sur scène," in *Théâtre: espace sonore, espace visual/Theater: Sound Space, Visual Space*, eds Christine Hamon-Siréjol and Anne Surgers (Lyon: Presses Universitaires de Lyon & FIRT/IFRT, 2003), 71.
51 Alan Licht, *Sound Art: Beyond Music, between Categories* (New York: Rizzoli International Publications, 2007), 43. Also in Chris Salter, *Entangled: Technology and the Transformation of Performance* (Cambridge: The MIT Press, 2010) 188–91.
52 Laurence Shyer, *Robert Wilson and His Collaborators* (New York: Theatre Communication Group, 1989), 235.
53 Ibid., 326.
54 Lehmann, *Postdramatic Theatre*, 156.
55 Quoted in Elinor Fuchs, *The Death of Character* (Bloomington and Indianapolis: Indiana University Press, 1996), 93.
56 Artaud, *The Theatre and Its Double*, 125.
57 Ibid., 90.
58 Lehmann, *Postdramatic Theatre*, 148.
59 Helga Finter, "Experimental Theatre and Semiology of Theatre: The Theatricalization of Voice," *Modern Drama* 26 (1983): 504
60 Quoted in Gérard Conio, "Les sonorités de Kandinsky et la synthese des arts," *L'Avant garde russe et la synthese des arts* (Lausanne: L'Age d'homme, 1990), 110.
61 See www.ubu.com/ubu/wilson_opera.html, last accessed 17 January 2011.

EPILOGUE

1 Lehmann, *Postdramatic Theatre*, 148.
2 Ibid., 148.
3 Lehmann, "Word and Stage in Postdramatic Theatre," in *Drama and/after Postmodernism*, 47–8.
4 Ibid.

Bibliography

Allain, Paul and Jen Harvie, eds. *The Routledge Companion to Theatre and Performance*. London and New York: Routledge, 2006.

Alström, Torbjörn. "The Voice in the Mask." *The Drama Review* 48, no. 2 (2004): 133–5.

Andrews, Benedict. "Christoph Marthaler: In the Meantime." http://www.realtimearts.net/article/issue76/8246. Last accessed 20 January 2012.

Apollonio, Umbro, ed. *Futurist Manifestos*. London: Thames and Hudson, 1973.

Aristotle. *Metaphysics*. Translated by John Warrington. London: Dent, 1956.

Arndt, Walter. Forward to *Songs from the Gallows* by Christian Morgenstern. New Haven: Yale University Press, 1993.

Arnheim, Rudolf. *Radio: The Art of Sound*. Translated by Herbert Read. London: Faber & Faber, 1936.

Artaud, Antonin. *Collected Works*. Translated by Victor Corti. London: Calder and Boyars, 1968.

– *Selected Writings*. Edited by Susan Sontag, translated by Helen Weaver. New York: Farrar, Straus and Giroux, 1976.

– *The Theatre and Its Double*. Translated by Mary Caroline Richards. New York: Grove Press, 1958.

Attali, Jacques. *Noise: The Political Economy of Music*. Minneapolis: University of Minnesota Press, 1985.

Bahn, Willard ed. *Italian Futurist Poetry*. Toronto: University of Toronto Press, 2005.

Ball, Hugo. *Flight out of Time: A Dada Diary*. Edited and translated by John Elderfield. Berkeley: University of California Press, 1996.

Barba, Eugenio. "The Deep Order Called Turbulence: The Three Faces of Dramaturgy." *The Drama Review* 44, no. 4 (Winter 2000): 56–66.

– "The Nature of Dramaturgy: Describing Actions at Work." *New Theatre Quarterly* 1 (1985): 75–8.

Barden, Garett. "Method in Philosophy." In *The New Bergson*, edited by John Mullarkey, 32–41. New York: Manchester University Press, 1999.

Barooshian, Vahan D. *Russian Cubo-Futurism 1910–1930: A Study in Avant-Gardism*. The Hague and Paris: Mouton, 1974.

Barthes, Roland. *The Responsibility of Forms: Critical Essays on Music, Art, and Representation*. Translated by Richard Howard. New York: Hill and Wang, 1985.

Bean, Robert. "Polyphonic Aurality and John Cage." In *Aural Cultures*, edited by Jim Drobnick, 127–49. Toronto: YYZ Books, 1994.

Bely, Andrey. "The Magic of Words." *Selected Essays of Andrey Bely*, edited and translated by Steven Cassedy, 93–111. Berkeley: University of California Press, 1985.

Benedetti, Robert. "Reconstructing 'Victory over the Sun.'" *The Drama Review* 28, no. 3 (Autumn 1984): 17–30.

Benjamin, Walter. "On the Mimetic Faculty." In *Reflections: Essays, Aphorisms, Autobiographical Writing*, edited by Peter Demetz, 333–6. New York: Schocken Books, 1986.

Berghaus, Günter. *Avant-Garde Performance: Live Events and Electronic Technologies*. New York: Palgrave Macmillan, 2005.

– "A Theatre of Image, Sound and Motion: On Synaesthesia and the Idea of Total Work of Art." *Maske und Kothurn* 32, no. 2 (1986): 7–28.

– "Dada Theatre or the Genesis of Anti-bourgeois Performance Art." *German Life and Letters* 38, no. 4 (1985): 293–312.

– *Italian Futurist Theatre, 1900–1944*. New York: Clarendon Press, 1997.

Bernstein, Charles, ed. *Close Listening: Poetry and the Performed Word*. New York and Oxford: Oxford University Press, 1998.

Bertini, Simona. *Marinetti e le 'eroiche serate'* (con antologia di testi). Novara: Interlinea edizioni, 2002.

Blago Bung Blago Bung Bosso Fataka: First Texts of German Dada. Translated by Malcolm Green. London: Atlas Press, 1995.

Blum, Cinzia Sartini. *The Other Modernism: F.T. Marinetti's Futurist Fiction of Power*. Los Angeles: University of California Press, 1996.

Bowlt, John E., ed. *Russian Art of the Avant-Garde: Theory and Criticism, 1902–1934*. New York: Viking Press, 1976.

Brook, Peter. *Empty Space*. London: MacGibbon & Kee, 1968.

Brown, Ross. *Sound: A Reader in Theatre Practice*. London: Palgrave MacMillan, 2010.

Burrows, David. *Sound, Speech, Music*. Amherst: University of Massachusetts Press, 1990.

Cage, John. *Silence: Lectures and Writings*. Middletown: Wesleyan University Press, 1961.

Calinescu, Matei. *Five Faces of Modernity: Modernism, Avant-Garde, Decadence, Kitsch, Postmodernism*. Durham: Duke University Press, 1987.

Cangiullo, Francesco. *Le serate futuriste: romanzo storico vissuto*. Milano: Ceschina, 1961.

Castelucci, Claudia, Romeo Castelucci, Chiara Guidi, Joe Kelleher, and Nicholas Ridout. *The Theatre of Socìetas Raffaello Sanzio*. New York and London: Routledge, 2007.

Cavarero, Adriana. *For More Than One Voice: Toward a Philosophy of Vocal Expression*. Translated by Paul Kottman. Stanford: Stanford University Press, 2005.

Chapman, Raymond. *The Treatment of Sounds in Language and Literature*. Oxford: Blackwell and Deutsch, 1984.

Compton, Susan P. *The World Backwards: Russian Futurist Books 1912–16*. London: British Museum Publications, 1978.

Conio, Gérard. "Les sonorités de Kandinsky et la synthese des arts." In *L'Avant garde russe et la synthese des arts*, edited by Gérard Conio, 106–12. Lausanne: L'Age d'homme, 1990.

Connor, Steven. "Feel the Noise: Excess, Affect and the Acoustic." In *Emotion in Postmodernism*, edited by Gerhard Hoffman and Alfred Hornung, 147–63. Heidelberg: Universitätsverlag C. Winter, 1997.

– "The Modern Auditory I." In *Rewriting the Self: Histories from the Renaissance to the Present*, edited by Roy Porter, 203–24. London: Routledge, 1997.

– "The Strains of the Voice," www.bbk.ac.uk/english/skc/strains. Last accessed 21 July 2012.

Churchill, Caryl. *Skriker*. In *Plays, 3*, introduced by the author. London: Nick Hern Books, 1998.

Davies, Hugh. "The Sound World, Instruments and Music of Luigi Russolo: The Expanding Medium." *Resonance* 2, no. 2 (Summer 1994) at http://creative games.org.uk/modules/Art_Technology/theory/authors/hugh_davies.htm. Last accessed 18 January 2012.

Derrida, Jacques. *Writing and Difference*. Translated by Alan Bass. Chicago: University of Chicago Press, 1978.

Descartes, René. *Discourse on Method, Optics, Geometry, and Meteorology*. Translated by Paul J. Olscamp. Indianapolis: Bobbs-Merrill, 1965.

D'Harnoncourt, Anne. *Futurism and the International Avant-Garde*. Philadelphia: Philadelphia Museum of Art, 1980.

Di Bello, Patrizia and Gabriel Koureas, eds. *Art, History and the Senses*. Surrey and Burlington: Ashgate, 2010.

Di Benedetto, Stephen. *The Provocation of the Senses in Contemporary Theatre*. New York and London: Routledge, 2010.

Dixon, Steve. *Futurism e-visited*. http://people.brunel.ac.uk/bst/3no2/Papers/Steve%20Dixon.htm. Last accessed 20 August 2011.

Drobnick, Jim, ed. *Aural Cultures*. Toronto: YYZ Books, 1994.

Erickson, John D. *Dada: Performance, Poetry, and Art*. Boston: Twayne, 1984.

Erickson, Jon. "The Language of Presence: Sound Poetry and Artaud." *boundary 2* 14, no. 1/2 (Autumn 1985–Winter 1986): 279–90.

Erlmann, Veit, ed. *Hearing Cultures: Essays on Sound, Listening and Modernity*. Oxford and New York: Berg, 2004.

Eruli, Brunella. "The Space of Emotions." http://www.dramforum.com/?articleid=32. Last accessed 16 May 2006.

Federman, Raymond. "The Language of Dada: Intermedia of Words." *Dada/Surrealism* 2 (1972): 19–22.

Fédida, Pierre. *Le Corps, le texte et la scène*. Paris: Delarge, 1983.

Finter, Helga. "Experimental Theatre and Semiology of Theatre: The Theatricalization of Voice." *Modern Drama* 26, no. 4 (1983): 501–17.

– "Mime de voix, mime de corps: L'intervocalité sur scène." In *Théâtre: espace sonore, espace visual / Theater: sound space, visual space*, edited by Christine Hamon-Siréjol and Anne Surgers, 71–89. Lyon: Presses Universitaires de Lyon & FIRT/IFRT, 2003.

Fischer-Lichte, Erika. "The Avant-garde and the Semiotics of the Antitextual Theatre." In *Contours of the Theatrical Avant-garde*, edited by James M. Harding, 79–96. Ann Arbor: University of Michigan Press, 2000.

– *The Transformative Power of Performance: A New Aesthetics*. Translated by Saskya Iris Jain. London and New York: Routledge, 2008.

Flam, Jack and Miriam Deutch, eds. *Primitivism and Twentieth-Century Art: A Documentary History*. Berkeley: University of California Press, 2003.

Folejewski, Zbigniew. *Futurism and Its Place in the Development of Modern Poetry: A Comparative Study and Anthology*. Ottawa: University of Ottawa Press, 1980.

Fonti, Daniela. "Depero 'mimismagico' (mimica, declamazione, teatro cabaret, marionette) e motorumorismo." In *Depero: Dal Futurismo alla Casa d'Arte*, Il catalogo. Milano: Ed. Charta e MART, 1994.

Fuchs, Elinor. *The Death of Character*. Bloomington and Indianapolis: Indiana University Press, 1996.

Gardner, Lyn. "The Watery Part of the World." *The Guardian*, 28 June 2003.

Goldberg, Rose Lee. *Performance Art. From Futurism to the Present*. London: Thames and Hudson. 1988.

Goldwater, Robert. *Primitivisim in Modern Art*. New York: Vintage Books, 1967.

Gordon, Mel, ed. *Dada Performance*. New York: PAJ Publications, 1987.

– ed. *Expressionist Texts*. New York: Performing Arts Books, 1986.

– "Songs from the Museum of the Future: Russian Sound Creation 1910–1930." In *Wireless Imagination: Sound, Radio, and the Avant-Garde*, edited by Douglas Kahn and Gregory Whitehead, 197–245. Cambridge: MIT Press, 1992.

Gordon, R.S. "The Italian Futurist Theatre: A Reappraisal." *Modern Language Revue* (London), 85, no. 2 (1990): 349–61.

Greenwood, Emily. "Sounding Out Homer: Christopher Logue's Acoustic Homer." http://journal.oraltradition.org/files/articles/24ii/14_24.2.pdf. Last accessed 20 May 2010.

Hausmann, Raoul. *Courrier Dada*, édition établie par Marc Dachy. Paris: Éditions Allia, 2004.

Helmholtz, Hermann von. *On the Sensations of Tone as a Physiological Basis for the Theory of Music*. Translated by Alexander J. Ellis. New York: Dover Publications, 1954.

Holmberg, Arthur. *The Theatre of Robert Wilson*. New York: Cambridge University Press, 1996.

Hulten, Pontus. *Futurism and Futurisms*. London: Thames and Hudson, 1992.

Ihde, Don. *Listening and Voice: A Phenomenology of Sound*. Athens, Ohio: Ohio University Press, 1976.

– *Sense and Significance*. Pittsburgh: Duquesne University Press, 1973.

Innes, Christopher. *Avant Garde Theatre, 1892–1992*. London: Routledge, 1966.

– "In the Beginning Was the Word: Text versus Performance." In *The Performance Text*, edited by Domenico Pietropaolo, 9–19. Ottawa: Legas, 1997.

Janacek, Gerald. *Zaum: The Transrational Poetry of Russian Futurism*. San Diego: San Diego State University Press, 1996.

Jestrovic, Silvija. *Theatre of Estrangement: Theory, Practice, Ideology*. Toronto: University of Toronto Press, 2006.

Jürs-Munby, Karen. "The Resistant Text in Postdramatic Theatre: Performing Elfriede Jelinek's *Sprachflächen*." *Performance Research: A Journal of the Performing Arts* 14, no. 1 (2009): 46–56.

Kahn, Douglas. *Noise, Water, Meat: A History of Sound in the Arts*. Cambridge: MIT Press, 1999.

Kandinsky, Wassily and Franc Mark, eds. *Blaue Reiter Almanach*. Translated by Henning Falkenstein. New York: Viking Press, 1974.

– *Complete Writings on Art*. Edited by Kenneth C. Lindsay and Peter Vergo. Boston: G.K. Hall & Co., 1982.

Kantor, Tadeusz. *A Journey through Other Spaces: Essays and Manifestos, 1944–1990*. Edited and translated by Michal Kobialka. Berkeley: University of California Press, 1993.

Kaun, Alexander. *Soviet Poets and Poetry*. Berkeley: California University Press, 1943.

Kelly, Caleb, ed. *Sound*. London and Cambridge: Whitechapel Gallery and MIT Press, 2011.

Kendrick, Lynne and David Roesner, eds. *Theatre Noise: The Sound of Performance*. Cambridge: Cambridge Scholars Publishing, 2011.

Khlebnikov, Velimir. *Collected Works*. Vol. 1–3. Edited by Charlotte Douglas, translated by Paul Schmidt. Cambridge: Harvard University Press, 1987.

– *Snake Train: Poetry and Prose*. Edited and translated by Gary Kern. Ann Arbor: Ardis, 1976.

– *The King of Time: Selected Writings of the Russian Futurian*. Edited by Charlotte Douglas, translated by Paul Schmidt. Cambridge: Harvard University Press, 1985.

Kimbrough, Andrew M. *Dramatic Theories of Voice in the Twentieth Century*. Amherst: Cambria Press, 2011.

Kim-Cohen, Seth. *In the Blink of an Ear: Toward a Non-Cochlear Sonic Art*. New York and London: Continuum, 2009.

Kirby, Michael. *A Formalist Theatre*. Philadelphia: University of Pennsylvania Press, 1987.

– *Futurist Performance*. New York: PAJ Publications, 1986.

Kostelanetz, Richard. *On Innovative Performance(s): Three Decades of Recollections of Alternative Theatre*. Jefferson: McFarland & Co., 1994.

– "Text-sound Art: A Survey." *Performing Arts Journal* 2, no 2 (1977): 61–70.

Kristeva, Julia. *Revolution in Poetic Language*. Translated by Margaret Waller. New York: Columbia University Press, 1984.

Kruchenykh, Alexei. *Our Arrival*. Moscow: Archive of Russian Avantgarde – RA, 1995.

– *Victory over the Sun*. Translated by Ewa Bartos and Victoria Nes Kirby. *The Drama Review* 15, no. 4 (Autumn 1971): 107–25.

Kuhns, David F. *German Expressionist Theatre: The Actor and the Stage*. Cambridge: Cambridge University Press, 1997.

LaBelle, Brandon. *Acoustic Territories: Sound Culture and Everyday Life*. New York: Continuum, 2010.

Lawton, Anna and Herbert Eagle, eds and trans. *Words in Revolution: Russian Futurist Manifestoes 1912–1928*. Washington: New Academia Publishing, 2004. Reprint from *Russian Futurism through Its Manifestos, 1912–1928*. Ithaca: Cornell University Press, 1988.

Lehmann, Hans-Thies. *Postdramatic Theatre*. Translated by Karen Jürs-Munby. New York: Routledge, 2006.

– "Word and Stage in Postdramatic Theatre." In *Drama and/after Postmodernism;*

Contemporary Drama in English, vol. 14, 37–54. Trier: Wissenschaftlicher Verlag, 2007.

Lehmann, Hans-Thies and Patrick Primavesi. "Dramaturgy on Shifting Grounds." *Performance Research* 14, no. 3 (2009): 3–6.

Levi, Erik. "Futurist Influences upon Early Twentieth-century Music." In *International Futurism in Arts and Literature*, edited by Günter Berghaus, 322–52. Berlin and New York: Walter de Gruyter, 2000.

Licht, Alan. *Sound Art: Beyond Music, Between Categories*. New York: Rizzoli International Publications, 2007.

Lista, Giovanni. *La scène futuriste*. Paris: Editions du Centre national de la recherche scientifique, 1989.

– ed. *Le Théâtre futurist italien, anthologie critique*, vol. 1–2. Lausanne: La Cité/L'Age d'Homme, 1976.

Livshits, Benedikt. *The One and a Half-Eyed Archer*. Translated by John E. Bowlt. Newtonville: Oriental Research Partners, 1976.

Malevich, Kazimir. *Essays on Art*. Edited by Troels Andersen. Copenhagen: Borgen, 1968.

– "From Cubism and Futurism to Suprematism: The New Painterly Realism." In *Russian Art of the Avant-Garde: Theory and Criticism, 1902–1934*, edited by John E. Bowlt, 116–35. New York: Viking Press, 1976.

Malina, Judith. "Directing 'The Brig.'" In *The Brig* by Kenneth H. Brown, 85–107. New York: Hill and Wang, 1965.

Maranka, Bonnie. *Theatre of Images*. New York: Drama Book Specialists, 1977.

Marinelli, Donald. *Origins of Futurist Theatricality: The Early Life and Career of F.T. Marinetti*. Pittsburgh: University of Pittsburgh Press, 1987.

Marinetti, F.T. *Critical Writings*. Edited by Günter Berghaus, translated by Doug Thompson. New York: Farrar, 2006.

– "Marinetti's Short Plays." Translated by Victoria Nes Kirby. *The Drama Review* 17, no. 4 (1973): 113–25.

– *Selected Writings*. Edited by R.W. Flint. Translated by R.W. Flint and Arthur A. Cappotelli. New York: Farrar, Straus and Giroux, 1972.

Marinetti, F.T. and Pino Mansata. "La Radia." In *Wireless Imagination: Sound, Radio, and the Avant-Garde*, edited by Douglas Kahn and George Whitehead, 265–9. Cambridge: MIT Press, 1992.

Markov, Vladimir. *Russian Futurism: A History*. Berkeley: University of California Press, 1968.

Martin, Marianne W. "Futurism, Unanimism and Apollinaire." *Art Journal* 28, no. 3 (Spring, 1969): 258–68.

Matejka, Ladislav and Krystyna Pomorska, eds. *Reading in Russian Poetics: Formalist and Structuralist Views*. Cambridge: MIT Press, 1971.

McCaffery, Steve. *Carnival* (the second panel 1970–75). Toronto: Coach House Press, 1976.

– "From Phonic to Sonic: The Emergence of the Audio-poem." In *Sound States: Innovative Poetics and Acoustical Technologies*, edited by Adelaide Kirby Morris. Chapel Hill: University of North Carolina Press, 1997.

McCaffery, Steve and bpNichol, eds. *Sound Poetry: A Catalogue*. Underwich Editions, Toronto, 1978.

– "Voice in Extremis." In *Prior to Meaning: The Protosemantic and Poetics*. Evanston: Northwestern University Press, 2001.

Menna, Filiberto. *Prampolini*. Rome: De Luca Editore, 1967.

Merleau-Ponty, Maurice. *The Primacy of Perception*. Edited and translated by James M. Edie. Evanston: Northwestern University Press, 1964.

Middleton, Christopher. "The Rise of Primitivism and Its Relevance to the Poetry of Expressionism and Dada." In *Bolshevism in Art and Other Expository Writings*, 23–37. Manchester: Carcanet New Press, 1978.

Moholy-Nagy, László. *Vision in Motion*. Chicago: P. Theobald, 1969.

Morey, Miguel and Carmen Prado. *Robert Wilson*. Barcelona: Ediciones Poligrafa, 2003.

Motherwell, Robert. *The Dada Painters and Poets: An Anthology*. Cambridge: Harvard University Press, 1981.

Nadotti, Maria. "Teatro d'artista: Conversazione de Robert Wilson." *Teatro in Europa*, no. 7, 1990.

Nietzsche, Friedrich Wilhelm. *Ecce Homo* and *The Birth of Tragedy*. Translated by Clifton P. Fadiman. New York : Modern Library, 1927.

Nilsson, Nils Åke. "How to Translate Avant-garde Poetry: Some Attempts with Khlebnikov's 'Incantation by Laughter.'" In *Velimir Khlebnikov: A Stockholm Symposium*, 133–50. Stockholm: University of Stockholm, 1985.

– "Kruchonykh's Poem 'Dyr bul shchyl.'" *Scando-Slavica* 24 (1979): 139–48.

Nudds, Matthew and Casey O'Callaghan, eds. *Sounds and Perception: New Philosophical Essays*. Oxford and New York: Oxford University Press, 2009.

O'Callaghan, Casey. *Sounds: A Philosophical Theory*. Oxford: Oxford University Press, 2007.

Oja, Carol. "George Antheil's Ballet Mécanique and Transatlantic Modernism." In *A Modern Mosaic: Art and Modernism in the United States*, edited by Townsend Ludington, 175–202. Chapel Hill: University of North Carolina Press, 2000.

Ong, Walter J. *Orality and Literacy: The Technologizing of the Word*. London: Routledge, 2002.

Oosterling, Henk. "Hypo-critical Theatre: Hollandia's Intermedial Multiverse." *Performance Research 'Navigations'* 6, no.3 (Winter 2001): 61–6.

Orban, Clara. *The Culture of Fragments: Words and Images in Futurism and Surrealism*. Atlanta: Rodopi, 1997.

Pam, Dorothy. "[Kokoschka's] Murderer, the Women's Hope." *The Drama Review* 67 (September 1975), 5–12.

Pavis, Patrice. *Analyzing Performance*. Translated by David Williams. Ann Arbor: The University of Michigan Press, 2003.

– *Languages of the Stage: Essays in the Semiology of the Theatre*. New York: PAJ Publishing, 1982.

– "The State of Current Theatre Research," *Applied Semiotics/Sémiotique appliquée* 1, no 3 (1997): 203–30.

Perloff, Marjorie. *The Futurist Moment: Avant-Garde, Avant Guerre, and the Language of Rupture*. Chicago and London: University of Chicago Press, 1986.

– "John Cage's Living Theatre." In *Against Theatre: Creative Destruction on the Modernist Stage*, edited by Martin Puchner and Alan Ackerman, 133–48. New York: Palgrave, 2006.

– "The Music of Verbal Space: John Cage's 'What you Say …'" In *Sound States: Innovative Poetics and Acoustical Technologies*, edited by Adelaide Kirby Morris, 129–49. Chapel Hill and London: University of North Carolina Press, 1997.

– *Poetry On & Off the Page: Essays for Emergent Occasions*. Evanston: Northwestern University Press, 1998.

Pioli, Richard J., ed. and trans. *Stung by Salt and War: Creative Texts of the Italian Avant-Gardist F.T. Marinetti*. New York: Peter Lang, 1987.

Pomorska, Krystyna. *Russian Formalist Theory and Its Poetic Ambience*. The Hague and Paris: Mouton, 1968.

Rainey, Lawrence, Christine Poggi, and Laura Wittman, eds. *Futurism: An anthology*. New Haven and London: Yale University Press, 2009.

Rebstock, Matthias and David Roesner, eds. *Composed Theatre: Aesthetics, Practices, Processes*. Bristol and Chicago: Intellect, 2012.

Richter, Hans. *Dada: Art and Anti-Art*. Translated by David Britt. London and New York: Thames and Hudson, 1965.

Roesner, David. "The Politics of the Polyphony of Performance: Musicalization in Contemporary German Theatre." *Contemporary Theatre Review* 18, no. 1 (2008): 44–55.

Roshwald Aviel and Richard Stites. *European Culture in the Great War: The Arts, Entertainment and Propaganda, 1914–1918*. Cambridge: Cambridge University Press, 2002.

Ruf, Frederick J. *Entangled Voices: Genre and the Religious Construction of Self*. New York: Oxford University Press, 1997.

Russolo, Luigi. *The Art of Noises*. Translated and edited by Barclay Brown. New York: Pendragon Press, 1986.

Salter, Chris. *Entangled: Technology and the Transformation of Performance*. Cambridge: MIT Press, 2010.

Salzman, Eric and Thomas Desi. *The New Music Theater: Seeing the Voice, Hearing the Body*. New York: Oxford University Press, 2008.

Sangild, Torben. *The Aesthetics of Noise*. Copenhagen: Datanom, 2002.

Schafer, Murray. "I've Never Seen a Sound." In *S:ON – Le son dans l'art contemporain canadien/Sound in Contemporary Canadian Art*, edited by Nicole Gingras, 66–71. Sherbrooke: Éditions Artextes, 2003.

Scheie, Timothy. "Voyage au Bout de la Nuit." *Theatre Journal* 52, no.1 (March 2000): 128–29.

Schiff, Christopher. "Banging on the Windowpane: Sound in Early Surrealism." In *Wireless Imagination: Sound, Radio and the Avant-Garde*, edited by Douglas Kahn and Gregory Whitehead, 139–91. Cambridge: MIT Press, 1992.

Schlemmer, Oskar, Laszlo Moholy-Nagy, and Farkas Molnár. *The Theatre of the Bauhaus*. Edited by Walter Gropius, translated by Arthur S. Wensinger. Baltimore: John Hopkins University Press, 1996.

Schöning, Klaus. "The Contours of Acoustic Art." *Theatre Journal* 43, no. 3, Radio Drama (October 1991): 307–24.

Schwitters, Kurt. *PPPPPP: Poems, Performances, Pieces, Proses, Plays, Poetics*. Edited and translated by Jerome Rothenberg and Pierre Joris. Philadelphia: Temple University Press, 1993.

Serafin, Stefania. "Russolo's Intonarumori: Acoustical Description and Real-time Simulation Using Physical Models" in *Generate and Test: Proceedings of the Australasian Computer Music Conference*, 2005. www.acma.asn.au/acmc05/acmc05-132-135.pdf. Last accessed 20 January 2012.

Shklovsky, Viktor. "On Poetry and Trans-Sense Language." Translated by Gerald Janecek and Peter Mayer. *October* 34 (Autumn 1985): 3–24.

– "The Resurrection of the Word." In *Russian Formalism: A Collection of Articles and Texts in Translation*, edited and translated by Stephan Bann and John Bowlt, 41–7. Edinburgh: Scottish Academic Press, 1973.

Shyer, Laurence. *Robert Wilson and his Collaborators*. New York: Theatre Communication Group, 1989.

Smith, A.C.H. *Orghast at Persepolis: An Account of the Experiment in Theatre Directed by Peter Brook and Written by Ted Hughes*. London: Methuen, 1972.

Sterne, Jonathan. *The Audible Past: Cultural Origins of Sound Reproduction*. Durham: Duke University Press, 2003.

Szondi, Peter. *Theory of the Modern Drama: A Critical Edition*. Edited and translated by Michael Hays. Minneapolis: University of Minnesota Press, 1987.

Tassel, Janet. "Staging a Kandinsky Dream." *New York Times*, 7 February 1982.

Tomashevsky, K. "Victory over the Sun." *The Drama Review* 15, no. 4 (Autumn 1971): 92–106.

Trimingham, Melissa. *The Theatre of the Bauhaus: the Modern and Postmodern Stage of Oskar Schlemmer*. New York: Routledge, 2011.

Verstraete, Pieter. 2009. *The Frequency of Imagination: Auditory Distress and Aurality in Contemporary Music Theatre*, http://exeter.academia.edu/PieterVerstraete/Books. Last accessed 10 February 2012.

Violi, Patrizia, ed. *Phonosymbolism and Poetic Language*. Turnhout, Belgium: Brepols, 2000.

Voegelin, Salomé. *Listening to Noise and Silence: Towards a Philosophy of Sound Art*. New York and London: Continuum, 2010.

Vovolis, Thanos. "The Voice and the Mask in Ancient Greek Tragedy." In *Soundscapes*, edited by Larry Sider et al., 83–102. London and New York: Wallflower Press, 2003.

Webster, Michael. *Reading Visual Poetry after Futurism: Marinetti, Apollinaire, Schwitters, Cummings*. New York: Peter Lang, 1995.

– "Words-in-Freedom and the Oral Tradition." *Visible Language* 23 (Winter 1989): 65–87.

Welton, Martin. "Seeing Nothing: Now Hear This ..." In *The Senses in Performance*, edited by Sally Barnes and André Lepecki, 146–55. New York: Routledge, 2007.

Wessendorf, Markus. "The Postdramatic Theatre of Richard Maxwell." *Norsk Shakespeare—og teatertidsskrift* (Oslo) 1/2006: 29–33. http://www2.hawaii.edu/~wessendo/Maxwell.htm

White, John. *Literary Futurism: Aspects of the First Avant-Garde*. Oxford: Clarendon Press, 1990.

Wilson, Robert. *The Théater of Images*. New York: Harper, 1984.

Index